D1507324

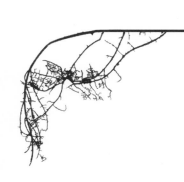

the world

and the wild

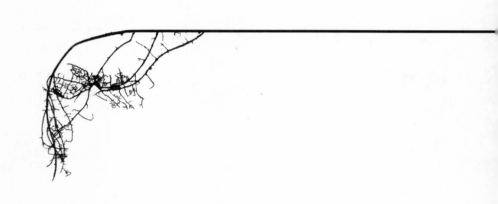

the world

edited by
david rothenberg
marta ulvaeus

and the wild

LIBRARY
FRANKLIN PIERCE COLLEGE
RINDGE, NH 03461

the university of arizona press   tucson

First printing
The University of Arizona Press
© 2001 Terra Nova
All rights reserved
∞ This book is printed on acid-free, archival-quality paper.
Manufactured in the United States of America

06 05 04 03 02 01   6 5 4 3 2 1

Library of Congress Cataloging-in-Publication Data
The world and the wild / edited by David Rothenberg and Marta Ulvaeus.
p. cm.
Includes bibliographical references and index.
ISBN 0-8165-2063-1 (pbk: alk. paper)
1. Nature conservation—Economic aspects.   2. Nature conservation—
Philosophy.   I. Rothenberg, David, 1962–II. Ulvaeus, Marta.
QH775.w667   2001
333.7´2–dc21   00-009968

British Library Cataloguing-in-Publication Data
A catalogue record for this book is available
from the British Library.

Publication of this book is made possible in part by a grant
from the publication program of the J. M. Kaplan Fund.

QH
75
W667
.N
2001

contents

VANCE G. MARTIN

foreword
whither world wilderness?

"Young man, wilderness is a moral issue, and I can assure you that the World Bank does not concern itself with moral issues. We build economies in developing nations. Good day." Clearly, the French vice-president of the World Bank had declared an end to our meeting. It was 1984, and I was trying to do the Bank a favor.

At that time, the World Bank was being protested and picketed for financing the destruction of much of the environment of developing nations, most visibly rain forests. As many of you may remember, *The Ecologist* magazine even published a special issue (with the help of David Rothenberg and others) denouncing the Bank's environmental practices. We proposed that the Bank participate in the Fourth World Wilderness Congress and help spearhead the WILD Foundation's concept of a world conservation bank. By using various financial instruments to innovatively address the protection of biological diversity, save wildlands, and improve environmental quality, the World Bank could possibly mend its ways. Wildlands and their dependent communities would benefit. A win-win situation, we thought. Apparently not.

Despite its rather summary dismissal of us at that early stage, the Bank did eventually agree to participate in the Fourth World Wilderness Congress (Colorado, 1987). Eventually (with the help of the small but growing environmental department at the World Bank, the World Resources Institute, and others), the concept of the world conservation bank became the Global Environmental Facility (GEF), a $1.3 billion fund within the World Bank. Was the future of wilderness in developing nations thereby secured? I only wish that it were so.

In addition to the GEF, during the last ten years the World Bank and other institutions have established many new mechanisms, organizations, and policies to address the loss of environmental quality. Despite these necessary and excellent changes, the development engine is still powered by high-octane capitalist fuel, without nearly enough of that necessary additive, *respect for nature*. In lieu of this value-laden additive, businessmen and politicians have been content only to tinker with the speed of destruction: they call it "sustainable development." But the car continues to careen madly. The problem is apparently the loose nut behind the steering wheel.

In the face of this, whither wilderness? Is the idea fated to stay in wealthy industrialized nations only? Some argue that it is a luxury concept and that it doesn't travel well in other classes. This is exacerbated by the fact that the economic model adopted by developing nations (or "emerging economies," as they are now called) is that of an overly consumptive America that seems unable to limit its consumption of natural resources.

The World Wilderness Congress (WWC) began in 1977 as a response to this dilemma and has purposefully applied a holistic approach to its search for solutions. Emulating the diverse template of wilderness itself, the WWC insists on combining the work of artists, philosophers, and indigenous people with those of scientists, businessmen, and politicians in an attempt to reformulate the fuel for that pesky engine of development. The WWC has met on six occasions—in South Africa, Australia, Scotland, the United States, and Norway, and most recently in Bangalore, India, October 1998.

The Sixth WWC was the first time the Congress convened in Asia, and it helped in many specific ways to galvanize the debate, the research, and the action necessary to protect and sustain wilderness (and dependent local communities) in Asia.

Through this twenty-eight-year series of Congress meetings, as the idea of wilderness slowly becomes a land-use reality in numerous countries, a pattern has emerged that appears similar in both rich and less-rich countries. This pattern is evident in Zimbabwe and Namibia, for example, where wilderness zones have appeared in communal lands and national parks. The common pattern is not economics but rather a priority that is placed on cultural heritage and a tacit acceptance (or subjective understanding) of the need to allow a part of Nature to do its thing.

That French vice-president of the World Bank was right, in part, when he said that wilderness is a moral issue. It is other things also, of course, but wilderness fundamentally exists as much as a personal landscape as it does a functioning ecosystem. However, as an indicator of human sanity, wilderness leads a perilous existence. Therefore, the need for philosophical discussion and clarity is just as great in the international wilderness debate as is the need for concrete action. We need to understand and communicate the relationship we have, or desire, with the wild nature we seek to protect—a very important step if we are to fix that loose nut behind the wheel.

The wwc and the wild Foundation are pleased to collaborate with David Rothenberg and the contributors to this volume in an exploration of the promise, the difficulty, and the questions inherent in understanding the role of wilderness in developing countries. We have all been on this trail for a while. We welcome your input and participation.

DAVID ROTHENBERG

<u>introduction</u>
wilderness in the rest of the world

A few years ago, the heat was on in the rising world awareness of the disappearing rain forests. We had rock stars touring with Yanomamo Indians, conservation biologists warning us how every day many species vanish forever. The bankers came up with the magnanimous notion of swapping debt for nature. "All right, don't worry about paying us back," they said to the developing nations. "Put aside some of your land, and we'll forgive and forget." There must have been a catch somewhere.

Then came the backlash. Aerial photographs from far up in space—a patchwork forest, a wilderness decimated by clear-cutting and human greed. Which distant jungle was this? Turns out it was the U.S. Pacific Northwest, the stage for the worst forest razing anywhere on earth. "What right have you," asked the governments of the south, "to preach of morality in our treatment of the natural world when you are wreaking such havoc on your own lands? Work out your own problems before you tell us what to do."

There has always been an irony in the idea of wilderness that is exported around the world as an indication of global, total concern: once again the rich countries are dictating what the poor countries should do. How much of this desire to save the wild is just one more instance of colonialism? And how much of it is a genuinely altruistic hope to save something that belongs to all of us, to be valued and cared for in many different ways?

Should lions, wolves, and bears continue to be perceived as a threat? Or should they be preserved no matter what? Tigers are still feared by Indians and Siberians and basically by all the people who live in close proximity to the few that remain in the wild. Is this the legacy of generations of cultural animosity akin to that of the Big Bad Wolf? Or is there something they know that we don't? Certainly, the dangerous creatures in nature are now nearly eradicated. So we in our safe places try to re-create the wild; we learn to venerate it as something sublime, a difference that dwarfs us without threatening us. We are secure, so we want to preserve some opportunity, real or imagined, for danger—like the old thundering appeal of the *sublime*, that great wild immensity that is beloved due to its safe distance from us.

And because we want the wild to be necessary, we say all sorts of things about it. In *The Abstract Wild* (University of Arizona Press, 1996), the best book to appear in recent years on the paradox of wildness, Jack Turner writes that the problem with wildness is that we abstract it, try to manage it, enumerate it, turn it into five-year plans. This dissipates its power even as we try to sustain it. Wildness is ineffable, elusive, impossible to contain in words or designs.

A fine, attractive, romantic idea, but how culture-bound is it? What form does the appreciation for the wild take in other cultures, among other peoples? I think of my return from the wilds of the Torngat mountains of northern Labrador, after I and three others had been fetched by floatplane back from nine days on a remote lake hundreds of miles from any other human beings. In the bar at the outpost of Kuujjuaq, northern Quebec, while having breakfast, I described the beauty of it all to an Inuit man who was sitting next to me, listing all the animals we had seen and noting how unafraid of humans they had seemed. I told of a rabbit, a large brown snowshoe hare that had hopped right up to me and sniffed my feet. "And?" said the man, in anticipation. "And what?" I countered. He shook his head: "You mean you didn't shoot it?"

How could I? I thought. It was the furthest thing from my mind at the time. You see, I was caught in wonder, not the raw mechanics of survival. We ecologists bask in the wild and are suspicious of those who mine it for sustenance. Civilization breeds our love of the great expanses of the world. But are we one civilization, or many?

Each culture has its own agenda, even as we gradually blur together in a unified planetary trek toward completely linked commerce and communication and possible destruction. If we want to encourage everyone to care about the wild, that "wildness" ought to be appropriate to each specific situation and consequently will look different from the varied perspectives of our world's myriad peoples. It should not be imposed from far away, becoming yet another colonialist or imperialist act. If there is to be any expansive agreement, it must come as the consensus of many voices, so that we may all learn from one another as we strive to engender respect for the earth.

What cannot be stressed enough is that we must be wary of totalizing approaches to the problem in which the primacy of the preservation of wilderness is not only assumed but is considered to be obvious. Wilderness is essential for the perpetuation of this planet, but it has never been the only thing worth fighting for. It is no substitute for the improvement of living conditions, human rights, economic stability, or fair government, all of which should be part of our progress as human beings.

Never will all of us learn to have the same relation to the natural world. And never will all of us like the same art, the same music, the same poetry. Diversity is part of the strength of any meaningful cause—diversity mixed with specific strategy. But recognizing the value of the wild is only a beginning.

We must cultivate a blend of urgency and openness in our response to the wild. Vanishing wildlands must be safeguarded immediately, all over the world. At the same time, we need to be sensitive to the fact that this wildness, and the necessary respect for it, might take different forms for those brought up to consider nature in other ways. Some have battled nature to secure a stronghold of civilization; others have revered its fragile resilience as a kind of sacred danger.

Although wilderness is necessary, we need to be safe enough from its threatening aspect to want to save it. Enough peoples all over the globe are struggling just to survive, and the training of the appreciation for wilderness must be seen as part of this struggle, even one of the reasons that the fight must go on. If wilderness truly is a need, we must explain why it is a need and not just another of many unrealizable fantasies.

Never have we depended on nature as much as we do now, and there has never been so little of it to love. Care, concern, education, admonishment—there are many tools in the quest to save what is authentically more-than-human.

This book is based on a collection of essays first assembled as a special issue of the journal *Terra Nova* (vol. 3, no. 3) in advance of the Sixth World Wilderness Congress (WWC), which is held once every four years. Organized by the WILD Foundation, under the direction of Vance Martin, the event has its origins in the International Wilderness Leadership School of Ian Player, based in South Africa. (We have included in this book an excerpt from his memoir of his remarkable, radical collaboration with Zulu naturalist Magqubu Ntombela in apartheid South Africa.) Most significant about this far-flung gathering of environmental activists, wildland and wildlife managers, environmental policymakers, and politicians is that it demonstrates that the fate of wilderness is a concern not just of rich colonial countries, and that this concern ought to be part of the guiding philosophy of any progressive and newly developing nation.

The contemporary concept of wilderness may have emerged out of the peculiarities of American history, but it is now evolving into an idea that will be useful worldwide. At the conference in Bangalore, I was heartened to find that the notion of wilderness has supporters all over the world, people who come from all levels of education, opportunity, and status. The idea of wildness needs to find resonance with both indigenous peoples' practices and local agricultural practices. For some native peoples, respect for the combined fragility and resilience of nature is an integral part of their cultural knowledge, while in other cases this is something new to learn.

At the conference in Bangalore, it was my role to show how philosophy could be relevant to a very practical and immediate discussion. Every philosopher ought to ask how her discipline is relevant so as to avoid being caught up in the conceptual spirals that can be the hallmark of the discipline. D. T. Suzuki once said, "This is what I love about philosophy—No one wins." It is Hermann Hesse's glass-bead game of concepts, the free flow of the test of ideas—fun, frustrating, endless, beautiful at its best, nitpicking and cold at its worst. "Philosophers," warned Keats, "are the kind who would pull off angels' wings." We are not satisfied with belief. Although we claim to want to explain things, we remain best at asking questions.

Environmental philosophy, however, is *applied* philosophy, which means it uses this questioning approach ostensibly to help solve real-world problems, in this case the clarification of how humanity should relate to the natural world. At the Sixth WWC in Bangalore, the challenge was to help decide how humanity should relate to the *wildness* in the natural world. We examined the fate of wilderness as an idea, attempting to define the wild place as something that can be understood and cared for in all parts of the world, as a concept that may change fluidly as it is reinterpreted within many cultural and political systems.

The wild resides somewhere in the hearts of all living beings, humans included. It conjures a sense of danger, a sense of reverence for nature in its purest form, as well as a sense of caring for something that is delicate and fragile, easy to ruin. There are people who dwell in the wild, but to love it is to acknowledge a value that goes beyond that which is human. The wild is more expansive, something that requires effort for humans to participate in, while the rest of nature embraces and inhabits it much more easily. That is the fate of humanity—to have to struggle to be compatible with and accommodate nature after our own human nature has cast us out.

The love of wilderness and the desire to maintain it are part of humanity's rise toward a less selfish state. It is a sign of our growing ability to look beyond ourselves, to expand our care to aspects of nature that are important not because they are useful to us but because we respect them beyond the limitations of use—the love of wilderness as something precious and worthy as part of the march of civilization. Our human culture is stronger for having seen the need to recognize it.

But I don't think wilderness is the only part of nature worth respecting and attempting to explain. Viewing nature in terms of wilderness, while perhaps not the most crucial, is one of many significant ways we can relate to the world around us. It is necessary to say this because just as the wild lands have been besieged by those forces in our world's culture that consider nature in terms of its potential for use, the *idea* of wilderness also has come under conceptual siege. Sometimes the attack comes from unexpected places, namely from the pulpits of historians and philosophers who say they are *for* the environment but *against* wilderness. These thinkers consider wilderness to be a narrow and exclusionary frame of reference for interpreting the natural world, one that is not representative of the real, diverse, and changing ways human beings throughout history have worked with the land.

In the pages of *The New York Times Magazine* and in his anthology *Uncommon Ground,* environmental historian William Cronon has decried the idea of wilderness as something naïve and unrealistic for those people who actually work with the land. According to him, its greatest fault is that it separates humanity from nature, perpetuating the illusion that we are separate enough from nature to draw boundaries around pieces of it to keep ourselves out. He asks instead for an environmental ethic and aesthetic based on respect not for the wild reserves thousand of miles from our homes but for the trees in our backyard, for the health of the family farm, for the understanding of exactly where our food comes from. For Cronon, wilderness exists only as an idea, an idea developed for the benefit of those who live in cities isolated from nature, where they can imagine whatever they will of the mountains.[1]

For several years now, environmental philosopher J. Baird Callicott has advocated the argument that belief in wilderness is a kind of old-time religion, based on backward colonial American ideas about separating humanity from nature. As such, he considers wilderness to be too limited a concept to warrant the inordinate amount of attention it has received from environmental philosophers in the first century of our discipline. It's time, according to Callicott, that we move beyond this naïve separation between ourselves and our surroundings and instead focus on sustainable development and biodiversity.

Callicott believes that "implicit in the most passionate pleas for wilderness preservation is a complacency about what passes for civilization."[2] An interesting notion, but I don't believe it for a second. Only a civilization that is somewhat enlightened could believe that there is value in saving wild country for its own sake. This desire is not a simplistic idyll from bygone days; it arose out of our era. And the fact that some of us care to save such lands signals a step in the right direction. While it ought not be the only kind of environmental sentiment that receives philosophical attention, it needs to be brought into the broader debate regarding what kind of relationship humanity should have with nature. It should not be set aside as a deviant path.

When it comes to saving wild country, Callicott suggests that instead of discussing such woolly concepts as wilderness we should set up "biodiversity reserves" to save endangered species and whole ecosystems in the name of science. That is all fine and good, but the concept of biodiversity is no less culturally constructed than the idea of wilderness. And, to me, wilderness continues to be a much richer and more valuable concept, one that might need some overhauling but that should be developed rather than set aside in favor of more positivist approaches.

Even more perplexing is the suggestion that sustainable development might somehow replace concern for wilderness. The Brundtland Commission, organized by the United Nations in the mid-1980s to define sustainable development, described it as "meeting the needs of the present without compromising the ability of the future to meet its own needs," which I consider to be a thinly veiled avoidance of our moral responsibility to future generations.[3] If we believe in and care about the future, we will have to make decisions on behalf of that future, rather than passively letting it take its own path. If we decide we want to preserve wilderness in perpetuity, as our forebears in conservation had the insight to do, we have to risk claiming to know what's best for the future. Modern UN and World Bank schemers are too slippery for such real moral commitment.

Sure, sustainable development is a useful concept in trying to elucidate plans for change around the world in the coming decades, but it is no substitute for a genuine respect for nature. It is really a suggested approach to an entirely different problem: how to foster continued international growth with economic profit for all involved, growth that can continue to proceed without exerting undue pressure on the environment.

Wilderness is something else, an idea that has stood the test of time. Throughout history, the wilderness has represented for many a source of spiritual experience and challenge. From Moses to Muir, many have found it necessary to get away from the civilization that shaped them in order to catch a glimpse of the God who so often slinks from the details of the constructed human world. Yet this has never been the only place to see God. It is one of many places where we can touch the greatness that is inherent in the fabric of this world.

But wilderness philosophy is not wilderness religion, and the philosopher who supports wilderness should not dismiss critiques of the idea of wilderness as blasphemy. The responsible philosopher of the wild won't just love it in silence but will be able to combine his support with relentless questioning. I stand behind the *intention* underlying the critical efforts of Cronon and Callicott, which is to caution against the totalizing tendencies of some all-or-nothing wilderness demagogues, but I protest the negativity of their tones. Intellectuals seem more prone to say no than to say yes to anything, for that is the way we are trained to think. We must challenge ourselves to turn that skepticism into support so that we may refine possibilities and honestly change the world.

It is imperative that we question the idea of wilderness so that we can defend it more forcefully rather than hasten its conceptual destruction. To that end, I offer three basic critiques of the idea of wilderness that deserve thoughtful consideration by all supporters of the wild:

1. *Wilderness comes from civilization, and it is an idea that makes sense only in connection with culture.* I agree. There was no need to worry about preserving the wilderness when it was perceived as a formidable and dangerous force against which humanity feebly defended itself in order to subsist. Times have changed. We have proliferated across the planet. Most of us no longer fear the wild, but we lament its passing.

This is not mere romanticism; it is an achievement. We are now able to care about something that is not primarily of use to us. We can love it for its difference. And while this may make nature something separate from the mainstream of human slash-and-burn mentality and activity, this nature is still a part of nature, our source. It is no place we can return to easily, after our long and hard cultural evolution, but it is a pure part of the environment that we might now be able to integrate somehow into our complicated lives.

The need for us to love the wilderness has resulted from a history of thought that has promoted a separation between humanity and nature—an unfortunate path we have taken. Yet the wild will surely prevail in the end, long after humanity, like all dominating species, passes beyond our time of domination to become a footnote to natural history. So we need not worry about its ultimate survival. Our challenge is to see if we can be compatible with its present state of health, and I sincerely hope we are up to the task.

We must be careful not to take this model for identifying wilderness, which is based on a dichotomy between humans and nature, as the *only* way or even the most important way we as a species relate to the environment.

2. *The preservation of wilderness has never been the only goal of the environmental movement, or its most important goal.* True, it may seem to be the most dramatic, the most obvious, or the most photogenic goal, but it should be understood as one end of the spectrum of a diverse movement whose purpose is to encourage our species to reflect carefully on our dependence on and attitude toward the vast world we inhabit.

We must never let concern for wilderness distract us from concern for the immediate ways human beings depend on a healthy environment for sustenance, taking care to design our habitations so they do not cumulatively pollute and degrade the surroundings. I would even admit that protecting where we live is more directly important to most of us in our day-to-day lives than the saving of wilderness. But knowing that the wilderness is out there and safe may be more symbolically important. Many Americans are happy to know that there are national parks that have been established to protect forever the most spectacular examples of our natural heritage. We like to believe that our country holds such places to be self-evidently sacred even though much money might be made mining them, logging them, or selling them into commercial tourist slavery. But saving a few areas does not mean calling for an end to all commerce.

I hope that more and more countries in the world will come to recognize that singling out some areas to be set aside as wilderness is a realistic course of action. It does not mean that we place the rights of nature above those of people but that people as a whole decide that sometimes nature must be given its own chance. Yet the problems faced by the diverse countries of the world in defining wilderness might vary substantially from what America has had to face.

3. *Wilderness does not always mean a place without people.* There are many examples of indigenous peoples who have managed to maintain a delicate balance with nature. But what is often overlooked is that it is only because of small populations that the land has been shielded from overharvesting. Nevertheless, there is much to be gained by learning from these peoples how to live intimately with our surroundings. It is unfortunate

that often the struggle of indigenous peoples for land sovereignty is pitted against the safeguarding of the wild, obscuring the real issue.

Frequently, the people who work closely with wildlands are gatherers or traders, buying and selling what they find there. Setting aside a place as wilderness does take it out of the marketplace, and this often sets it against the interests of the people who live nearby and whose livelihoods depend on having access to the land. They must be compensated and should not be punished for having used the land. And they must be brought into discussions of why wilderness can matter to all of us. Although they might sometimes be put in charge of monitoring the newly demarcated areas, there are cases in which they might not be the ones who know best how to manage the land.

The lives of indigenous peoples are changing. And their hunting and harvesting practices are changing. These changes will have to be accompanied by an increasing respect for the wild. While there might not have been the need in the past for the languages of some of these peoples to include a word for wilderness, perhaps there is that need today. Many of these cultures have long-held values and beliefs revering nature, which inform how they interact with their surroundings. Each tribe, region, culture, and country must outline its own way to deal with most certain change. Although having the common goal of caring for the wild might bring the world's peoples together from time to time, each people must be free to find its own route through the problem.

The presence and activities of people who have tended the land responsibly for generations are permitted in some wilderness areas. In other places where the situation is more fragile, this might not be realistic. Each case deserves separate consideration.

Scientific knowledge cannot save the wilderness. Although conservation biologists have clearly established the value of biodiversity, it might not resonate for many who are only vaguely familiar with this specialized term. In contrast, the wild is an idea whose evocative power makes it much more compelling. We cannot resist it. Science and its exacting language can only support our love for the wild, not replace it.

Economics cannot save the wilderness. The wild may depend on funding from the nations' budgets, but it cannot be quantified or reduced to number-crunching. The safeguarding of wild places cannot be financially justified based on cost-benefit analyses. But how dare we put a price on those wild places that remain in the world, whose value is inestimable?

Nor can the wilderness be saved by management. Drawing a line on a map might be practical for demarcating the wild areas that are to be patrolled and governed by laws. But legislation cannot confine wildness—for the cordoned-off land to thrive, the unprotected fringe areas also must remain healthy. It is unfortunate that we require laws to keep us in check. But this is a sad fact of the irreconcilability of humans with nature: left to our own devices, most humans just don't know how to fit in.

Philosophy certainly can't save the wilderness, especially if it only pokes thorns in the sides of everyone else's beliefs and arguments. Throughout history, ideas may have changed the world, but they haven't been its salvation. Will humility be its saving grace— if we just dare to step back and tread lightly but seriously across this planet? Will education save the wild if we simply teach more and more people to consider caring? Will poetry save the wild if we learn to bend language as far as it can go so that we can express it most beautifully? As Swedish poet Tomas Tranströmer writes, "The wild does not have words."[4] We don't have much time. We have to do everything, and nothing, acting always with both passion and concern.

Go out there. See what you know. Come back with more. But don't forget to come back. We need all of you in some way. None of these approaches *alone* will do enough to save the wild, but if they all acknowledge their own limitations and the contributions of other, quite different ways of seeing the wild, then hopefully something can be done.

The goal of our present anthology is to reinvigorate the effort to understand, reveal, and save wilderness beyond the usual futile polarities.

Zeese Papanikolas shows how the contemporary idea of wilderness has roots in the Romantic era, when paintings had much more power to change the way people think. Sahotra Sarkar presents an Indian take on social ecology, saying that the subcontinent is a place with a very long tradition of people interacting with a multispecies habitat. But Philip Cafaro and Monish Verma argue that saving a whole species at the brink of disappearance still takes precedence over particular human populations that may be upset by new wildland reserves. Edward Whitesell argues that conservation is truly a place for "both-and" logic. We must save both endangered species and endangered cultures. Their mutual safety need not conflict.

Often wildness looms at the brink of the world's large cities. Tom Vanderbilt reports on what an increasingly likely eruption from towering Popocatépetl would do to Mexico City and how people are dealing with this ferocious sense of nature so close to where they live. Shall the wildlands be managed in detail or should they be left well enough alone? Evan Eisenberg suggests that a looser, more improvisatory approach might be truer to the ambiguity that characterizes natural order. He calls it "earth jazz."

While we play the changes, Pramod Parajuli joins the band, from Nepal, with the chorus, "No nature without social justice." Antonio Diegues brings the same cautious support for the idea of wilderness to bear on the Amazon of Brazil, where myths of wilderness often gloss over the complex cultural forces and different kinds of human settlement that affect the fragile lands. It's not just a question of indigenous people versus exploitative industries—there are many other layers of possible social and governmental involvement.

Our future ecology must be deep, embracing the human and the beyond-human. Three case studies from Africa show that defenders of the wild are by no means always in agreement. David Western explains how the creation of the Amoboseli Reserve in the Kenyan savanna was possible only through the active initiative of the local Maasai, who preserve the natural environment as they preserve their own culture and show how humanity and nature thrive together through the practice of ancient wild pastoral traditions. John Terborgh counters with the view that while native-run reserves might be a nice idea, what really works is top-down management, legal muscle, and a park agency with real power to enforce the protection of nature against the local populations' tendency to exhaust the land and poach the wildlife. According to him, we can't rely upon voluntary compliance. Meanwhile, Ian Player describes the added difficulty of working to preserve the wild in apartheid South Africa. Against all odds, he forged an inspiring partnership with Zulu expert Magqubu Ntombela, a friendship that crossed social barriers to fight for the nature that both men believed in.

Meanwhile, William Bevis tells the compelling story of Bruno Manser, the Swiss activist who lived with the Penan of Malaysia. The Penan have long subsisted in the oldest rain forest on the planet, in Sarawak, a state in the north of the island of Borneo. Each year, millions of acres of their land is cleared. Manser's courage and commitment in helping the Penan are legendary, but is his involvement necessary for people in the rest of the world to register the suffering of this unique culture? And, in the end, will they be seduced by the possibility of material wealth accompanying development, as has happened in so many cases the world over?

Sometimes money speaks louder than protest. Dan Imhoff tells the impressive tale of Doug Tompkins, a former sportswear executive who is now using his fortune to purchase millions of acres of unspoiled Chilean forest. Can he get the local people to trust his intentions and dreams? After a few difficult years, as time goes on, he is gaining respect in his adopted home. Kathleen Harrison describes the profound knowledge of healing plants and practices of the Mazatecs, for whom the botanical and spiritual worlds are interdependent. As the road of progress is being built through their mountainous terrain, its attendant changes follow close behind, some of which threaten that ancient wisdom, while others provide resources to enable its continuation. It is important that we respect and support the people in such places as well as the wild resources whose healing power only they may have learned. Damien Aragabali closes the book with his warning that, more often than not, colonialism is likely to draw traditional societies *away* from their ancient codes that include respect for the wild. In the pursuit of development, foreign powers demonstrate little regard for the rules that have guided human and natural life in Papua New Guinea for centuries: we trample on their taboos.

Wilderness is a reality to fight for, only one of many kinds of nature we can uphold. It should not be placed in opposition to human presence, but its persistence leads us to question the values at the core of the many human cultures that live on and with this earth. For no matter how much damage we do, nature does endure. As Robert Service concluded, "the wild will win in the end."

Be willing to change your views when you learn how others see and engage with the world. The distant wildness is a far cry from the nature lived within. The array of cultures in this world can teach all of us. However much power we usurp, however much we think we know about things, we—the sort of people who might pick up this book, this self-selected group—will remain a minority. And it's no easy task to get through to that vast, unstoppable, diverse, rich, interesting, constantly transforming rest of the world.

At the same time, we must be careful not to romanticize the supposed paradise of fantasized remote and idyllic ways of life other than our own. What was it, then, that started progress in motion in the first place? A fundamental human flaw that prevents us from being satisfied with what we have? This may be the greatest human tragedy, that in the long run we are not satisfied with local ecological subsistence "ecotopias." If such worlds ever existed, we sadly left them.

The history of ecological solution is a history of the future. We will not find the perfect environmental answer in anyone's past. Certainly, we'll come across a few clues here and there but no perfect social models to be nostalgic for. No previous society has had to confront environmental problems on the scale we must face as the millennium turns. We won't be able to hold on to our precious old ways—not any of us. All of our relationships with nature and with one another are subject to change. The concept of wilderness must change so that it is relevant to many cultures, and those of us dedicated to its preservation must learn more and better ways to translate the word into different worlds. Wilderness need not be dogma; it can be an open and free kind of place that we must ensure the future will still accommodate. If wilderness does not exist in the whole world's diverse futures, it exists nowhere at all.

NOTES

Portions of this essay were adapted from David Rothenberg, "Why Wild Philosophy?" *International Journal of Wilderness* 5/5 (1999): 4–8.

1   See William Cronon, ed., *Uncommon Ground: Toward Reinventing Nature* (New York: Norton, 1995) and William Cronon, "The Trouble with Wilderness: A Response," *Environmental History* 1/1 (1996). For a response, see "Who's Naive about Nature?" Review of *Uncommon Ground*, ed. William Cronon, *Amicus Journal* (Spring 1996): 41–44.
2   J. Baird Callicott, "The Wilderness Idea Revisited," in J. Baird Callicott and Michael Nelson, eds., *The Great, New, Wilderness Debate* (Athens: University of Georgia Press, 1998), p. 339.
3   World Commission on Environment and Development, Gro Harlem Brundtland, chair, *Our Common Future* (Oxford University Press, 1987).
4   Tomas Tranströmer, *Selected Poems*, Robert Hass, ed. (Hopewell, NJ: Ecco Press, 1987), p. 159.

the world

and the wild

1 how can four trees make a jungle?

One afternoon in March 1994, our neighbor Mr. Tularam Gahire came to visit Ajamvari Khetipati, our experimental farm in Saradanagar, Chitwan, Nepal. He told us that he had heard about a new "American" or "Japanese" farm being started there and wanted to see it for himself.[1] We had established this farm as part of an action-research project on agroecological knowledge with a research grant from the MacArthur Foundation. The idea was to diversify a two-acre stretch of land in such a way that it would produce enough to meet all the food, fiber, fodder, firewood, and other household-related needs of an average Nepali peasant family. Tularam also owns about a two-acre piece of land nearby. He is a member of one of the families who migrated to Chitwan from the hills about three decades ago. I gave him a tour and told him about our plans to plant many varieties of trees and also put aside one-tenth of the land for pasture. Near the end of the tour, Tularam began to show his disapproval of the way I was planting trees on my land. Let me share with you a slice of the conversation that we had over tea:

TULARAM: I really like the idea of native species of trees that you have planted. After a few years, that section [pointing toward the southeastern part of the farm] might look like a Chitwan jungle I used to see when I migrated to Chitwan twenty-eight years ago.

PRAMOD: That is the idea. I want to make sure that we do not have to destroy the forest in order to farm. Farming and forestry can work together so that a peasant can derive all the wood and biomass from within his or her own farm.

TULARAM: But I still don't understand why you are planting hundreds of trees on the farm. Maybe I am *abujh* [stupid]. But does it not make sense to plant just three or four kinds of trees such as *baans* [bamboo], *pipal, bar,* and *swaami* [all members of the ficus family found widely in rural Nepal]? Excuse me for being such an abujh.

PRAMOD: I would like to plant fewer trees too, if it would make a jungle.

TULARAM: I think it would make good jungle in the long run.

PRAMOD: It would? How so? How can four trees make a jungle?

TULARAM: People say that you are a learned man. You have become a professor. But I will have to tell you my *chaar-paise buddhi* [four-cents' wisdom]. I hope you do not think I am a Pakhe [a person from a remote hill].

PRAMOD: Please tell me. I am really curious.

TULARAM: If you have those four trees in the four corners of your field, don't you think the birds would come? Then what would the birds do?

PRAMOD: I like to hear birds chirping in the morning. I am not against birds, you know. Even *dhukur* [doves] and *titra* [grouse] have begun to come to the farm. I feel so happy about it. Yes, I want hundreds of birds to live on this farm.

TULARAM: This is where the trick is. When birds come, they also bring lots of seeds from the Chitwan jungle. When they *bisti* [defecate], they will drop it in your field. Then you will get as many kinds of trees as you want, all natural, and solid from bird droppings. These saplings are not weak like those you have brought from the forest department depot. That is how forests are grown.

PRAMOD: What an idea! I am just ashamed of myself for not thinking even that much. Looks like my *buddhi* has to be sharpened.

TULARAM: Not sharpened, but deepened. I do not mean to discourage you. What you have done by using your personal farm as a demonstration is nevertheless a great idea. But why try too hard, when there are easier ways of doing things?

Tularam's sharp commentary on my "missionary zeal" or rather, as they say in Nepali, a *vikase sapana* (dream of developing) to reforest my farm brings up a host of questions that pertain to the theme of this volume. On the one hand, his native critique of planned forestry points to the perennial conflict between forest department or demonstration farms and the peasants' own view regarding the selection of species of trees. Throughout South Asia, we have heard about the conflicts between "government trees" and "people's trees." His remarks could be considered a challenge to the mainstream discourses of forest use and afforestation, nature conservation and protection. On the other, it motivates me to explore what might be a peasant discourse about the wild and wilderness, nature use and nature conservation.

The dominant discourses about national parks and sanctuaries echo an overwhelming fear of poaching and wanton destruction of nature by hungry peasants, forest dwellers, and ignorant villagers. Thus the top-heavy missions of nature conservation often have been carried out either by ejecting the peasant from the area or by subsuming his or her existence within the imperatives of biodiversity conservation. For those of us in the agrarian communities of rural South Asia, protecting nature from human use is not a workable option. The way I see it, the only option we have is to use and interact with nature in a healthy, balanced way. Based on what I learned while growing up in the mountains of central Nepal and what I have witnessed in the Jharkhand region of India, as well as in many other peasant societies around the world, I cannot bifurcate "nature" from "culture" or the "domesticated" from the "wild." It seems to me that mainstream notions of wild and wilderness are primarily a product of the industrial economy and Cartesian rationality.

A nature that is "pure" no longer exists. For the peasants, what exists is a continuum of farm and forest, commons and pastures. Unlike the fantasies of the urbanites and city-bred environmentalists who do not directly depend on nature's economy, civilization and the wild are not considered as distinct entities in the peasant economy. Rather, the human and natural entities form parts of a whole that is bound by a variety of functions and relationships. Historically, farming has been perhaps the first step toward setting humans apart from nature, if we take nature in the primordial sense. But from the peasant point of view, I would venture to say that the clearing of land for cultivating crops is the first moment in "naturalizing culture" as well as "culturizing nature."

William Cronon's observation in *Uncommon Ground* that "an environmental ethic should tell us more about using nature than about not using it" rings a true chord for the people I will be discussing in terms of "ecological ethnicity." Ecological ethnicity is a social category that refers to those people who have developed a respectful use of the natural resources and consequently a commitment to creating and preserving a technology that interacts with local ecosystems in a sustainable manner. It is a land-based ethnicity that in some cases might correspond with ethnicities based on blood, race, or language ties and identities, but these are not necessarily the primary source of identification. Within the rubric of ecological ethnicity I include peasants, indigenous peoples, rural inhabitants, fisherfolk, forest dwellers, nomadic shepherds, and a host of people marginalized by development projects and the programs of environmental modernization. Ecological ethnicity is a politically charged concept in the sense that the survival of these specific ways of life calls for a degree of autonomous governance for devising appropriate ownership over the biotic wealth, the commons, and the communities. These ecological ethnicities are linked with, and have to be theorized within, the ecological field. Ecology is the matrix in which ethnicity is reproduced as well as altered.[2]

Ecological ethnicities have shown that an ecosystem can be conserved and restored while growing crops, earning incomes, and enjoying life. For example, in the United States, the oyster growers of Willapa Bay in Washington have become active guardians of water quality. Wild mushroom growers and collectors have also become guardians of healthy, intact, diverse vegetation in forests. Some fish-processing communities produce a variety of products including organic fertilizer and fish meal, and in turn, the fertilizer is sold to cranberry growers. The notion of the "foodshed" could be considered to be one of the threads that connect producers with the soil, human collectivity with nonhuman collectivity, and nature with culture. Like a wilderness preserve, a foodshed might be based on proximity, locality, and regionality. It can be defined flexibly as being built around boundaries set by plant communities, soil types, a watershed, a valley, or a mountain range. But unlike a preserve or a park, a foodshed includes the people—both producers and consumers—living within it. These people and their communities are not isolated entities but are connected to one another through regional markets and exchange networks. The boundaries of a foodshed are not there to prevent humans from entering it. Rather, they mark the distinct profile of the ecosystem so that the technologies of production and consumption can be refashioned accordingly.

Food is a key consideration in this new social arrangement because what we eat, where the food comes from, and what kind of technology has been used to produce it can teach us about how we relate to the earth and how we relate to one another. A movement called community-supported agriculture (CSA) illustrates the ways consumers and producers could be linked by a commitment to an ecosystem. Participants in a CSA or a foodshed not only mutually ensure that the animals and plants they bring to their tables are treated well, they also educate themselves about their eating habits. It is a commitment to becoming attentive to the processes that transform soil and human labor into sources of energy for life. It is a way of ensuring that the farmers who work for them will not be forced to abandon farming because of competition from agribusiness giants or be forced to use toxic sprays in their fields, whose chemicals cause deadly diseases or infertility.

This vision is very different from the way the so-called broiler belt is organized in the United States today or how the tomatoes and lettuces we eat in North America are grown in Mexican and Guatemalan farms that displace the indigenous *ejido* land system and *milpa* agriculture. Milpa agriculture is one of the most efficient ways of maintaining diversity in the fields. In Chiapas, a milpa might contain as many as seventy-nine different food and fiber crops.[3]

Mahatma Gandhi preached and practiced a "voluntary agrarian simplicity" as an alternative to the model of mass production and mass consumption in India. In the United States, Aldo Leopold and Wendell Berry articulated a "land ethic." Among others, Berry—a farmer-poet from Kentucky—argued that we cannot preserve wildness by making wilderness preserves. Informed by an agroecological ethic in which we consider agriculture as the art of producing food locally while at the same time being stewards of the fields and forests as one single unit of production, a more tenable and enduring way of preserving nature might be possible. The preservation of nature would be combined with farming methods that replenish the land, returning what is vital back to nature.

Among ecological ethnicities there is a constant fine-tuning of human needs according to the dynamics of an ecosystem and simultaneously an effort to alter nature according to new social dynamics. The key feature governing this delicate human-nature interaction is the acceptance that humans cannot survive at the expense of nature. At the same time, the so-called wilderness cannot survive without humans creating a balance between who uses it, how it is used, and for what purpose. In the absence of this delicate balance, we find the kind of dilemma the deep ecology movement has faced globally. In the U.S. Northwest, loggers have lost their employment when nature lovers have tried to save the spotted owl; in the Amazon, rubber-tappers have lost their source of subsistence when their habitat was fenced off as wildlife or biodiversity preserves.

Who Saves Whom?

Perhaps my views are informed by the way I grew up in the rural landscape of mountainous Nepal. Having been born to a peasant family in a remote mountain village in midwestern Nepal, I grew up in the hilly country that straddles terraced farms and

FIGURE I. A typical household integrating farm and forest in Nepal. (Pramod Parajuli)

forests, mountains and river valleys. The landscape that figured strongly in my child-hood consciousness included the Himalayan range of Macchapuchhare (the famous Fishtail mountain overlooking the Pokhara town) and Annapurna (the mountain sup-posed to be the abode of grain harvests) in the north. To my mind, and for other peas-ants of this region, the fields, crops, climate, and our own lives as peasants were inex-tricably linked. I often wondered if the Himalayas and other mountains belonged to me and if I had to protect them. Or was it the other way around? I had no doubt that I belonged to the mountains and that they were protecting me. Similarly, the Mende rice cultivators in Sierra Leone live from the forest but do not see themselves as standing over it, either to exploit or to conserve it. For them the forest is not "out there" as an endangered piece of land. They do not see themselves as called upon to "save the for-est," as the conservationists do. Instead, Paul Richards has found that in local eyes, the relationship is the other way around—the community is under the protection of the forest.[4]

But I am not merely trying to project a harmonious picture of a remote mountain village life. Many cracks in our so-called Shangri-la tranquility had surfaced by the early 1960s when I was growing up. I vividly recall my mother telling me that we were approaching a *yuga* (a time period or historical episode) in which cows would no longer stand on four legs. There would be one-footed cows roaming the streets. She told me that during the Satya Yuga, cows had four legs, but they gradually lost another leg during each of the next two yugas, the Dwapar and Treta Yugas. My father, who is a pandit, later suggested that in the Vedas (the most ancient texts for the Hindus), there is mention of the one-footed bull being alive in the Kali Yuga.

I often wonder what relevance my mother's metaphor of the one-legged cow could have for today. For her, the one-legged cow was a sure sign of the upcoming erosion of moral ecology. Her Kali Yuga epitomized a period when avarice and profit-motivated shortsightedness overrode the long-term sense of responsibility and care. However, in her interpretation of the cyclic cosmic wave of the world, the idea of a one-footed cow was not a permanent feature but a passing phenomenon. She inculcated in me the sense that even this most horrible symptom could be altered.

As I understand it today, my mother's alerting story might refer to how the market economy is overwhelming the nature-based economy or how a social capital of nurturing is being overshadowed by the market economy of profit. Today, in the age of what I call the "ecological phase of capital," the relationship between the market economy and wilderness or other sources of biotic wealth is a key area of concern. The perspectives of my childhood now offer me insight as I contemplate notions of the wild and wilderness, "forest" and farm, civilization and modern environment, and their rise and fall in the currents of global capital. Little did I know during my childhood that at some point in my life, farms, forests, and the wild would be devalued and contested—demanded for the circulation of capital as well as needed to provide the biomass for peasant life. This particular rupture in my own reality sets the context for my present thinking with respect to what I have called the "sociality of nature" and the "naturalness of the social."

As my colleague Frederique Apffel-Marglin has suggested, the nature-culture divide, embedded in Cartesian rationality, implies a severing of the emotions and sensibilities one feels in relation to one's immediate space. Although such a rationality might have been most instrumental to serve the industrial mode of production, it is incapable of enveloping the performative and rhetorical functions of magic and ritual in peasant life. It is built upon the dualism of efficacious, instrumental action versus rhetorical and/or performative action. In peasant cultures, humans are not the only agents for rationality; other beings are equally active in cognition and dialogue. There is no such strict division between the material and the ideational, the subject and the object, the literal and the symbolic. In other words, "there is no ontological cleft between the world and the mind."[5]

The separation between the "wild" and the "domestic" is at the core of industrial life. In contemporary suburban life, the overtly denaturalized mall offers the gadgets that are of the cultural realm, while the parks and sanctuaries are supposed to offer "raw" nature. But the park is not a break from urban life; it is the extension of it in a different form. As Shiv Visvanathan comments,

> It is the economics of aesthetics that captures the two basic roles of the park today. There is first the relation of production to consumption and second of production to preservation. Here nature is preserved not only to be consumed by tourists but kept in reserve for later industrial use. Preservation thus combines both the function of maintenance for later production and consumption through leisure and recreation.[6]

This is the model to which environmental organizations such as the Nature Conservancy and the Sierra Club subscribe. For them, humanity stands out, and what remains is the environment. The struggle is to save a piece of the environment for future generations so that they can either enjoy it in their leisure time or use it to learn about the almost extinct biotic world.

In my own home district of Chitwan, Nepal, this "arcadia" and "laboratory" mode of nature conservation—in this case, the temptation to protect wildlife for profit from tourism—has caused many predicaments and much unintended human suffering.

Crocodiles Eat the Fish and Tourist Dollars Eat the Crocodile

Today, the pervasiveness of a particular idea of wilderness is rather daunting. Not only are the parks and sanctuaries, wilderness and biological reserves, sprouting up all over North America, they have also begun to spread like locusts in the so-called developing countries as well. So far, 3.2 percent of the earth's land surface has already been closed for natural parks and sanctuaries and other reserves. According to one estimate, India has already created 66 national parks and 421 sanctuaries spread over 25 biotic provinces and covering 3.3 percent of its land. And there are future plans to increase this to 147 national parks and 633 sanctuaries, covering 5.6 percent of the country's land. India's dilemma is that within a mere 2 percent of the world's land area, it hosts 15 percent of the world's human population and 14 percent of the world's livestock population.

So far, Nepal has created fourteen protected areas, covering at least 10 percent of the country's land mass, and there are plans to extend these protected areas. Part of Nepal's showcase of nature conservation is its first established park, the Royal Chitwan National Park (RCNP). Established in 1973, this park covers an area of 932 square kilometers within the Chitwan district. Among other restrictions it has imposed on residents who live adjacent to it, the park has banned fishing rights to traditional fisherfolk, such as the Mushars, Botes, Kumhals, and Darais. These are the groups of indigenous peoples who opted to live in the river valleys and eke out their livelihoods from the bounties of the rivers and the nearby forests. Before bridges were built, these people worked as ferrymen and had developed extensive knowledge about the currents and contours of the rivers and the seasonal upstream and downstream movements of the fish. They used to fish abundantly for themselves as well as for other populations in exchange for grain. Now they have been denied fishing rights under the pretext that their fish harvesting would reduce the number of fish to such an extent that crocodiles would not have enough to eat and consequently would decline in number. Peasants of Chitwan have expressed their dilemma in the following commentary: "Crocodiles eat our fish, and the tourist dollars eat the crocodile."

The RCNP has also imposed restrictions on the grazing rights of other peasant communities, creating a fodder shortage for domestic animals. Again, most hard-hit by these restrictions are the Kumhals, Botes, Tharus, and Darais, whose large number of cattle is the basis of their agrarian economy. Keeping hundreds of cattle and putting them in different parts of their land was the best way to fertilize the fields. And these cattle were nourished in the *gauchars* (the area for cattle grazing—*gau* meaning "cow" and *char* meaning "where they graze"). These pastures, usually located between the river and the forest, were considered common lands and were regulated according to the rules of the community. As these commons and forests were annexed into the RCNP, peasants were adversely caught up in the "high-input, low-output" spiral of modern agriculture. Buddhi Ram Darai, a landholder farmer from the Darai ethnic group, comments on this transformation:

> As far as I can remember, we were not using chemicals in agricultural production. People used to have plenty of cattle, and therefore they had enough fertilizer for their land. My family had four to five hundred cattle. We used to put the cattle out in the land for some days. That process is called *molne* [literally, "to fertilize the soil"]. Even the wild animals were thought to make the land fertile. In this process, we keep the animals in some portion of the land for some time then shift them into another portion until the whole field gets fertilized.
>
> Once we started to use chemical fertilizer, the yield was very good for the first few years. After that, the production started to decline. My father then thought that they should not use chemical fertilizer. We reverted back to the old system of putting the cattle out in the land. But after the government started its agricultural extension pro-

gram, we again started to use the chemicals. Some extension workers from Gram Vikas [Village Development] came and stayed with us. They told us about the chemical fertilizer and why it is good for farming. They even gave us the fertilizer for free. Meanwhile, grazing lands were occupied, and we couldn't keep enough cattle to produce enough manure.

A drastic reduction in the circulation of organic matter in the soil resulted from the enclosure of the commons. Darais, Tharus, and Kumhals told me that they had to reduce the number of cattle from an average of about one hundred per household to merely three or four within a short period of time, between 1955 and 1960. With the closing off of the commons for the park and with settlers from the hills laying claim to parts of the land, their livelihood and community structure, which revolves around a mixture of herding, farming, fishing, hunting, and gathering, has been seriously threatened.

Paradoxically, although Tharus are denied access to pastureland in the RCNP, they are called on to participate in the park in another capacity. One of the main features supplied by the RCNP is the much-publicized spectacle of watching the tiger come to hunt the timid buffalo. Yet the tigers of the Chitwan Valley can be elusive in the absence of propitiation by Tharu priests. Bikram Gurao (one of the surviving Tharu priests) told me this in the summer of 1996:

> About ten years ago, tigers stopped coming to the site where the buffalo were being kept for them. This disturbed the tourist industry because this ritualized scene was one of the main attractions of the Tiger Tops industry. The manager then called on me to ask if I could do something to make the tigers come. I propitiated the sites with the traditional Tharu ritual, and instantly a dozen tigers began to roar. The Tiger Tops business continued as usual. I hope the Tiger Tops managers know that tigers do not come after tourist dollars; they still belong to Tharus.

Tharus believe that the tigers and other animals in the Chitwan Park are still linked to them in a magical symbiosis. Akin to my mother's sense of the changing and decaying of the *yugas,* Tharus are witnessing the "whirlwinding" of their world—their belief of the Rapti Valley (also known as Chitwan) as an area of abundance being turned upside down. Tharus told us about the many caves that had protected their settlements from floods. Tharu settlements are interspersed between the Rapti and Narayani River systems. When monsoon floods approached their settlements, they told us, drums were beaten inside the caves, and the people could hear it. The Churia hill range located south of the Rapti River was their grazing land, which today is enclosed within the Royal Chitwan National Park. As for my mother, the whole *yuga* has changed for them as well. Many have also forgotten the magic that helped them befriend this swampy and forested area of the Rapti Valley.

The Sacred and the Profane

Seen from the peasant perspective, Indian ecological historian Ramachandra Guha identifies two fundamental flaws in the modern model of nature conservation. First, it confuses the American frontier ethic—what one might call "cut-and-run" agriculture and grazing—with agriculture as a culture, a traditional mode of livelihood. Second, it is symptomatic of the sharp separation of the material and spiritual domains in wilderness thinking. It artificially separates what is considered as the "human realm" from what is a "natural realm." Not only is this model reductionist and thus unfit for the rest of the world, it has caused disastrous consequences as well.

For a majority of people who eke out their livelihoods from nature's economy, the widely held ideas that nature can be preserved in wilderness and that wilderness is what is untouched by humans are simply untenable. Historical examples clearly illustrate that this notion of nature is very much a cultural construct. As William Cronon has commented, "The removal of Indians to create an 'uninhabited wilderness' [in nineteenth-century United States]—uninhabited as never before in the human history of the place—reminds us just how invented, just how constructed, the American wilderness really is."[7] A parallel can be found in India's history, when the British colonial administration began to suggest the enclosing of forests using the rationale that Adivasi (tribals) and rural peasants had kept *sarna* groves. But the notion of sarna and that of a protected park or sanctuary are far from the same; they embody different intents, contents, and functions. With regard to the sacred grove of the goddess Harachandi in coastal Orissa, Frederique Apffel-Marglin and I have commented that it would be wrong to say that this so-called sacred grove is sacred because the trees are the goddess and cannot be cut for use. The trees are indeed the goddess, but so are the earth and the sea, and these are definitely used by farmers and fishermen. The earth and the sea can also be qualified by the word *sacred* since they are worshiped not only in the form of the goddess Harachandi in her temple, but also directly with offerings in the fields at various moments in the agricultural cycle or with offerings to the sea.[8]

The sacredness of these groves cannot be taken as a proof of nonutilitarian attitudes or practices. Herein lies a profound difference between forest preserves, parks, wildlife sanctuaries, and other biodiversity preserves, on the one hand, and the sacred groves of the peasant economy, on the other. Although both the sacred grove and modern preserves are set aside and not used for human consumption, the sacred grove differs emphatically in its relation to those parts of the environment that are used for human ends. Sacred groves are in fact the sites where the community as a whole performs rituals and regenerates itself during every annual crop or tree cycle.

With all due respect to John Muir's and Edward Abbey's uncompromising visions in favor of nature conservation, their urge to protect a nature that is "untouched" is not affordable in rural South Asia. Muir, in his love for pristine nature, wrote that "sheep were locusts with hoofs" and that "Native Americans are nature pillagers." It is becoming very clear that we will not be able to "keep the Yosemite as it was" without perpetuating the already tenuous logic of social justice. Ecological ethnicities seem to offer a different message: "No nature without social justice." Obviously, there is no hope of saving nature without a proper guarantee of social justice for those who produce directly from nature's economy.

Nurturing and Being Nurtured

How then do ecological ethnicities make sense of the nature-culture divide? What is for them the appropriate technology of nature use? Let me try to illustrate this by using the rubric of "relational" and "rational." In the relational mode, a preference is given to the ethic of care and the cultivation of a reciprocal relationship between humans' need to create a "culture out of nature" and perhaps nature's need to be nurtured by humans. I am borrowing the metaphor of "nurturing" from intellectuals in the Andean Peasant Technologies Project (PRATEC), who have articulated a Peruvian peasant discourse in which Andean peasant technology is interpreted as a marker of civilization that is attuned not to the modernist ideas of the nature-culture divide but to a relationship of nurturing.⁹ By a nurturing relationship, they mean that peasants can function only as midwives and nurturers in their *chacras* (cultivated fields) so as to be birthed and nurtured in return by Pachamama, the mother earth, as well as all the *apus* (sacred mountains) and other sacred beings. Life is a constant process of nurturing and letting oneself be nurtured among peoples and the many beings of the *pacha* (local world)— the sun, the moon, the constellations, the plants, the animals, the clouds, the winds, the rainbows, and so on.

Such a view demonstrates the recognition of nature's subjectivity—as opposed to the Judeo-Christian and capitalist tradition in which nature is merely an object for human intervention and commodification. According to Eduardo Grillo, an Andean peasant community is not simply a human environment; rather, it comprises all who live together in proximity. Nor is a *chacra* merely the place where the soil, the water, the microclimate, and the plants are nurtured; it is also the ritual space where humans converse and reciprocate with the deities, the ancestors, and all the elements of the natural world.[10]

Such practices of care and renewal between humans and their "farm-forest-pasture continuum" offer new insights for the long-standing debates over nature and culture. The discussion then is not necessarily limited to whether nature determines culture or whether nature is simply a cultural construction. What becomes significant are the precise areas of intersection and interdependence between the two. While ecological anthropologists have emphasized that nature is shaping culture, cultural anthropologists have insisted that culture imposed its own meaning on nature. However, both are informed by the notion of a nature-culture divide that is at the heart of the modernist paradigm; both positions have become engaged in a deadlocked battle over semantics and corresponding interpretations, obfuscating any understanding of how nature and culture might actually intersect and interpenetrate.[11]

This notion of nurturing is not predicated on accurate human predictions about the intricacies of natural phenomena; it is the conversation and mutual understanding between human collectivities and nonhuman collectivities. Situated as mutual nurturers, humans cannot treat nature merely as "sublime" or "divine" either. Maybe what links them is the notion of a community where human collectivities and nonhuman collectivities dwell together and nurture each other. Thus we might replace the notion of nature conservation with the notion of a community of nature users and preservers. This would shift the ground on which the "nature talk" of the conservation discourse stands. For this sort of nature talk still points its finger at overpopulation and identifies ecological ethnicities as "overbreeders" or practitioners of slash-and-burn agriculture.

The Art and Aesthetic of Dwelling on the Land

Perhaps Wendell Berry's observations in *Home Economics* resonate much closer to the sentiments of ecological ethnicities. He writes that we cannot live in nature without altering it: "The only thing we have to preserve nature with is culture; the only thing we have to preserve wildness with is domesticity." If people cannot live in nature without changing it, people cannot preserve wildness by making wilderness reserves either. So, according to Berry, the only option we have is to use nature without abusing it—to use it and, through that mode of use, to enhance it. A wilderness ethic must be tied to what we produce, what we eat, and how we live in communities. Forest economies can thrive if value is added to the forest through small, local, nonpolluting industries. A community can enhance the diversity of its forest species while also finding ways to make furniture and tools using those diverse species of trees. In other words, wild and domestic culture can and must coexist.

Aldo Leopold's call for a "land ethic" and Mahatma Gandhi's plea for "voluntary agrarian simplicity" are also premised on humans' enduring but careful interaction with nature. In other words, as Guha has aptly stated, an agroecological mode searches for "a golden mean of stewardship and sustainable use."[12] Gandhi's selective dismissal of the British romantic tradition might be instructive to highlight some key differences I am posing between the "relational" and the "rational." As David Arnold and Ramachandra Guha note,

> Gandhi's ashram at Sevagram could not have been further, in an intellectual as in a scenic sense, from Ruskin's lakeside home at Brantwood. Rather, Gandhi's environmentalism had its roots in a deep antipathy to urban civilization and a belief in self-sufficiency, in self-abnegation and denial rather than wasteful consumption. Gandhi was not going back to nature but to the village and to the peasantry as the heart and soul of India, to rural asceticism and harmony as against urban bustle and industrial life.[13]

In Chitwan Nepal, Jharkhand in India, and the Peruvian Andes, the "relational" is privileged over the "rational." Julio Valladolid of PRATEC has documented how the Andean peasants predict whether a certain agricultural cycle is going to get enough rain or not by looking at the flowering of the cactus. The role that Tularam Gahire attributes to wild birds in Nepal for regenerating a robust forest in the farm indicates a similar kind of modest participation of humans in the larger natural order. These examples suggest to me that human technologies can be fine-tuned to earth's technologies.

Such peasant practices and technologies try to balance the agroecosystems with the larger ecosystem—an art of balancing the parts with the whole. For ecological historian Donald Worster, an ecosystem is a subset of the global economy of nature—a local or regional system of plants and animals working together to create the means of survival. An agroecosystem, as the name suggests, is an ecosystem reorganized for agricultural purposes. It is a domesticated ecosystem, which entails a restructuring of the trophic processes in nature, that is, the processes of food and energy flow in the economy of living organisms.[14] Obviously, an agroecosystem has to alter an ecosystem. The productive energies in one ecosystem might be forced to serve more exclusively a set of conscious purposes often located outside it—namely, the feeding and prospering of a group of humans. However, in order to survive for very long, the agroecosystem must achieve a balance between what it draws out and what it returns to the larger ecosystem. Today, achieving this precise balance is the key struggle for ethnoecological communities as they are pushed head-on to face the monetization of the very basis of their lives—land, soil, plants, earthworms, and seeds. The fact that over five million Adivasi and Dalit women in India eke out their very livelihoods by selling firewood and forest products in the market demonstrates the seriousness of the situation.

Ecological activists in South Asia are coming to realize that the ecological ethnicities are losing at both ends in the battle between environmentalists and pro-development people. Medha Patkar, the leader of the Narmada Bachao Andolan, is confronting the dilemma in the Narmada Valley. She wonders whether conservationists who talk of wildlife protection, on one hand, and use toilet paper, plastic, and air conditioning, on the other, can be credible. The Adivasi's concerns are entirely different and are sometimes inconceivable to the city-bred activists. Medha Patkar states,

> What the tribals are saying today is, don't kick us out of the national parks and sanctuaries because you are the ones who have already destroyed the forest. The little which remains today is because we are living here as nonconsuming protectors, users but not ambitious users like you. The whole problem is basically one of lifestyle. There can be no solution unless the conflicts between lifestyles, between immediate and future interests, are resolved. Because even when a certain section of the population says the wildlife and forest should be preserved, they have not changed their basic vision of life.

Restoration of the Ecosystem or the Renewal of Community?

In the way ecological ethnicities are positioned today vis-à-vis the global economy, the renewal of nature and the renewal of local culture have become inextricable. The duality of this enterprise has made the task extremely complex and perhaps an unachievable goal. As Shiv Visvanathan comments, the choice is between putting nature in the hands of the state and the nature-conservation bureaucracy for "restoration" or giving it back to the community for "renewal." If the former strategy reduces the park problem to a strictly managerial one, the latter strategy makes it a question of livelihood, dwelling, survival, and human rights. In the so-called free-market spaces of the global body politic, the questions of who saves nature, who nurtures it, and who gets nurtured by it are becoming unavoidable. Even if we give it the fullest benefit of the doubt, the bureaucratic management strategy might restore the ecosystem but cannot renew it—in the sense of *renewal* as a process of keeping both natural and human labor intact in the local community. Visvanathan's distinction between restoration and renewal is analogous to the distinction I have made between the rational and the relational:

> You restore a painting or a church like a material artifact. But in general, culture—and also nature—cannot be "restored" in this sense. They have to be renewed. Renewal is never totally cyclical. It seeks to recover what there was but is also open to novelty by combination.[15]

For ecological ethnicities, "nature" is the place where they work, live, and play, produce and reproduce; it is integral to their lives. Thus, as much as nature can be constructed through dominant discourses and priorities, a people's version of nature also can be reclaimed through environmental action and struggle. For example, if the fisherfolk of Chitwan regained access to the rivers for fishing and their economy was able to continue, the very idea of who owns the fish in the Narayani and Rapti Rivers would eventually have to change. Then their new mode of nature use might also alter the tourist economy. In this new organization of fishing, the power of the tourist economy to determine the species composition of a region would be redefined.

Ultimately, it seems, the challenge is in integrating the wild, wilderness, and the land in our bodies as well as our minds. Having "land in our mind" is not as easy as it sounds, especially in overproducing and overconsuming societies. According to Scott Sanders, a bioregional consciousness means bearing your place in mind, keeping track of its conditions and needs, committing yourself to its care.

It is indeed ironic that humankind has once again tried to solve the so-called crisis of nature without really recognizing how much of "us" is involved in that nature. It is perhaps the separation of "us" from nature that bewilders our approach to nature. In 1970, radical environmentalists Theodore Roszak and Paul Shepard hoped that ecology would be a subversive science, for it was supposed to be sensible, holistic, receptive, trustful, and deeply grounded in aesthetic intuition. It was considered to be a radical deviation from traditional sciences. By 1998, upon publication of the special issue of *Terra Nova*—twenty-six years after the first Earth Day and more than half a decade after the Earth Summit—it had become obvious that ecology has not turned out to be such a subversive science. Perhaps ecology failed in this regard because it could not transcend the very nature-culture divide embedded in the scientific tradition and instead became yet another science in which humans are set apart from nature. In the uphill struggle to achieve legitimacy for ecological concerns, perhaps we accepted that what environmentalists defend is the environment but not nature.

Raymond Williams has aptly noted that the decisive form of human struggle is the resistance to capitalism. However, the preceding discussions indicate that those acts of resistance, including the desire to save nature or preserve wilderness, are futile because they are not informed or equipped with an alternative vision that does not subscribe to a rationality in which culture and nature, human needs and nature's processes, are seen as separate concerns.

Isn't it ironic, asks Neil Evernden, that we consider the California condor saved when it is in captivity? He goes on to argue that the California condor can be considered saved in captivity only if we define a California condor as a feather-crusted bundle of meat. But if our concept of the condor includes its context, then it has not been saved at all because we have accepted the destruction of the creature's habitat, the creature's place. And once that place is gone, the animal, too, in its contextual sense, is gone.

It is akin to saying that some aspect of the culture of the Adivasi in India or the fisherfolk in the Chitwan Valley might be useful or fashionable to display in a museum or in the tourist industry, but that the survival and continuation of their culture as a living and thriving way of life does not warrant protection or acknowledgment. And indeed, the Tharus and Botes are invited to Tiger Tops in Chitwan to perform "authentic" Tharu dances for tourists, and the Tharu *guraons* (priests) are invited to bring the tigers back, but the Tharus as such have been excluded from the park. As the saying goes in Mexico, the dominant mind-set might appreciate "the Indian dress to look at but not the Indian who wears it." That is why every effort is being made to "Mexicanize the Indians" rather than to "Indianize the Mexicans." By the same logic, the plans for creating wilderness preserves designed to save the tigers or the rhinos will simply be cosmetic dressing and museum displays unless these projects also save the fisherfolk, forest dwellers, and peasants with whom they have shared these habitats for centuries.

NOTES

1 Although our research team (which included coresearcher Elizabeth Enslin and research associates Anil Bhattarai and Jagannath Adhikary) started this farm to create a model of a sustainable Nepali peasant farm, people still considered it an "American" or "Japanese" experiment. This popular conception might have evolved because I had just returned to

Chitwan after having spent a long period of time in the United States or because people associated our work with two other earlier permaculture experiments in adjacent villages.

2 See Pramod Parajuli, "Ecological Ethnicity in the Making: Developmentalist Hegemonies and Emergent Identities in India," *Identities: Global Studies in Culture and Power* 3/1–2 (1996): 15–59; and idem, "Beyond Capitalized Nature: Ecological Ethnicity as an Arena of Conflict in the Regime of Globalization," *Ecumene: A Journal of Environment, Culture, Meaning* 5/2 (1998): 186–217.

3 George Collier and Elizabeth Quaratiello, *Basta! Land and Zapatista Rebellion in Chiapas* (Oakland, CA: Food First, 1994), p. 44.

4 Paul Richards, "Saving the Rainforest? Contested Futures in Conservation," in Sandra Wallman, ed., *Contemporary Futures: Perspectives from Social Anthropology* (London: Routledge, 1992), pp. 139–52.

5 Frederique Apffel-Marglin, "Introduction: Rationality and the World," in Frederique Apffel-Marglin and Steve Marglin, eds., *Decolonizing Knowledge: From Development to Dialogue* (New York: Clarendon Press, 1996), p. 9.

6 Shiv Visvanathan, "Footnotes to Vavilov: An Essay on Gene Diversity," in Frederique Apffel-Marglin and Steve Marglin, eds., *Decolonizing Knowledge: From Development to Dialogue* (New York: Clarendon Press, 1996), pp. 335–36.

7 William Cronon, "The Trouble with Wilderness; or Getting back to the Wrong Nature," in William Cronon, ed., *Uncommon Ground: Toward Reinventing Nature* (New York: W. W. Norton, 1996), p. 79.

8 See Frederique Apffel-Marglin and Pramod Parajuli, "Sacred Grove and Ecology: Ritual and Science," in Mary Evelyn Tucker and Christopher Chapple, eds., *Hinduism and Ecology* (Cambridge, MA: Center for the Study of World Religions, Harvard University, 2000).

9 See Frederique Apffel-Marglin with PRATEC (Andean Peasant Technologies Project), eds., *The Spirit of Regeneration: Andean Culture Confronting Western Notions of Development* (London: Zed Books, 1998).

10 Eduardo Grillo Fernandez, "Development or Cultural Affirmation in the Andes?" in ibid., pp. 124–45.

11 See P. Parajuli, "Discourse on Knowledge, Dialogue and Diversity: Peasant Worldviews and the Science of Conservation," *Worldviews: An International Journal of Environment, Culture and Meaning* 1/3 (1997): 189–210.

12 Ramachandra Guha, "Toward a Cross-Cultural Environmental Ethic," *Alternatives* 15 (1990): 434.

13 David Arnold and Ramachandra Guha, "Introduction: Themes and Issues in the Environmental History of South Asia," in David Arnold and Ramachandra Guha, eds., *Nature, Culture and Imperialism: Essays on the Environmental History of South Asia* (Delhi: Oxford University Press, 1995), p. 19.

14 Donald Worster, *The Wealth of Nature* (New York: Oxford University Press, 1993), p. 52.

15 Shiv Visvanathan, "From Dudhwa with Love," *Seminar* 426 (1995): 18.

Few people even know the definition of the term "West"; and where is its location?—
phantom-like it flies before us as we travel.   —GEORGE CATLIN

2   the unpaintable west

Figures in a Landscape

What do the figures in George Caleb Bingham's painting *Fur Traders Descending the
Missouri* mean? An old man, a boy, a bear cub chained to the prow of a pirogue floating
downstream on a calm river in some golden morning of a past that no longer has a
history.[1]

They gaze at us. The boy leans on a skin-covered box that holds the cache of furs,
his chin rests on his hand, a gun is under one arm, a mallard he has shot beside him.
His face is dreamy, sweet. The old man glares at us. The smoke from his short pipe
drifts behind him. The bear looks at us with the mute stare of animals that we can
neither enter nor interpret. The reflections extend themselves from the bottom of the
boat, lose their outlines in the smooth water.

Because of the reflections we don't know if the painter George Caleb Bingham saw
them or simply imagined them.

Stillness

The rift the boy's gun has made in the morning has closed. Mist blurs the lines between sky and tree-lined shore and water. Or maybe sky and shore and water are only
now forming themselves in that gold of a morning, composing themselves out of this
stillness.

FIGURE 2. George Caleb Bingham, *Fur Traders Descending the Missouri*, 1845, oil on canvas. (The Metropolitan Museum of Art, Morris K. Jesup Fund, 1933 [33.61])

The river will run beyond the frame the canvas has made of this moment.[2] Flow on down to the shanties along the wharves of St. Louis, to the cheap hotels and eating houses, the dives and the river women. For now we have only the stillness.

Yet a tension remains underneath the painting's resolution. The snags—the chained animal and the disturbing glare of the old man—evoke an unpainted presence at the edges of the canvas. Rivers come from somewhere, too. And so, in order to tell one story, I will begin with another.

The Great Unknown

In the fall of 1804, where the Knife River flows into the Missouri in the present state of North Dakota, the American explorers Meriwether Lewis and William Clark reached the earth lodges of the Mandan Indians. It was here, among these friendly farmers and buffalo hunters, that they would stay through the winter, preparing for the expedition into the Great Unknown, to the Missouri headwaters and across the divide into the waters of the Columbia and, they hoped, as far as the Pacific Coast. They had reached the edge of an imaginary landscape. Beyond the Mandans there were only things they had heard tell of. The Stony Mountains. The river the French called the Rochejhone. Another river called the Oregon, which mapmakers thought would provide the long-sought inland passage to India. For everything was conjecture.

That spring, with a complement of picked men, a store of medicines and trade goods for the Indians, a collapsible boat, Clark's slave York, a French-Canadian transla-tor named Toussaint Charbonneau, Charbonneau's young Shoshone wife, and the son who had been born to her in the Mandan lodges that winter, Lewis and Clark set out from the lodges of the Mandan. They would see the rivers feeding into the Missouri—the Knife, the Rochejhone, the Milk, the River That Scolds All Others. The Rocky Moun-tains. Finally, the Columbia itself. And then the Pacific Ocean.

Their project was to make the imaginary landscape real. So at every opportunity they measured, they observed, they drew. And they wrote. Always they wrote. In sand-storms, attacked by mosquitos, weakened from dysentery, bitten by fleas, cold, hungry, they wrote. They wrote when the ink froze in their pens. And when the expedition ended in St. Louis two and a half years later, after the balls and the dinners and the speeches, they were still writing.

Constantly, a running thread through the journals, with their careful descriptions of new animal and plant life, of the Indians, their habits, of the geography of new plains and mountains and the rivers that fed the great Missouri, is the theme of won-der.

It was the essential purpose of the expedition to describe this wonder. Sitting across from each other, the whites and the Indians interrogated each other through the me-dium of maps, a kind of language beyond words. Maps smudged with charcoal from the fire on elk skins or on reed mats or traced with sticks in the sand, embedded with the memories of the Indians of cold and heat, of hungry bivouacs and plains plentiful with meat, of sights seen at eye level and canoe level and from the backs of their po-nies. Then William Clark dipped his quill in ink and drew the symbols on a page of his journal, coordinating what he had seen with the observations of the planets and the stars. Thus they knew where they were, and from whence they had come.

Or did they? For they were entering a world of such strangeness that once, Meriwether Lewis, hunting on the Medicine River, pursued by grizzlies and buffalo, missing shots at bobcat, thought it might be a dream. (The spines of prickly pear jabbing into the soles of his feet through his moccasins, reminded him it wasn't.) Always they matched what they had heard—told by Indians to other Indians, then translated through the French Canadians—with what they saw. And always what they saw was new.

Meriwether Lewis at the Great Falls of the Missouri:

> after wrighting this imperfect discription I again viewed the falls and was so much disgusted with the imperfect idea which it conveyed of the scene that I determined to draw my pen across it and begin agin, but then reflected that I could not perhaps succeed better than pening the first impressions of the mind; I wished for the pencil of Salvator Rosa or the pen of Thompson, that I might be enabled to give to the enlightened world some just idea of this truly magnifficent and sublimely grand object, which has from the commencement of time been concealed from the view of civilized man; but this was fruitless and vain.[3]

Beautifull. Grand. Sublime. Specticle. Confronting the magnitude of this new landscape, the language of observation gives way to the poetics of the late eighteenth century. It was Clark, the less literary of the two captains, who called one scene of river and ravines *romantick.*

There is always, for the reader, a special poignancy in these journals. For if we see these scenes through the eyes of Meriwether Lewis and William Clark, we see them as well with our own: the poignancy of these first views of wonder, of the first meetings with tribes who had never seen a white man before, is that they are doomed at the moment of their telling. It will never be new again.

The Beautiful and the Sublime

To name something means to have it in your power. Meditating on his recent discoveries at the Great Falls of the Missouri, Lewis compares two scenes:

> ... nor could I for some time determine on which of those two great cataracts [Colter Falls and Rainbow Falls] to bestoe the palm, on this [Colter Falls] or that which I had discovered yesterday; at length I determined between these two great rivals for glory that this was *pleasingly beautifull,* while the other was *sublimely grand.*[4]

In adopting the categories of eighteenth-century aesthetics to attempt to describe this landscape, Lewis sets up a dialectic that has, imbedded in its terms, a meditation on power.

The sublime, that reminder of the awesome grandeur of God, of the littleness and contingency of man, cannot be possessed. Indeed, the sublime possesses you. The author of the sublime is the masculine god who engraves the words of the laws with his finger on the tables of stone: to gaze on the terrible infinite without the mediation of a prophet or the veil of aesthetic distance is to perish. It is only beauty that can be gazed upon without such distancing. And beauty, for Edmund Burke, who fixed these terms for his generation, is above all things feminine:

> Observe that part of a beautiful woman where she is perhaps the most beautiful, about the neck and breasts; the smoothness; the softness; the easy and insensible swell; the variety of the surface, which is never for the smallest space the same; the deceitful maze, through which the unsteady eye slides giddily, without knowing where to fix, or whither it is carried.[5]

To gaze on the beautiful is to possess it. But, says Burke—and the statement is surprising—it is not commonly imagined how near love approaches to contempt.

Meriwether Lewis and William Clark came to the Great Unknown to map, to describe, to name. Because they came as men of science, and, when they were overcome by splendor, as poets, they did not defile what they saw, but the very naming of that wonder, in its innocence and joy, began the process of its destruction. Henceforth known, the wilderness was ready to be exploited. After an arduous trek across the divide and the dangerous descent of the rapids of the Columbia, in a village near Vancouver, Washington, the captains met Indians wearing sailor jackets and overalls, with muskets and tin powder flasks. Beyond the falls of the Columbia, they met their own language. It was the name *J. Bowman*, tattooed on the arm of an Indian woman. Already they had begun to hear a few words of English from the Indians. Soon they heard more: *musquit, powder, shot, nife, damned rascal, sun of a bitch*. Lewis, the soldier, knew very well what Burke had meant about love and contempt: when the Wahkakum women of the Columbia Valley knelt, their cedar bark aprons parted, and what the Americans called "the battery of Venus" was, in Lewis's words, "not altogether impervious to the penetrating eye of the amorite." Even in Eden such batteries were not to be stormed without casualties. In his stores of medical supplies Meriwether Lewis carried four pewter penis syringes.[6]

The *Philosophe*

In the mind of Thomas Jefferson were stately rooms, with busts of Newton, Bacon, and Locke, fiddles, gadgets, cabinets of curiosities, labor-saving devices; libraries of books; porches opening to graceful gardens; and well-ordered fields. The farms tilled by free men fell off into a contested frontier of rough pioneers, distillers of whiskey, breakers of raw land, and then, beyond the Mississippi, a vast unknown—a map with no mountain chains, no arabesques of rivers or stippled forests or tranquil lakes—a blank that extended beyond the Stony Mountains.

Because he was a man of the Enlightenment, Reason shone its ray into the unknown. And so, from his vast reading, Jefferson filled this emptiness beyond the Mississippi with smoking volcanoes and mountains of pure salt, with the lumbering forms of mastodons and giant sloths (in the great chain of being there were no links missing, no final extinctions). And somewhere there was a passage that would open the new republic to its destiny on the shores of the Pacific and that little strip of coast just beginning to be known to English and American sea captains, where the Columbia emptied into the Western Sea.

Lurking about the margins of Jefferson's mind, troubling its moral scheme—a kind of momentary cloud passing across the sunny clarity of his thought—were the slaves. Waiting at table, running errands, padding about the house—did he see in the faces of his secret family, his slave children, a suggestion of his own? Best not to speculate. A powerful mind has powerful locks to put on its out-of-the-way closets and storage-rooms. Unlike the slaves, the Indians, the aboriginal people of the land, interested Jefferson. As with many another Virginia planter, there was a twig for Pocahontas on his family tree, and he assiduously collected Indian vocabularies. For the Indians he had a place in his imaginary landscape.

So, like whites before him, Jefferson sent out medals and certificates and gifts—glass beads, kettles, fishhooks, and blankets—and men in blue coats and brass buttons to announce that the Indian peoples of the new land had a new father. A loving and kindly father, indeed, whose other face was coercion, displacement, threat. Settled on their neat farms in that American pastoral that was Jefferson's dream, blending and perhaps intermarrying with whites whose habits they had adopted and whose religion they now shared, these settled Indians (of course they would be in debt to the white traders) would have much land to sell. And if the red men would not civilize themselves and would not sell, well, as Jefferson pointed out to William Henry Harrison, on the Indiana frontier, the other side of love was fear:

> we presume that our strength and their weakness is now so visible that they must see we have only to shut our hand to crush them, and that all our liberalities to them proceed from motives of pure humanity only. Should any tribe be fool-hardy enough to take up the hatchet at any time, the seizing of the whole country of that tribe, and driving them across the Mississippi, as the only condition of peace, would be an example to others, and a furtherance to our final consolidation.[7]

Having ripped ourselves from the terrible grasp of Mother England, it remained to conquer Mother Nature, and her red children.

The light of Reason that emanated from Jefferson's study made its way across the far reaches of the Missouri watershed, sought an opening through the Stony Mountains, pushed on to the Western Sea, to the horizon of Asia: there, at the edge of the continent, in November of 1805, a handful of American soldiers, a few French-Canadian hunters, a Shoshone Indian woman, and a black slave voted on where to make their winter quarters.

Coming Home

O! how horriable is the day waves brakeing with great violence against the Shore throwing the Water into our Camp &c. all wet and confined to our Shelters.
   —WILLIAM CLARK (November 22, 1805)

The rain continues, with Tremendious gusts of wind, which is Tremendious. The winds violent. Trees falling in every direction, whorl winds, with gusts of rain Hail & Thunder, This kind of weather lasted all day, Certainly one of the worst days that ever was!   —WILLIAM CLARK (December 16, 1805)

It rained all winter long. . . . Rain and more rain in the huddle of shelters they built inside a stockade on the banks of the Lewis and Clark. And the horrible roaring of the waves on the seacoast, and the fleas, and the poor elk. And the miserable Indians with their flattened heads, squatting like frogs around them smoking and farting and clucking their untranslatable language. And the smoke stinging their eyes, and the clothes rotting, and the blankets rotting, and the damp. And the eternal rain. The captain's store of trinkets had shrunk to a few handfuls, and the Indians were unimpressed with the merchandise. They higgled for days over a handful of roots.

Since the expedition's start, Sacagawea had been feeding the men, finding stores of wild artichokes that mice had hidden in the earth, probing for roots with a digging stick, discovering wild licorice, white apples, wild currants—medicinal plants for the men who were constantly sick from malnourishment, bad water, and spoiled food.

When the vote was taken about the expedition's winter quarters, Clark noted in his tally "Janey in favour of a place where there is plenty of Potas." Somewhere along the route, he had taken to calling Sacagawea "Janey." The "Potas"—potatoes—were the *wappato* roots that would become the expedition's staple. Later that November, Sacagawea gave Clark a piece of bread made from flour she had been saving for her child. It was the first bread he had had for months. The flour had become wet and the bread was sour. Clark found it delicious.

At Christmas the captains distributed meager gifts: tobacco for the men who smoked; for those who didn't, a handkerchief. Lewis gave Clark a shirt, drawers, socks. Another of the men gave him a small basket. Sacagawea gave him two dozen white weasel tails.

That spring she had fallen deathly ill, and the captains had doctored her. Once, when Charbonneau had struck her, Clark had intervened. She had not forgotten him.

On the January 6, Clark set out with a party in two canoes to see a whale that had reportedly been washed up at the seashore and perhaps take some of its flesh. While Clark was making his way to the seacoast, on the other side of the continent, Thomas Jefferson, the president of the United States, composed a letter to his children the Cherokees, who had lately visited him, about the virtues of the settled life that they had begun to take up. Already the Cherokees had made much progress. They would need corn mills (Jefferson was big on these), then they would need laws. Then they would need judges. Soon, they would be white. Or something like that. . . . Jefferson sat warm in his study, dreaming of virtuous Cherokees. At Fort Clatsop one of the expedition's men almost had his throat cut by an Indian who wanted to rob him. On the same day, Lewis reported that Clark had reached the great beached whale and found that it had been stripped of every edible part, leaving nothing but a vast skeleton. On the 23rd of March, the corps of volunteers for North Western Discovery started out for home.

Near the end of their journey, after more than two years of hardship in the wilderness, of near-starvation, of clothes that rotted on their backs in the endless rain, and of forced marches and broken pirogues and backbreaking portages, they met in the Mandan villages where they had spent their first winter two trappers from Illinois, who talked John Colter (later becoming perhaps the first white man to see the Yellowstone geysers) into turning back up the river from whence he'd come on a trapping expedition. Henceforth, known, the wilderness was ready to be exploited.

Journey's End

By the 14th of August 1806, the Lewis and Clark expedition had returned to the Mandan villages. Six days later, while floating down the Missouri, Clark took the time to write Charbonneau. There is a poignant urgency in the letter. He was urgent for Sacagawea's security and for the future of her boy, who was in some manner his other self. Clark goes on to offer Charbonneau a piece of land, horses, cows, and hogs if he wishes to live with white people, a horse if he wants to visit his friends in Montreal. He offers much more. He concludes the letter:

> Wishing you and your family great suckcess & with anxious expectations of seing my little danceing boy Baptiest I shall remain your Friend William Clark[8]

On the shores of the Pacific, Sacagawea had taken bread from her child and given it to Clark. Now, floating back to the civilizition of St. Louis, Clark remembered her and the boy. He was no longer a child in the wilderness, but its conqueror.

What Clark had so urgently wished for came to pass. In 1808, Sacagawea and Charbonneau brought the boy to Clark in St. Louis. There Charbonneau tried and failed to settle. We see the last of Sacagawea in the summer of 1811. A journalist on his way up the Missouri to Fort Manuel found himself on the Fur Company steamer with her and Charbonneau:

> The woman, a good creature, of mild and gentle disposition, was greatly attached to the whites, whose manners and airs she tries to imitate; but she had become sickly, and longed to revisit her native country; her husband, also, who had spent many years among the Indians, was become weary of a civilized life.[9]

As it happened, she was going upriver to die. On December 20, 1812, a Missouri Fur Company clerk at Fort Manuel noted in his journal the death from putrid fever of Charbonneau's Snake squaw: "She was a good and the best woman in the fort, aged about 25 years. She left a fine infant girl." Once, importunate, she had demanded to go with the canoes to the Great Water that she had traveled so long to see, and a great fish washed up on its shore. Six years later, dressed in a white woman's clothes, she had died between the world she had been born into and the one she had helped to create.

Toussaint Charbonneau accompanied a few expeditions, including that of Maxmilian of Wied to the upper Missouri in 1833. In 1838, at the age of eighty, he married once more. The girl was a captive Assiniboin of fourteen. There is an account of the magnificent chivaree the men of Fort Clark gave him, with drums, pans, kettles all beating and guns firing. The old man went to bed with his young wife, the fort's clerk wrote, "with the intention of doing his best." What he was, he remained: profane, half-savage, a lover of women, a good hand with *boudin.* He could live no other way. Charbonneau died penniless the following year. It is he or his ghost who stares out at us from Bingham's canvas—brutal, tough, smoking his short pipe—having seen things upriver and in St. Louis perhaps left unsaid.

And what of the boy, his son? Baptiste, or Pomp, or Pompei, as Clark would call him, was adopted by Clark and educated in St. Louis at Catholic schools. Then he turned to the life of the hunter. He might have been a figure out of a romance: the free-spirited child of nature who turns his back on civilization and its charms and returns to the forest. At the age of eighteen, he met young Prince Paul of Württemberg in a traders' village at the mouth of the Kansas. He went to Europe with the prince, traveling, hunting, and learning languages for six years. By 1829 he was back in the West.

He was at the famous trappers' rendezvous of 1833 on the Green River. In 1846, with the coming of the Mexican War, he became a guide for the Mormon Battalion, and at war's end he became *alcalde* of the Mission San Luis Rey. But his half-Indian status did not serve him, for he was sickened by the enslavement of the mission Indians and was implicated in an aborted revolt. The frontier shrank around him, and he went north with the gold fever of '48. The Placer County, California, Directory of 1861 lists him as a clerk in an Auburn hotel, another bit of human debris left beached at the end of the gold rush. In the spring of 1866, he went gold hunting again. He died of pneumonia in eastern Oregon after crossing a swollen stream on the way to Montana.

Destiny

Forty years after Lewis and Clark arrived at the Pacific, when Bingham painted *Fur Traders Descending the Missouri,* the land that the Corps of Discovery had mapped had been criss-crossed by white trappers and empire-builders. The Osage warrior lurking above the river in battle paint, whom Bingham had painted as *Fur Traders'* pendant, had become a nostalgic reminder of a savage past. It is as if, in the bustle of commerce, he had simply become irrelevant. The fur trade had entered its long decline. The streams that flowed down from the Rockies had been trapped out, and much of the game had been driven off. In Europe, the fashion in gentlemen's hats had changed from beaver to silk. The last rendezvous of the fur trappers had been held in 1840. Smallpox, introduced by the Fur Company steamer, had made of the lodges of the friendly Mandan, where Lewis and Clark had spent the winter of 1804–5, one vast desolation. "The scene was horrible," an eyewitness wrote Albert Gallatin in about 1837,

> the large level prairie surrounding the Village had been converted into one great grave yard, whilst hundreds of (loathsome) carcasses . . . lay mouldering on the surface of the earth, emitting fetid exhalations which poisoned the surrounding atmosphere—and made it quite sickening even at a distance of several miles. . . . Thirty one [M]andans only were living at the time I passed their villages."[10]

Soon the buffalo on which the plains tribes' way of life depended would be virtually gone as well, killed by hide hunters, contract hunters for the railroads, United States policy, and the Indians themselves to make way for the cattle that would supplant them. George Catlin, who had traveled through the West painting the Indians, heard of a large band of Sioux who arrived at a fur company fort with the tongues of 1,400 freshly slaughtered buffalo. They traded the tongues for a few gallons of whisky.

The Uses of Nostalgia

The friendly and flowing savage, who is he?
Is he waiting for civilization, or past it and mastering it?
—WALT WHITMAN

Perhaps, we think, it is something like this the old man in Bingham's painting has seen; for he stares out at us with a look of suspicion, bitterness. He looks out of a past and into our future, into Bingham's future as well, for by the time the painting was made, such pirogues were a rarity on the Missouri, and even the great rafts that Bingham was to paint, ornamented with dancing raftsmen and raffish idlers, were already being supplanted by steamboats with their drumming pistons, their churning paddle wheels, and their fire-belching boilers.

Yet Bingham, the Whig, who had stumped for steamboats and railroads and Henry Clay, and who had painted campaign banners for the Indian-fighter William Henry Harrison (if the stories are true, at the Battle of the Thames, Harrison's army inscribed his victory over Tecumseh on a different sort of canvas—the flayed skin of the Indian prophet), painted this sour old man, this chained bear. Painted them, but placed between them, as if to link them and to pacify the terrible aggressions that they stood for, a boy.

Did such a boy belong there, really, at all? He is of a different order than the man and the bear. He wears the same gaudy cloth shirt as his father but the fringed leather pants of the savage world. The chained bear cub at the other end of the pirogue stands for a part of nature that has been subjugated, bounded, named. The boy is both the chained bear cub and the white man's son. Posed between two gazes—the numb gaze of nature that only exists, only suffers, and the gaze of his father, the gaze of history and consciousness—he dreams. The gun loosens in his grasp. He is a figure from the pastoral, from the historyless world of myth, where time stands still.

Remove the boy from the painting. It becomes a different picture. Paradoxical. Disturbing. The old man's glare becomes a question. The bear silhouetted against that golden sky becomes ominous, doubled by its shadow, which hangs darkly from the waterline of the heavily laden boat. Everything is a dissonance—the figures at either end of the boat pull away from each other. A chained animal and a bitter old man.

Bingham's original title for the painting, *French Trader and His Half-Breed Son*, confirms what we have known about the old man and the boy at our first view of the painting. But there is something unpainted here, an absence. If we see a father and son in the pirogue, where is the boy's mother?

Bingham might have painted her. She might have been another version of the coy and sentimental Indian maiden of Alfred Jacob Miller's *Trapper's Bride.*[11] ("I saw the marriage of the trapper in the far-/west," Walt Whitman wrote, in the same vein, "the bride was a red girl . . . / She had long eyelashes, her head was bare, her coarse straight/ locks descended upon her voluptuous limbs and reach'd/to her feet . . . ")[12] But Bingham does not paint her. Her absence calls up a deeper resonance, more complicated, and more disturbing. [13]

"I believe," wrote Alexis de Tocqueville in 1835,

> that the Indian nations of North America are doomed to perish, and that whenever the Europeans shall be established on the shores of the Pacific Ocean, that race of men will have ceased to exist. The Indians had only the alternative of war or civilization: in other words, they must either destroy the Europeans, or become their equals."[14]

But, of course, the Indians, as Tocqueville could well foresee, could neither destroy the Europeans nor become their equals. They were fated, so he thought, to disappear. Thus the Indian woman, who makes the missing third of this family, is necessarily unpaintable. To give that missing Indian mother in the Bingham painting the presence she demands calls up all too well her claim to this wilderness out of which the trappers have come and the furs they have ransacked from it; calls up the bloodshed of war for the land, the forced removals, the endless betrayals of treaties. But, perhaps more disturbing, the presence of the Indian woman would call up the longing for her, the joining of two races, and the annihilation, in this act, of the boundary between civilized man and savage. Longing for that lost maternal world of nature that the Indian woman represented could turn into the nightmare fear of being devoured by it. Tocqueville quotes Louis XIV's governor of Canada:

> It has long been believed that in order to civilize the savages we ought to draw them nearer to us. But there is every reason to suppose we have been mistaken. Those that have been brought into contact with us have not become French, and the French who have lived among them are changed into savages, affecting to dress and live like them.[15]

"Woe to them that have trespassed against God and taken strange wives of the people of the land" (Ezra 10:2). The savage white Indian lay loitering on the margins of civilization, bearing within his drink-sodden form a wilderness of panic, disorder, and the linguistic chaos of a desperate pidgin: "The Great Renegade" Simon Girty, and Walt Whitman's Half-Breed, and Poe's bestial Dirk Peters.[16]

So that sexual and romantic longing for unspoiled nature that is imbedded in the pastoral must remain unspecified. Generalized. A longing for connection with a feminine landscape that was, in fact, being ravaged, and whose innocence, the theme of Bingham's painting, had been destroyed.

This missing, maternal nature is the world of the river and its source that Bingham has chosen to suggest by the misty outlines of the few trees, the soft lights and shades and golden colors of his landscape. It is the world of seventeenth-century landscape painter Claude Lorrain, a landscape sugggesting a mythologized past beyond history. But the myth of the pastoral always has in it the seeds of its own destruction. To call up its maternal presence is always to call up the pain of its loss. The other side of our longing is our fear and our contempt for the fragility of the very things we have destroyed. Thus the pastoral must exist in that timeless world of a suppressed history— its nostalgic longings must be expressed but not fulfilled. Once all that is missing is glimpsed, or even imagined, the pastoral enters the world of history and time and thus ceases to be functional. Its method is the perpetual delay of reverie. In a sense, then, the old man, the boy, paddling out of the Great Unknown, might be seen to have triumphed over their dependence on this maternal nature, which they have left forever behind them.

Meriwether Lewis died in 1809, probably by his own hand, in a tavern on the Natchez Trace. William Clark, more successful in his life and in his death, died in 1838. And Jefferson, who had sent them to map the Great Unknown, died in 1826. He did not live to see his children, the industrious Cherokees, driven from their farms and settlements along the Trail of Tears. With the coming of the Mexican War, the republic he had helped to found became an empire, and soon the men who had had a taste of battle at Palo Alto and Cerro Gordo and Chapultepec were leading armies in a fratricidal war—a war that Jefferson had feared and had predicted—which marked the end of his dream of a democratic agrarian republic. Three years after Baptiste Charbonneau's death, the continent that he had traversed as an infant on his mother's back was pulled together by the steel tracks of the transcontinental railroad. The Civil War would rip itself across the contradictions that could not forever be submerged beneath Jefferson's vision of the land. And the vast interior of America would be opened up to exploitation on a scale never imagined by Jefferson or the men he had sent out to learn its limits. The dream of a pastoral land that lay beyond the settlements lived only in paintings. The beautiful image of an old trapper, a boy, and a chained bear is one of those—a relic of a time when the pastoral vision and all it hoped for and all it obscured could be painted in the guise of a boy musing in a pirogue headed downstream to a civilization he should never reach.

Best leave this boy to dream, the gun loose in the crook of his arm, the duck he has killed forgotten, in the reverie of an eternal adolescence. Behind him, beyond the frame of the picture, a she-bear rages for her stolen cub.

NOTES

1   The mysterious animal on the pirogue has been variously identified as a bear, a fox, and even a cat. But in *Trappers' Return*, his 1851 reworking of the painting, Bingham clearly shows that the animal is a bear cub. See Nancy Rash's note on the subject in *The Painting and Politics of George Caleb Bingham* (New Haven, CT: Yale University Press, 1991), p. 239.

2   The painting itself might have been inspired by the sort of vignette incorporated in the panoramas, popular in Bingham's era, such as John Banvard's "three mile long moving panorama" of a journey down the Missouri and Mississippi Rivers to the Gulf. See Angela Miller, "The Mechanisms of the Market and the Invention of Western Regionalism: The Example of George Caleb Bingham," in David C. Miller, ed. *American Iconology: New Approaches to Nineteenth-Century Art and Literature* (New Haven, CT: Yale University Press, 1993), p. 116.

3   Reuben Gold Thwaites, ed., *Original Journals of the Lewis and Clark Expedition, 1804–1806, in 7 Volumes, with Atlas* (New York: Dodd, Mead and Company, 1904), vol. 2, pp. 149–50. Hereafter referred to as *Lewis and Clark*.

4   *Lewis and Clark*, vol. 2, part 1, p. 154.

5   Edmund Burke, *A Philosophical Enquiry into the Origin of Our Ideas of the Sublime and Beautiful* (Oxford: Oxford University Press), p. 115.

6   Donald Jackson, ed., *Letters of the Lewis and Clark Expedition with Related Documents, 1983–1854,* 2d ed.(Urbana: University of Illinois Press, 1978), vol. 1, p. 74.

7   Jefferson to Governor William Henry Harrison, February 27, 1803, in Merrill D. Peterson, ed. *Thomas Jefferson, Writings* (New York: Library of America, 1984), pp. 1118–19.

8   *Lewis and Clark*, vol. 7, pp. 329–30.

9   Henry M. Brackenridge, *Journal of a Voyage up the Missouri River in 1811*, quoted in Harold P. Howard, *Sacajawea* (Norman: University of Oklahoma Press, 1971), p. 157.

10 Quoted in Bernard W. Sheehan, *Seeds of Extinction: Jeffersonian Philanthropy and the American Indian* (Chapel Hill: University of North Carolina Press, 1973), p. 229.

11 See Dawn Glanz, *How the West Was Drawn: American Art and the Settling of the Frontier* (Ann Arbor: UMI Research Press, 1982), p. 44.

12 Walt Whitman, "Song of Myself," from *Leaves of Grass*.

13 To get a hint of what Bingham left unexpressed, you need only examine the painting by Bingham's contemporary Charles Deas, *The Trapper and His Family*, completed the same

year as *Fur Traders Descending the Missouri* and perhaps its source. Under the grotesque comedy of the frontier family who inhabits the chaos of pots and pans and robes of an overladen canoe—the trapper with his battered stovepipe hat, his Indian wife, and their heterogenous brats—is a desperate fear. They are paddling furiously, not toward the new civlization of racial amalgamation that Jefferson and others had wished for them, but backward, back to a despoiled wilderness upstream. See Miller, *Mechanisms of the Market*, pp. 119–20. See also Rash, *Painting and Politics,* pp. 50–51.

14 Alexis de Tocqueville, *Democracy in America,* trans. Philips Bradley (New York: A. A. Knopf, 1945), vol. 1, p. 342.

15 Ibid., pp. 345–46.

16 Robert S. Tilton (in *Pocahontas: The Evolution of an American Narrative* [Cambridge, Cambridge University Press, 1994], p. 64) quotes Natty Bumppo in James Fenimore Cooper's *Prairie:* "the half-and-halfs that one meets in these distant districts are altogether more barbarous than the real savage."

3 restoring wilderness or reclaiming forests?

The rapidly increasing pace of biological extinctions throughout much of the world since the 1950s is by now acknowledged to be one of the most pressing of environmental problems. Extinction is a natural evolutionary process, but the current extinction rate is estimated to be several orders of magnitude higher than the "background" rate inferred from the fossil record. Responses to the decline of biological diversity due to these extinctions have varied from global conventions to local community actions. At the global level, the potentially most far-reaching action has been the adoption of the UN Convention on Biological Diversity at the so-called Earth Summit in Rio de Janeiro in June 1992. At the more local level, responses have varied from the tiny but largely successful Community Baboon Sanctuary of Belize, owned and managed privately for profit from tourism, to the giant national parks of the United States maintained at considerable cost to the taxpayer.

The dominant model of biological conservation everywhere is the national park: human exclusion from reserves designated for other species. The plausibility of this model arises from the fact that many extinctions are known to have been caused by human activities such as hunting, deforestation, and industrial pollution. During the last fifteen years, additional support has come from a new and highly fashionable science, conservation biology, which emerged in the United States in the 1980s. Devoted to the conservation of all biological diversity, rather than to the conservation and effective use of any specific resource, it is easily distinguishable from scientific forestry, fisheries biology, and so on, which nonetheless have some claim to be its intellectual antecedents. By being a goal-oriented, prescriptive science routinely operating under the veil of uncertainty, it is equally distinguishable from traditional (descriptive) ecology.

The debates that dominated conservation biology during its early years included the optimal size and shape of a reserve (such as a national park), whether one large reserve is preferable to several small ones with the same total area, whether establishing corridors linking reserves is an effective use of resources, and so on. These debates often generated more heat than light and were eventually realized to concern questions with no noncontextual answers. Meanwhile, conservation biology also saw the development of many potentially powerful techniques to assess the extinction risk faced by small populations.

But what the overwhelming focus of these debates on the design of national parks ignored was that such parks had become purported reservoirs of self-sustaining biological diversity almost by coincidence. Humans were implicated in many extinctions; national parks excluded humans—from these premises it was inferred that the best general strategy for conserving biological diversity was to set up national parks. That national parks in the United States and elsewhere had traditionally been set up either for aesthetic reasons (to protect landscapes of outstanding beauty or cultural interest) or to protect specific species for recreation (hunting, wildlife tourism, and so on) was not acknowledged.

Evidence that challenged the assumption that national parks resulted in self-sustaining biological diversity was also ignored. There are known instances where human exclusion by the creation of national parks has been detrimental to biological diversity. One of the best known is the Serengeti Plain in Tanzania and Kenya. The Serengeti ecosystem and the adjoining Ngorongo crater are home to about 20 percent of Africa's large mammals, including many herbivore species, almost all of Africa's large carnivore species, as well as 450 bird species. Detailed research has shown that pastoralists, livestock, and wildlife have coexisted in the area for over two thousand years; that the pastoralists' grazing and burning practices have created and maintained the landscape that is now so valued by conservationists; and that the presence of the pastoralists and their livestock has no measurable negative impact on wildlife populations or soil erosion. Nevertheless, starting in 1951, much of the area was allocated to national parks. By then it was even known that human absence and the absence of grazing livestock led to the conversion of grasslands into woodlands, which are unsuitable to the herbivores ultimately responsible for the region's diversity (by both their own presence and by their role as prey for carnivores).

The systematic modeling of such human-habitat interactions never became part of conservation biology in the United States. But if American-style conservation biology— and, unless explicitly otherwise indicated, *conservation biology* will be used to refer to the U.S. version—represents the ethos of nature thriving only in human absence, the contrary view that human living patterns and the natural world are inextricably inter- twined, at least in surviving traditional societies, has been embodied in a radically different science of biological conservation that emerged in India, also in the 1980s. That science is social ecology. Social ecology claims that traditional societies require a high diversity of natural resources and that those such societies that persist have done so only because they have managed to evolve cultural and utilization practices to main- tain this diversity. Consequently, ensuring the survival of these practices is the optimal method for conserving biological diversity.

American-style conservation biology and the Indian version of social ecology are not the only available approaches to biological conservation. They represent two ex- treme ends of ideologies about interactions between humans and nonhuman biota, and both have well-articulated theoretical frameworks. Most other approaches fall within the spectrum of possibilities defined by these traditions at each end.[1] There are other versions of conservation biology, in particular an Australian version, which rejects much of the analytic framework developed in the United States. There are also other versions of social ecology, particularly one developed by Mexican ecologists who, by drawing attention to the decline of neotropical rain forests in the early 1970s, were ironically responsible for helping to initiate the American-style conservation biology, which is inimical to their goals.

Birth of a Brave New Science

The (U.S.) Society for Conservation Biology was founded on May 8, 1985, in Ann Ar- bor, Michigan, at the end of the Second Conference on Conservation Biology. Two ad hoc committees, chaired by Jared Diamond and Peter Brussard, had met during the conference to discuss the need for a new society and a new journal. Following their reports, an informal motion to found the society was passed, and Michael E. Soulé was given the task of organizing it. The motion to start a journal also passed. That a suc- cessful journal, *Biological Conservation,* devoted to the same topic had been in existence since 1968 apparently went unnoticed.

From there, things moved quickly. In December 1985, Soulé published a long mani- festo, "What Is Conservation Biology?" in *BioScience,* the journal most visible to academic and nonacademic biologists in the United States. It defined the precepts of conservation biology for that broad audience. The first issue of the new journal *Conservation Biology* appeared in May 1987, and the first annual meeting of the society was held at Montana State University in June 1987.

Thus between 1985 and 1987 conservation biology emerged in the United States as an organized academic discipline. Its focus became *biodiversity*, a term that entered the everyday and scientific lexicons around 1988. It was created at some point during the organization of a National Forum on Biodiversity held in Washington, D.C., in September 1986. *Biodiversity*, shorthand for "biological diversity," was probably first used by Walter G. Rosen, one of the organizers of the forum. No one bothered to mark the boundaries of what counted as "biodiversity." The term passed from a hopeful neologism to the buzzword of the conservation movement with hardly any attention to what exactly it specified.

In 1989, Soulé and Kathryn A. Kohm published a primer on research priorities for the new field. It was catholic in its scope, including demography, ecology, genetics, island biogeography, public policy, and systematics as components of conservation biology. It called for massive biological surveys, especially in the neotropics, and for the circumvention of legal barriers to the use of U.S. funds for the purchase of land in other countries. In 1993, Richard B. Primack produced the first textbook of conservation biology, and in 1994, Gary K. Meffe and C. Ronald Carroll followed with a more comprehensive effort.

Meffe and Carroll begin their book by repeating what, in the United States, had become the central dogma of conservation biology—that human population growth is the cause of the decline of biological diversity—although, unlike many others at the forefront of the field, they mitigate this claim by explicitly admitting that it is not human numbers per se that matter, but patterns of habitation and consumption. A sketch of a history of biological conservation focusing entirely on the United States followed. Modern conservation biology—that is, the developments of the preceding decade—was declared as a "synthesis" of all past attempts.

A brave new science had been born. Its brief was no less than to halt the decline of "biodiversity."

Conservation Biology, Made in the U.S.A.

Soulé's 1985 manifesto, which aimed to delineate the foundations of conservation biology, provides two sets of postulates: a "functional" or "mechanistic" set and an "ethical" or "normative" set. Each postulate is accompanied by several "corollaries." Though these "corollaries" are supposed to be consequences of the postulates, most of them involve additional assumptions that also form part of the theoretical framework of conservation biology.

Soulé's four functional postulates are supposed to be "working propositions based partly on evidence, partly on theory, and partly on intuition [that] suggest rules for action." There are four normative postulates, as well, that, together, are supposed to constitute "an ethic of appropriate attitudes toward other forms of life—an ecosophy": (1) *"diversity of organisms is good"*; (2) *"ecological complexity is good"*—the most important "corollary" of this postulate is that wilderness is to be preferred over gardens; (3) *"evolution is good"*; and (4), the most fundamental of the normative postulates: *"biotic diversity has intrinsic value,* irrespective of its instrumental or utilitarian value." "In emphasizing the inherent value of nonhuman life," Soulé argues, this postulate "distinguishes the dualistic, exploitive [*sic*] world view from a more unitary perspective: Species have value in themselves, a value neither conferred nor revocable, but springing from a species' long evolutionary heritage and potential or even from the mere fact of its existence."[2]

Soulé's postulates continue to capture the operative presumptions of conservation biology in the United States. For scientific developments, the critical functional postulate was the third: *"Genetic and demographic processes have thresholds below which nonadaptive, random forces begin to prevail over adaptive, deterministic forces within populations."* It had important consequences not only for conservation policy, but also for the elaboration of a theoretical framework for conservation biology. If the targets of conservation are small populations, then stochastic (random) factors can dominate over deterministic factors (such as the ecological processes affecting fitness) in determining a population's fate. Island biogeography theory and population ecology suggested that small populations are critically subject to size fluctuations that occur because of demographic stochasticity, that is, size fluctuations due to chance differences in the mating success of individuals. Population genetics theory implied that individual genes (alleles) could decrease in frequency and disappear in small populations by chance, a process known as genetic "drift" (genetic stochasticity).

In a 1978 dissertation entitled "Determining Minimum Viable Population Sizes: A Case Study of the Grizzly Bear," Mark L. Shaffer provided a systematic framework for analyzing the effects of stochasticity on small populations. Besides demographic and genetic stochasticity, Shaffer distinguished environmental stochasticity (random environmental fluctuations that affect all members of a population) and catastrophes.

Using demographic and environmental stochasticity, he analyzed the grizzly bear populations in Yellowstone National Park. This analysis was extended by Michael E. Gilpin and Soulé, who coined the term *population viability analysis* (PVA) to describe analyses that estimate minimal viable populations.[3]

The crucial assumption in these analyses is that stochasticity is of paramount importance. Therefore, the only relevant population parameter is its size. Ecological details and population structure are deemed not to be relevant to the problem of determining the probability of a population's extinction or in recommending policies to avert that fate. This feature of conservation biology is captured by corollaries (b) and (c) of Soulé's third functional postulate: population size thresholds are specified independent of species or ecological context.

Risk assessment using PVA is remarkably powerful in an important way: because it is independent of ecological details, its techniques can be applied to almost all species without modification. With some justice, Shaffer could claim in 1994,

> Like physicists searching for a grand unified theory explaining how the four fundamental forces . . . interact to control the structure and fate of the universe, conservation biologists now seek their own grand unified theory explaining how habitat type, quality, quantity, and pattern interact to control the structures and fates of species. Population viability analysis (PVA) is the first expression of this quest.[4]

For practitioners and critics (such as the Australian ecologists) alike, PVA has come to symbolize conservation biology, made in the U.S.A.

Legislative and Cultural Contexts of U.S. Conservation Biology

Is PVA an appropriate response to the threat of impending extinctions? There are at least two grounds for caution, if not outright skepticism. First, precisely because small populations are subject to stochasticity, it is far from clear that scarce resources should be allocated toward their conservation rather than toward declining populations of threatened species except, perhaps, in the cases of species of known cultural, economic, or scientific interest. Second, even if an endangered population recovers sufficiently to be judged "viable" in terms of size, since it had been declining, there is no reason to suppose that a new decline will not occur unless the causes of the previous decline are identified and addressed. The greatest weakness of PVA is that it provides no method for doing this.

The dominance of PVA in conservation biology reflects the discipline's emergence in a very particular legislative context. As such it provides an intriguing example of the sociopolitical modulation of an emerging science. The decisive event was the passage of the Endangered Species Act (ESA) in 1973 at the end of a long history of U.S. federal conservationist legislation including the Endangered Species Preservation Acts (1966, 1969) and the National Environmental Policy Act (1969). Subsequent amendments to the ESA required not only the listing of threatened and endangered species but also the designation of critical habitats and the design of population recovery plans. Other legislation mandated measures even to prevent local extinctions of species. In particular, the 1976 National Forest Management Act required the U.S. Forest Service to maintain "viable populations" of native vertebrates in each national forest. These legislative measures were themselves a result of the heightened popular concern for the environment—including the problem of extinctions—that had emerged in the United States in the 1960s.

Since populations of threatened and endangered species are generally small, attempts to implement this legislation naturally lead to a focus on small populations. Gilpin and Soulé have perceptively noted that the term *minimum viable population* came into vogue probably because of the injunction to the U.S. Forest Service that was incorporated in the 1976 National Forest Management Act. The conservation and recovery plans required under the ESA (as amended) led almost inexorably to the risk assessment of small populations through stochastic analysis. That PVA would emerge in such a context should probably come as no surprise. What is perhaps more surprising is that PVA—rather than the analysis of deterministic causes for declines even in large populations, which are more likely to be reversible—has come to dominate conservation biology. But here, the very strength of the ESA, which is usually regarded as the strongest piece of conservationist legislation in the world, may be to blame. By legally mandating the protection of every population of every threatened or endangered species (and, sometimes, subspecies), the ESA directs scarce financial and human resources toward them, leaving little else for other conservation measures.

Biological critics of the ESA's species-based approach to conservation have often argued that this approach is a nonoptimal use of resources. If the target of conservation is biological diversity, attention to entire habitats is more important. This argument gained force in the 1970s, when general biological diversity emerged as the focus of concern. This shift also reflects a context peculiar to the United States. The post–World War II period saw a massive increase in neotropical forest destruction during the same period when U.S.-based tropical ecologists began to establish and expand their research programs in those forests. It was abundantly clear that the destruction of these forests, many of them with high species diversity in many taxa, was resulting in the extinction of species unknown to science. These could not be protected by species-specific efforts such as those envisioned by the ESA.

Rather, entire habitats merited concern. In a famous exhortation to his professional colleagues, Daniel H. Janzen urged that

> the real future of tropical ecology lies in whether, within our generation, the academic, social and commercial sectors can collaboratively preserve even small portions of tropical wildlands to be studied and used for understanding, for material gain, and for the intellectual development of the society in which the wildland is embedded. . . . If biologists want a tropics in which to biologize, they are going to have to buy it with care, energy, effort, strategy, tactics, time, and cash.[5]

Janzen's exhortation found a receptive audience. During the last decade, not only have neotropical forests emerged as the dominant experimental system for conservation biologists, but the image of endangered tropical rain forests has come to symbolize public concern for biological conservation all over Europe and neo-Europe, but especially in the United States.

In U.S. conservation biology, habitat and biodiversity conservation have been conflated with the preservation of wilderness. This is evident not only in the preferred U.S. conservation policy of creating national parks but also in Soulé's normative postulates for conservation biology (more specifically, in his assumption that wilderness is preferable to gardens). The extent of this conflation, its influence on the practice of conservation biology or on policy recommendation, and the question of whether it is justifiable or a continuation of a regrettable history remain deeply contested.

The first point to note is that *wilderness*, as a category of positive concern—as opposed to "waste" lands to be domesticated and exploited—is of recent and highly localized vintage. As the historian of "wilderness," Roderick Nash, puts it, "Friends of wilderness should remember that in terms of the entire history of man's relationships to nature, they are riding the crest of a very, very recent wave."[6] Though the origins of this concept of wilderness are usually traced back to eighteenth-century European romanticism, its relevant use in this context emerges only in the late nineteenth and early twentieth century, primarily in the United States, where wildernesses as uninhabited areas were generally created through the exclusion of indigenous residents and the erasure of their history. In the United States, the final stage of exclusion was achieved at the end of the last "Indian" wars, when the remnants of the First Nations were herded into reservations and their traditional habitats were declared to have been unoccupied by humans since the beginning of time. Recently, many scholars have shown that throughout much of North America, these habitats had been relatively stably modulated for centuries by the First Nations.

The process of exclusion and erasure had begun earlier, with the conquest and (direct and indirect) decimation of the First Nation populations by European settlers. Erasure means the denial of this history, through a systematic, if unconscious, reconstruction of memory, recasting the lands being occupied by the settlers as previously uninhabited. There are at least three likely explanations for the initiation of this erasure. First, European-introduced diseases led to precipitous declines in the First Nation populations, in turn leading to the abandonment of previously occupied habitats. Consequently, the Europeans saw uninhabited lands and assumed that their form owed nothing to anthropogenic factors. Second, the Europeans were so intent on occupying these habitats that they ignored obvious signs of previous occupation and use. Third, given the racist conceptualization of the First Nations as non- or subhuman, the settlers considered the land they occupied to have been previously unoccupied by humans.

As wilderness preservationism spread, especially in the early twentieth century, the immediate target was the creation of national parks for recreational use. The strategy of choice—and, in retrospect, a very effective one—was federal intervention, eventually imposed with the force of law. Concern for biological diversity played no role in the selection of U.S. national parks in the early decades of this century: the first swamp was so designated (the Everglades National Park) only in the 1940s, and there is still no national park dedicated to preserving grasslands. Rather, the parks were "sublime" landscapes (mountains, waterfalls, and so on) of deep aesthetic appeal to transient visitors, usually from an urban elite rather than from the surrounding rural population.

Since the 1970s, many wilderness preservationists in North America have also propounded a new ideology—deep ecology—whose goals are based on normative postulates that carry more weight than aesthetic preference. Deep ecology attributes "intrinsic values" to nonhuman species and, sometimes, to nonbiotic entities such as rivers and mountains. It thus attempts to provide allegedly ethical justifications for wilderness preservation. Deep ecology has gained support among conservation biologists: the attribution of intrinsic value to all species was Soulé's most important normative postulate, and Meffe and Carroll's textbook presents deep ecology as one of the normative foundations of conservation biology. Nevertheless, the philosophical basis for the assertion of intrinsic values to nonhuman entities remains suspect. Meanwhile, deep ecology and the associated program of wilderness preservation have provoked intense criticism from many angles, in particular from social ecologists.

Of Elephants and Humans

On January 29, 1985, residents of Bangalore (in southern India) found newspaper headlines screaming, "Elephants Invade City."[7] The previous morning, students of an engineering college in a Bangalore suburb had woken up to discover nine elephants outside their hostel. The elephants had walked some fifteen kilometers from their forest home, through cultivated fields, to the campus. This incident attracted attention only because it occurred so close to a major city. In India, elephant incursions into human habitats are routine and have occurred since the beginnings of recorded history. The *Gajasastra*, a fifth- or sixth-century B.C.E. Sanskrit text on elephant natural history, records how wild elephants invaded the kingdom of Anga and did considerable damage.

In India, wild elephants cause damage primarily in two ways: crop and livestock depredations and manslaughter. Crops that attract elephants include cereal grains, sugar cane, fruit trees, oil palm, and various legumes. In southern India, with an elephant population of about six to seven thousand, the crop damage between 1981 and 1983 was substantial; in eastern India, the loss was even greater. Besides damage to crops, elephants destroy houses and other property. Wild elephants kill thirty to fifty people each year in southern India, thirty to fifty in West Bengal, and over one hundred in the rest of the country. In southern India, about 45 percent of these deaths occur when elephants enter human habitats to raid crops; the rest occur in forests. No doubt the frequency of human-elephant encounters has increased as the natural habitat of elephants has been lost.

Elephants have been captured for domestication and hunted in India since the beginnings of recorded history. However, as ecologist Raman Sukumar argues, the fact that wild elephant populations survive in spite of the enormous cost to humans reflects a culture of relative tolerance for them. But this is only part of the explanation for the persistence of elephants. In Kautilya's *Arthasastra* (circa 300 B.C.E.–300 C.E.), the oldest extant text that contains detailed measures for the conservation of elephants, the animals are protected primarily to maintain a reliable elephant supply for imperial armies.

FIGURE 3. Captive Asian elephant, on the outskirts of New Delhi, India. (© Robert Radin)

The Asian elephant *(Elephas maximus)* is severely endangered, and its populations are very fragmented. About sixty-five thousand individuals remain worldwide, less than 10 percent of the number left of the better-known African bush elephant (*Loxodonta africana*). It took over a decade, starting in 1980, for social ecologists to devise the appropriate conservation strategy. The analysis was based on research in which the ecological and social factors causing population declines were identified and the ecological and social consequences of possible conservation measures were assessed.

There are two causes for the declines: habitat modification and slaughter. However, mere human presence in a habitat is not necessarily detrimental to elephant populations. As in the case of many other herbivorous mammals, secondary plant growth (due to modification of habitat) may be able to support larger elephant populations than primary climax plant communities. Shifting cultivation with a long rotation period (greater than ten-year cycles) does not significantly damage elephant habitat. Similarly, timber felling, if it follows sound forestry norms, also does not do measurable damage. By encouraging secondary growth, it may increase food availability. It is unclear whether bamboo or grass extraction (including grazing by domestic livestock) or occasional fires do any harm. (These factors may well harm species other than elephants, but this needs to be demonstrated through empirical studies.) In contrast, the establishment of forest plantations generally decreases the food supply of elephants even when the planted species—such as bamboo and several species of acacia—are part of the normal diet of elephants. The creation of water reservoirs often submerges suitable habitat and disturbs traditional migratory routes.

Populations of Asian elephants have also been reduced by the regular capture of elephants for domestication, by hunting—especially of male elephants for ivory—and by the killing of males and females in defense of agricultural crops. By the late twentieth century, illegal hunting for ivory had become the most significant of these factors. Unlike African bush elephants, only male Asian elephants have tusks. The fraction of males that have tusks varies from about 10 percent in Sri Lanka to almost 100 percent in southern India. Expectedly, poaching is insignificant in the former region and a serious problem in the latter.

Asian elephant populations are polygynous, and the fertility among males varies. The basic population unit is a "family" consisting of an adult female and its offspring, including females of all ages and prepubertal males. Adult males disperse from families and are solitary animals. They associate temporarily with family groups to mate with females in estrus. Given this breeding structure, if the sex ratio is not heavily biased against males, the removal of a fraction of the males would have little demographic impact on the population. Similarly, although there is no tangible evidence of this, one might suspect that such a removal would not have a significant influence on genetic variability within the population. Solitary adult males are far more likely to raid crops than members of female-led family groups, and because of its larger body size, a male will also consume about twice as much as a group member per raid. Sukumar estimates that an average male causes twenty times as much damage as an average group member. An investigation of 150 cases of human fatalities in southern India showed that adult males were responsible for 80 percent, even though they formed less than 10 percent of the population.

Ecologists generally believe that the aggressive behavior of males increases due to overcrowding from the loss of adequate habitat. In the absence of relevant controls, however, this can only be regarded as a conjecture. But it is at least plausible that a decrease in the availability of the elephants' natural food supply (as a result of habitat shrinkage) would lead elephants to forage for food in cultivated areas.

Based on his observations, Sukumar proposes a conservation strategy that consists of three parts: protection of adequate elephant habitat with an emphasis on its quality (this does not require complete human exclusion); adequate compensation for indi-

viduals who suffer from elephant depredations; and, if the sex ratio is not heavily biased against males, the removal of offending males. To some extent, such removal can
be effected by capture for domestication. In southern India, where almost all males are
tuskers, poaching for ivory has reduced the proportion of males to less than 10 percent. Further removal of males is not justified. However, where a lower frequency of
tuskers has led to a far less skewed sex ratio due to poaching, removal remains a reasonable option.

The Indian Version of Social Ecology

This elephant conservation strategy could hardly be more different than one based on
PVA and the establishment of national parks. The ingredients that went into devising
the strategy are a mixture of detailed ecological observations and explicit social policy
imperatives. There was no explicit analysis of stochasticity; rather, the emphasis was
on the quality of elephant *and human* habitat. Indian ecologists call this approach *social
ecology,* a term coined by the pioneering sociologist Radhakamal Mukerjee in 1942. But
the ecologically oriented sociology that Mukerjee envisioned found little resonance
with others in the colonial era, and social ecology, as an identifiable discipline, emerged
in India only in the 1980s.[8] One of its most influential proponents, Ramachandra
Guha, identifies five basic "categories" of social ecology: ecological infrastructure,
economy, social structure, polity, and culture. Social ecology consists of the study of
reciprocal relations between ecological infrastructure and the other categories. In practice, in the Indian context, social ecology has been uniformly directed toward social
justice.

The central tenet of Indian social ecology—the reason why it can claim to be a
science of biological conservation—is that societies that have a long tradition of interaction with a habitat, using only technologies that emerged in that habitat, will have
evolved cultural and resource utilization practices that lead to a sustainable use of that
habitat.[9] Societies that do not evolve such practices would disappear over time due to
resource exhaustion. Indian social ecologists, particularly Madhav Gadgil, have collected evidence supporting this claim since the early 1980s. They have also shown that
some human activities enhance biological diversity and have worked out the implications of this for conservation strategy.

For social ecology, the most pressing problem is that traditional living patterns are
increasingly being ruptured through the expropriation of local resources, the use of
new and successively more disruptive technologies, the loss of traditional control of

habitat, and so on. The culprits include colonizers, developers, and, of late, conservationists bent on turning living habitats into wilderness (for example, national parks), all usually acting with the authority of a distant state. Consequently, the political struggle for resident people's traditional rights is ipso facto a program for the conservation of biological diversity.

In social ecology, the models are generally qualitative descriptions of human-habitat relationships, based on systematic observation of traditional human-habitat interactions—outside India, this has usually been the province of anthropologists—and assessments of the biological consequences of these interactions. The major purpose is to identify practices that help maintain or enhance the resource being used: these are the practices to be encouraged. Even in India, such assessments, informed by "rules of thumb," have often failed to incorporate ecological knowledge sufficiently. Sukumar's work stands out as one of the few notable exceptions.

Gadgil and his collaborators have argued that in many regions of India, traditional religious practices may help preserve biological diversity and that traditional resource management practices help prevent the depletion of individual species. In the Western Ghats of India—one of the global "hot spots" of biological diversity identified by conservation biologists—the religious practice of setting aside sacred groves and ponds from which hunting is banned has resulted in the survival of a few patches of primary rain forest in an otherwise ecologically devastated region. Religious tradition has also protected some species of animals and plants completely (such as all species of ficus). Meanwhile, traditional management practices have led to resource utilization patterns where different societal segments specialize in harvesting specific resources, often preventing the overharvesting of any species. In India, these different societal segments are often constituted by different castes, and these resource utilization practices persist because of the inheritance of caste-based professions. Gadgil's most important recommendation is that these local traditions, and the local knowledge that accrues from them, be incorporated into conservation strategies.

Gadgil and Sukumar are beginning to have an impact on official Indian policies, which have so far largely continued the game-management practices introduced during the colonial era. Probably the most glaring of these was Project Tiger, the establishment in the early 1970s of fifteen tiger reserves as a conservation strategy that was supposed to prevent the extinction of the Bengal tiger *(Panthera tigris tigris)*. Initially, the international conservation community hailed this as a major success, since tiger populations increased. But this euphoria dissipated by the 1990s, when populations declined precipitously because of poaching. Social ecologists have been less than enthusiastic about Project Tiger. Guha puts their criticisms bluntly:

> Project Tiger . . . posits the interests of the tiger against those of poor peasants living in and around the reserve. . . . The initial impetus for setting up parks . . . came from two social groups, first, a class of ex-hunters turned conservationists belonging mostly to the declining Indian feudal elite and second, representatives of international agencies, such as the World Wildlife Fund (WWF) and the International Union for Conservation of Nature (IUCN), seeking to transplant the American system of national parks onto Indian soil.[10]

Guha has a point for even the most ardent national parks advocate: one of the major reasons why poaching has been impossible to eradicate in Indian national parks is the local people's resentment toward having been displaced or restricted from collecting minor forest produce (firewood, fodder, and so on). By explicitly incorporating human interests and not constraining traditional locally evolved human activities that do not demonstrably have a negative effect on the targets of conservation, social ecology aims to avoid all such conflicts of interest.

Colonial Social Forestry and Social Ecology

Why social ecology? Guha's answer is straightforward: "The Indian environmental movement has its genesis in . . . conflicts [over natural resources], in contrast to the West where aesthetic and biological concerns have been more important in creating a constituency for environmental protection."[11] In a pioneering ecological history of the Indian subcontinent, Gadgil and Guha develop the arguments underlying this answer. Conflicts emerged because of two interrelated sociopolitical factors: (1) Indian forests, some of which are high in plant endemism and diversity, have had relatively high population densities throughout recorded history, and patterns of existing biological diversity have coevolved with human habitation; and (2) the British colonial authorities initiated a program of "scientific forestry" that denied the customary rights of forest communities. Instead, forests were commercially exploited for timber, and large segments of the diverse forests were replaced by monoculture plantations. These policies were not only continued by the postcolonial Indian state, but, in the interest of industrial development, the exploitation was intensified. International agencies (including USAID) actively encouraged this process.

Before colonization, hunter-gatherers and shifting cultivators coexisted within communal forests, and nomadic pastoralists and settled agriculturalists also made use of the forest resources. Commercial use of the forests was largely confined to the collection of items such as ivory, cardamom, and pepper. Colonization marked an "ecological watershed." The East India Company (EIC) asserted state ownership over the forests, which constituted about 20 percent of the occupied land in 1800. The imperial agenda motivated the initial deforestation. After the depletion of the oak forests of Britain and Ireland and the loss of the timber resources of the American colonies in 1776, Indian teak, the most durable of ship-building timbers, became a primary concern for the Royal Navy during the Anglo-French wars. The assault began on the Malabar forests of western India and spread through the areas controlled by the EIC. After 1850, the expansion of the Indian railway network, which required timber for sleepers on the tracks, drove the deforestation.

The environmental consequences of massive deforestation became a matter of colonial concern in the 1850s and 1860s. Since Britain lacked expertise in forest management, German foresters were imported to establish a Forest Department in 1864. A draconian Indian Forest Act, which abolished centuries of customary use and communal control, was passed in 1878. By the 1890s, in some provinces the Forest Department controlled as much as 30 percent of the land; nationwide it controlled 20 percent. The main aim of the department was the production of large commercial timber. Mixed coniferous broad-leafed forests of the Himalayas were converted into pure coniferous forests. Rich evergreen rain forests of the Western Ghats were converted into single-species teak forests. In a later phase, tracts of forest were converted into tea, coffee, and other plantations. In the postcolonial era, eucalyptus emerged as the timber of choice in many areas.

There is a continuous history of resistance to the Forest Department from about 1870. Hunter-gatherers were the least organized, powerful, and numerous of the affected communities. Most of these communities were able to mount little organized resistance and either went into demographic decline or abandoned traditional living patterns. All other communities offered significant resistance. Neither the colonial nor the postcolonial authorities have been able to eradicate shifting cultivation though scientific forestry decrees, with little supporting evidence (then as now) that this practice is necessarily environmentally destructive.

The most significant resistance came from settled cultivator communities, particularly in the Himalayan regions of Uttar Pradesh. During the colonial era, revolts involving widespread violations of forest regulations and, sometimes, attacks on forest officials occurred in 1904, 1916, 1921, 1930, 1942, and 1944 to 1948. For the emergence of social ecology, the critical revolt in this region was the Chipko movement against commercial forestry, which started in 1973. This decentralized movement was sociologically important because of the mass participation of women and ecologically important, not only because it succeeded in ending commercial forestry in the region, but also because one of the participant groups initiated programs of noncommercial afforestation in degraded areas. All participant groups defended traditional use of the forests.

The success of Chipko encouraged the emergence of similar movements in many other areas. Environmentalism became part of the national political agenda. Most environmental movements interpreted their demands in political terms: the disputes were about the use and control of forests and other natural resources. Foresters and ecologists, with Gadgil being the most prominent of the latter, were called on to provide expert advice to the state on environmental consequences of both commercial and traditional patterns of resource use. The ecologists' verdict was almost uniformly in favor of traditional use. In a period of intense environmental activism, augmented by the devastating gas leak from the Union Carbide plant in Bhopal, they were probably happy to align themselves politically with the burgeoning environmental movements. If popular concern with extinctions helped conservation biology focus on small populations in the United States, in India, social ecology emphasized the reclaiming of the forests.

Conservation with a Human Face

Both conservation biology and social ecology are goal-oriented enterprises. However, the only specific goal that they share is the conservation of biological diversity. This is the ultimate goal of conservation biology. For social ecology, this goal must be achieved with social justice. In conservation biology, the value of biological diversity is underscored by the attribution of intrinsic value to all species; social ecology is explicitly anthropomorphic. Conservation biology focuses on wilderness because wilderness preservation is supposed to be the best guarantor of the conservation of "biodiversity," while social ecology focuses on those parts of the biota that are utilized as resources by local populations. "Throw the people out" is a hostile, but not entirely unfair, rendition of much of the policy prescriptions that have emerged from conservation biology. Social ecology begins with human welfare—throwing humans out is inimical to its ideology. Rather, the political struggle is between those who would reclaim the forests, *and maintain them,* and those who would destroy them.

What is perhaps most promising about the dialectic between social ecology and conservation biology is that their differences may potentially be used to enrich both traditions of conservation. For conservation biology, while consistency between intrinsic and anthropomorphic values may be impossible to achieve, a commitment to the intrinsic value of nonhuman species should not preclude adequate respect for human interests. The experience of social ecology provides two important lessons: a general strategy of starting with a model of a habitat that includes humans may lead to a more accurate biological description of a threatened ecosystem; and a recognition of human interests may lead to constructive resolutions for political conflicts over conservation— national parks do not work without local support.

Conversely, social ecology should admit that no ascription of intrinsic value is needed to justify attempts to conserve general biological diversity. Even if some species do not have immediate or future use value, Bryan G. Norton has pointed out that they have "transformative value": knowledge or interaction with them may change worldviews— scientific, cultural, or otherwise.[12] In acknowledging the importance of conserving certain species or habitats (sacred groves and ponds) for their religious value, social ecology implicitly recognizes the transformative values of species. This recognition could be extended to accept the social value of science. Conservation biology has two specific lessons. First, social ecology too easily assumes that traditional resource use is sustainable. Social ecology will have to borrow techniques from conservation biology and ecology to be able to assess the long-term effects of activities carried out by resident populations. And second, so far, social ecology has relied almost entirely on qualitative models. If populations fall low enough, social ecology might need to adopt quantitative analytic tools such as PVA in the effort to prevent extinctions.

Conservation biology and social ecology, as I have described here (that is, the United States and Indian variants), do not exhaust traditions of biological conservation. Gadgil and Fikret Berkes have compiled an extensive list of traditional resource-management systems around the world. These range from the control of watersheds by Swiss communes or the Nishga First Nation of British Columbia to the *dina* system of resource specialization in the inland delta of the River Niger in Mali. However, the particular practices that were outlined in this essay emerged in the Indian context of a conflict of interests between local communities and a colonial state. This circumstance does not hold everywhere. Comparative studies of these other conservation practices and the functional and normative frameworks of assumption under which they operate remain an important task for the future. Perhaps comparative studies of these traditions, which illuminate the unstated presumptions of each of them, will help generate less parochial, but nevertheless locally sensitive, modes of biological conservation that incorporate insights from a wide variety of social histories.

NOTES

1 This probably reflects the fact that the colonial Indian and U.S. models of scientific forestry and environmental management emerged by 1900 as the two dominant alternatives in much of the world. See R. H. Grove, "Colonial Conservation, Ecological Hegemony and Popular Resistance: Towards a Global Synthesis," in J. M. MacKenzie, ed., *Imperialism and the Natural World* (Manchester: Manchester University Press, 1990), pp. 15–50.

2 Michael E. Soulé, "What Is Conservation Biology?" *BioScience* 35 (1985): 727–34.

3 Michael E. Gilpin and Michael E. Soulé, "Minimum Viable Populations: Processes of Species Extinction," in M. E. Soulé, ed., *Conservation Biology: The Science of Scarcity and Diversity* (Sunderland, MA: Sinauer, 1986), pp. 19–34.

4 In Gary K. Meffe and C. Ronald Carroll, *Principles of Conservation Biology* (Sunderland, MA: Sinauer, 1994), p. 195.

5 Daniel H. Janzen, "The Future of Tropical Ecology," *Annual Review of Ecology and Systematics* 17 (1986): 305–6.

6 Roderick Nash, *Wilderness and the American Mind*, 2d ed. (New Haven: Yale University Press, 1973), p. xii.

7 See Raman Sukumar, "Wildlife-Human Conflict in India: An Ecological and Social Perspective," in R. Guha, ed., *Social Ecology* (Delhi: Oxford University Press, 1994), pp. 303–17; R. Sukumar, *The Asian Elephant: Ecology and Management* (Cambridge: Cambridge University Press, 1989); R. Sukumar, *Elephant Days and Nights: Ten Years with the Asian Elephant* (New Delhi: Oxford University Press, 1994); and R. Sukumar and M. Gadgil, "Male-Female Differences in Foraging on Crops by Asian Elephants," *Animal Behavior* 36 (1988): 1233–55.

8 Parallel developments, though with significantly less attention to scientific (that is, biological) ecology, occurred in the West around this time, under the rubrics of *political ecology* and *liberation ecology*. A different use of *social ecology* also emerged in North America in the 1970s. See Murray Bookchin, *The Philosophy of Social Ecology: Essays on Dialectical Naturalism*, 2d ed. (Montreal: Black Rose Books, 1995).

9 Mexican ecologists have also made this suggestion. See Arturo Gómez-Pompa and Andrea Kaus, "Taming the Wilderness Myth," *BioScience* 42/4 (1992): 271–79.

10 Ramachandra Guha, "Radical American Environmentalism and Wilderness Preservation: A Third World Critique," *Environmental Ethics* 11 (1989): 75.

11 Ramachandra Guha, "Introduction," in R. Guha, ed., *Social Ecology* (Delhi: Oxford University Press, 1994), p. 6.

12 See Bryan G. Norton, *Why Preserve Natural Variety?* (Princeton: Princeton University Press, 1987).

4   for indian wilderness

A *wilderness,* in one important definition, is a place that remains largely unmanaged and unmodified by human beings. Due to increased human numbers and technological power, only places mandated by law will remain as wildernesses in the coming centuries. If we wish to allow nature to remain wild in select areas, political authorities must set boundaries within which human numbers and human uses are limited and direct economic uses are largely excluded. For wilderness advocates, such restraint indicates proper respect for these places and for the individual organisms, particular communities, and biological species they protect.

Wilderness preservation gains support from two cornerstone positions of Western environmentalism, as it has developed over the past twenty years: first, the view articulated within environmental ethics, that wild, nonhuman nature, or at least some parts of it, has intrinsic value and therefore should be treated respectfully; second, the understanding developed within conservation biology that we have entered a period of massive anthropogenic extinction of biological species and biodiversity loss, that human economic activities are the major cause of this, and that landscape-level habitat preservation is essential for ameliorating it.

Recently, some writers have argued that wilderness preservation is a specifically American or Western preoccupation whose promotion in the Third World amounts to cultural imperialism. According to Ramachandra Guha, for example, wilderness preservation is inappropriate and unnecessary in the Third World, whose peoples face more pressing environmental issues centered on meeting basic human needs.[1] In effect,

Guha denies the intrinsic value of nonhuman nature and dismisses as unimportant the loss of biodiversity in the Third World.

In opposition to this well-intentioned anthropocentrism, we argue that nonhuman nature retains intrinsic value in the Third World, as in the First. Furthermore, biodiversity loss is not in the interests of Third World citizens but will lead to their material, intellectual, and spiritual impoverishment. To stem such loss, we advocate, with Guha, sustainable development for the poor and decreased consumption among the rich worldwide.

Is concern for wilderness preservation a luxury that the poor cannot afford? In a wide-ranging critique, Guha argues that

> the emphasis on wilderness is positively harmful when applied to the Third World. . . . The setting aside of wilderness areas has resulted in a direct transfer of resources from the poor to the rich. Thus, Project Tiger, a network of parks hailed by the international conservation community as an outstanding success, sharply posits the interests of the tiger against those of poor peasants living in and around the reserve. The designation of tiger reserves was made possible only by the physical displacement of existing villages and their inhabitants; their management requires the continuing exclusion of peasants and livestock . . . transplant[ing] the American system of national parks onto Indian soil. In no case have the needs of the local population been taken into account, and as in many parts of Africa, the designated wildands are managed primarily for the benefit of rich tourists.[2]

There is some truth in Guha's claims. Several of Project Tiger's reserves were built around the old hunting preserves of the Indian princely elite, from which the poor had long been excluded; others were set up on former state or communally owned lands, displacing numerous villages and causing real hardship to thousands. In either case, grazing and tree cutting in the core areas of the reserves were prohibited in order to both limit human-tiger conflicts and to preserve a fuller flora and fauna and a landscape more the result of natural forces than of human intervention. Many of the visitors to the reserves *were* wealthy outsiders, both Indian and foreign.

On the other hand, India's wild tigers were clearly headed for extinction when Project Tiger was undertaken: between 1900 and 1972, the year it was initiated, the population fell from between twenty and fifty thousand to eighteen hundred. Strictly limiting tiger hunting had not halted this decline. Habitat conservation was clearly necessary to protect the tigers over the long term. Given the requirements of tigers and their inevitable conflicts with humans, attempts to preserve them had to involve some displacement and restrictions on local inhabitants. Wildlife proponents used the setting aside of tiger habitat to simultaneously attempt to protect full complements of native species with their natural community and ecosystemic interactions.

Should Project Tiger have been attempted? Guha suggests not: it represented an unjust appropriation of the resources of poor people. At the same time, a focus on tigers went hand in hand with ignoring "environmental problems that impinge far more directly on the lives of the poor—e.g., fuel, fodder, water shortages, soil erosion, and air and water pollution . . . far more pressing environmental problems within the Third World."[3]

We disagree. Habitat preservation and restrictions on human economic use of this habitat were necessary and appropriate responses to the imminent extinction of the Bengal tiger. This would have been a great loss to the Indian people and the unjust destruction of an intrinsically valuable species. We do not accept the extinction of species as a "less pressing" problem than those mentioned by Guha because we do not accept his exclusive focus on human interests or his narrow definition of those interests.

At the same time, Project Tiger was carried out unjustly. It failed to adequately compensate displaced villagers. It failed to grant them an adequate share of the revenue that the parks produce or to allow them to make a living in other ways from the parks that had been set up in their midst. The same government that created the reserves arguably failed to secure access to necessary resources for displaced and adjacent inhabitants. Partly for these reasons, there has been great resistance to the reserves, which has undermined their effectiveness and led to bloodshed.

Project Tiger would have been both fairer and more successful had local people been given an interest in its success. Recently, wildlife managers in the Third World have been experimenting with numerous ways to give local people a stake in the success of wildlife and park conservation, with encouraging results. In Africa, these efforts have included disbursing a percentage of park revenues directly to local villages, increasing efforts to hire locals as guides and forest wardens, compensating for crop damage done by wildlife straying outside of parks, and giving local people input into the management of protected areas. In South America, Bolivia's Beni Preserve, created in the late 1980s, surrounds a core wilderness preserve with a forested area devoted to traditional, sustainable resource extraction. Surrounding the forested area is a section devoted to sustainable agriculture. This project thus makes room for both conservation and preservation of natural resources while fostering the economic interests of local people. In India, beginning in the late 1980s, the Rathambhore Foundation and other groups began working to promote sustainable development in the villages on the periphery of the Project Tiger reserves. This has included replanting denuded forests and improving fodder—to decrease pressure to graze and cut firewood within the reserves—as well as efforts to educate local children in natural history and conservation principles.

Justice demands that local people be treated with respect and that their interests be considered in all programs to protect wildlife and wildlands. But such respect and consideration will not solve all problems, particularly in a country as overpopulated as India (whose human population has increased from 280 million to 910 million in this century). If we want to preserve tigers or any wild beings or places, we will have to sacrifice some human interests. Subsistent graziers will have to graze livestock outside the parks. Wealthy sportsmen will have to give up hunting tigers. Visitors to the parks will not be allowed to roam freely but will have to be accompanied by guides. We believe strong efforts should be made to meet the basic needs of poor inhabitants adjacent to these parks. But where these needs conflict with measures that are necessary to preserve species, we believe they should be met in ways that preserve wild nature. This is where we part company with Guha.

In Project Tiger, promises of resettlement help were not fully met—an injustice. But even if they had been, real hardship would have occurred. People were moved out of their homes and off their lands, creating psychological hardship, which even generous resettlement efforts would only partly ameliorate. Unfortunately, it is not callous environmental imperialists who set "the interests of the tiger against those of poor peasants," but rather the realities "on the ground," including increasing human populations and the basic facts of tiger biology.[4]

Do only the rich visit the tiger reserves? Tax them and give the money to adjacent villages. Provide funds for local schoolchildren to visit the parks and learn about the wildlife. But do not let wrangles about which people enjoy or benefit from designated wildlands undermine efforts to protect them, because they deserve protection for the sake of their nonhuman inhabitants and for the sake of future generations of Indians. The grandchildren of today's subsistence farmers, and *their* grandchildren, will be able, it is hoped, to experience and appreciate these wild places. If we fail to protect them, we impoverish future generations.

A particularly difficult issue involves local control of resources. Guha praises the Chipko movement and similar grassroots organizations that "seek to wrest control of nature away from the state and the industrial sector and place it in the hands of rural communities who live within that environment but are increasingly denied access to it."[5] David Rothenberg, summarizing views at the Fifth World Wilderness Conference, wrote: "We [most conference participants] affirmed the right of local people to be given the chance to manage their own local resources; however, they, like everyone else, must show that their specific knowledge builds on what the world as a whole now knows about itself."[6] As a statement about the desirability of local versus hegemonic outside control, Rothenberg's statement is correct. Local people should control their own economic lives with a degree of freedom from faraway governments and corporations. And Guha is correct that current gross economic inequalities, both within and between nations, are unjust. But concern for human social justice and autonomy must be balanced by a recognition of the intrinsic value of the nonhuman beings who will be affected by human actions. If it is wrong for the U.S. Forest Service or Champion International Corporation to knowingly extinguish species, it is equally wrong for a group of villagers to do so.

What happens when principles of local control and nature preservation come into conflict? One of these valuable desiderata must go. We support top-down regulations mandating nature preservation, provided they meet three criteria: they are necessary to prevent the extinction of species or rare ecological communities; they provide fair compensation for affected individuals (individual people, not corporations); they respect basic human rights. We do not pretend that such regulations will not create real human hardship, but we believe they are necessary to preserve a rich human future.

Guha criticizes Western and especially American environmentalists for failing to address issues of social justice, especially overconsumption among the wealthy. Whether or not "overconsumption remains the unasked question of the American conservation movement,"[7] we agree with Guha that Americans' *answers* to this question have been selfish and inadequate. Both the wasteful and extravagant lifestyles of average Americans and the U.S. government's successful attempt to undermine efforts to combat global warming at the Kyoto Conference in December 1997 illustrate this clearly. Even when issues such as recycling or water conservation are addressed in the United States, discussion usually focuses on sustaining resources to facilitate more "development" to satisfy ever-increasing "needs." Such an approach both avoids tough conservation decisions and utterly fails to grasp the centrality and destructiveness of the U.S. place in the current world industrial system. Furthermore, even though Americans have successfully preserved important tracts of wildlands within their boundaries, their insatiable appetites condemn many more places within the United States and around the world to destruction.

Guha's calls for "renunciation and self-limitation" are thus entirely justified. But that is what we as societies and individuals do when we set aside wild areas. We renounce certain uses of certain places. Doubtless this is sometimes a matter of individuals with an interest in wilderness recreation seeking to limit the incompatible uses of others. Guha is right, then, that wilderness proponents must work to limit our own consumption or risk a justified charge of hypocrisy.

Consumer restraint among the wealthy is necessary to protect wild nature. But so are wilderness preserves. Both are necessary because with human populations and economies continuing to grow, explicit legal protection from human economic activities is the only way to secure the survival of many species and ecological communities. Guha doesn't face this issue squarely in his critique of wilderness. Are we not to have any nature reserves? Can we ever displace or seriously inconvenience human populations to safeguard wildlife? He asserts that the reserves set up by Project Tiger moved resources from the poor (subsistence farmers) to the rich (foreign tourists) but leaves aside an essential point: they preserved resources for the tigers.

But why should this matter? Why preserve tigers, or for that matter any of the hundreds of other plant and animal species listed in the International Union for Conservation of Nature *Red Data Books* as threatened and endangered on the Indian Subcontinent, the thousands listed as threatened and endangered around the world? We see two reasons. First, the goodness of the tiger itself: its beauty, its complexity, its ancient and unique natural history. There is something here that should compel our respect. Second, the goodness of a full, rich human life, which includes both knowledge of and personal connection to nature. If we do not preserve the tiger and the land, we close off important ties to the human past and possibilites for future human aesthetic, scientific, and spiritual development.

In their recent book *This Fissured Land* (University of California Press, 1993), Guha and coauthor Madhav Gadgil provide what they subtitle "an ecological history of India." This widely praised book contains not the briefest description of an animal or plant except as they figure as natural resources to be used in various ways or fought over by contending humans. It contains absolutely no natural history: no accounts of the evolution of India's flora and fauna, their ecological interactions, or the formation of characteristic natural communities. These lacunae are not accidental, nor are they artifacts of academic specialization; rather, they illustrate well the cramped and solipsistic worldview to which anthropocentrism leads. Such a view falsifies the past, narrows the present, and diminishes the future.

Guha argues that "the anthropocentric-biocentric distinction is largely spurious" in distinguishing between environmental positions,[8] but his own flawed analysis and truncated ecological history show the need to preserve this distinction. It is needed in order to give voice to the interests of nonhuman nature. It is needed in order to appreciate our genuine, but noneconomic, interests in wild nature—the interests of the poet, painter, scientist, dreamer, or seeker of religious visions. It is needed, most simply, in order to see nature at all. Proper environmental policy, both in India and America, will only become clear when we come to appreciate the nature and value of the many millions of species with whom we share the earth and when we can distinguish essential from inessential human interests, and genuine human interests from increased wealth and consumption.

With this we return to our original point: respect for nonhuman nature and an understanding of the threats facing it logically lead to strong support for wilderness preservation. To be successful, this must include continued expansion of nature preserves and limits to human consumption, mammonism, and numbers. It must also include, we believe, attention to the plight of the poor and a more just distribution of wealth worldwide. We should not sacrifice human rights or deny democratic processes to secure any of this, but neither should we apologize for "taking resources away from more pressing issues." This is the same arrogant anthropocentrism that has played such a great role in bringing us to the brink of the sixth great extinction spasm in the 3.5-billion-year history of life on earth: the first—if we continue on our current path— to be freely and consciously enacted by self-proclaimed *Homo sapiens sapiens*.

NOTES

1 Ramachandra Guha, "Radical American Environmentalism and Wilderness Preservation: A Third World Critique," *Environmental Ethics* 11 (1989): 71–83.
2 Ibid., p. 75.
3 Ibid., pp. 75–76.
4 Ibid., p. 75.
5 Ibid., p. 81.
6 David Rothenberg, ed., *Wild Ideas* (Minneapolis: University of Minnesota Press, 1995), p. xx.
7 Guha, "Radical American Environmentalism," p. 82.
8 Ibid., p. 83.

FIGURE 4. Long-necked gerunucks in Samburu, northern Kenya. (© Robert Radin)

5
of kilimanjaro
in the dust

The Ford Foundation hall, tucked in between the East African Herbarium and National Museums of Kenya, is small as lecture theaters go, its upper floor rising steeply toward the ceiling. The auditorium was packed and the atmosphere noisy with anticipation as I waited to give my findings on Amboseli at the request of the East African Natural History Society. It was eighteen months since I had begun work, and a newly released film titled *The Death of Amboseli* had put the reserve back in the international spotlight.

I felt hedged in and nervous after so long in the bush. Only a handful of black faces looked out from the crowd. Several prominent hunters, tour operators, and preservationists sat waiting to pounce. Researchers were a highly suspect bunch among the old wildlife hands, and my degree labeled me a boffin—a scientific egghead—regardless of my upbringing. It didn't help, knowing that a failure at today's function could scuttle my plan for Amboseli.

Flicking on the first slide, I began to describe the ecology of Amboseli, stressing the erratic pattern of migrations extending well beyond the reserve boundaries. Slide after slide showed large herds of zebra, wildebeest, buffalo, and elephants, dispensing a subliminal message that far from being dead, Amboseli was very much alive. To judge from the murmurs of approval, the message was hitting home, but the provocative point was yet to come.

"The Maasai fit into the picture much the same as wild species—and have done so for centuries," I hurried on, trying to quell the reaction to cattle and lay the ground for the conclusion.

"And what about the destruction of Amboseli's woodlands? I am sure this is what you've all come to hear about." I waited, letting expectations mount. Made famous by countless photos and tourist brochures, Amboseli's fever trees growing at the foot of Kilimanjaro had come to epitomize the African savannas to countless people around the world. Nothing did more to infuriate conservationists than to hear that the elegant trees were being destroyed by hungry hordes of Maasai cattle.

"Well, the Maasai are not destroying the woodlands. Overgrazing is not the cause of habitat loss."

"Look at the trees here," I continued, raising my voice above the shuffling. "This slide was shot in the center of the stock-free area. No cattle, but plenty of dead trees. And this shot? It was taken at the edge of the basin where there are thousands of cattle. Look. No dead trees. Why?"

The shuffling died down, and the room went quiet. I had no explanation for the loss of trees, but evidence did point to earlier treeless cycles. "Let me read the first written account of Amboseli made by the Scots explorer Joseph Thomson in 1883. 'Conceive of yourself standing in the center of the plain. In your immediate vicinity there is not a blade of grass to relieve the barren aspect of the damp muddy sand, which, impregnated with various salts, is unfavorable to the growth of any vegetation. Here and there, however, in the horizon are to be detected a few sheets of water, surrounded by rings of green grass, and a few straggling trees or scrubby bushes. . . . In spite of the desolate and barren aspect of the country, game is to be seen in marvelous abundance. . . . The question that naturally rises in one's mind is, How can such enormous numbers of large game live in this extraordinary desert?'"

I projected slide after slide to accompany the text, illustrating a contemporary Amboseli resembling the scene Thomson described eighty years earlier rather than the intervening years. "So what are the implications for conservation?" I continued with rising confidence, expanding on a plan hastily sketched in the dust a few weeks earlier.

The plan began to take shape at the tail end of 1968, a year after starting my research. In August of that year I had counted 20,000 cattle, 6,000 sheep and goats, 5,000 wildebeest, 3,700 zebra, 800 buffalo, 450 elephant, 60 rhinos, and 15,000 other animals packed into the 150 square miles of the Amboseli basin. The congestion caused conflicts, running the gamut from the amusing to the grotesque, from an elephant charging furiously through a bucking herd of donkeys, to a large python that swallowed two goats and terrified the Maasai. A Maasai elder horned by a rhino had dragged himself several kilometers homeward, only to be trailed and killed by a lion. Lions had also broken into the cattle camps up on the Eremito Ridge, killing several animals. Exacerbating the already volatile situation, the Maasai warriors, irate over rumors of a government takeover of the reserve, speared several rhinos in a show of protest. The *Los Angeles Times* ran an article decrying the killings and calling for action.

Conflict had become a way of life in Amboseli, and, for many, a way of death.

Tempers flared all round, with the government threatening to crack down on the Maasai, the tourists grouching about the invasion of cattle, and the Maasai angry at anyone who sided with wildlife.

Sindiyo ran himself ragged, trying to restrain the warriors from killing animals and animals from killing livestock. Oloitiptip made a bad situation impossible for the warden by brazenly poaching zebra and daring the rangers to stop him. Sindiyo fought hard to keep the Maasai out of the small wildlife sanctuary around Ol Tukai. The Maasai resented Sindiyo for banning cattle from their favorite swamps and accused him of caring more for wild animals and foreigners than for his own people. The Kajiado County Council came in for its own share of resentment for allocating the thirty-square-mile sanctuary to wildlife and tourists without consulting the Maasai. In fact the Maasai felt doubly cheated by this latest slight, having resisted the efforts of the national parks only to fall victim to their own council.

The final straw came when the government banned tourists from photographing the Maasai under the pretext that it was tantamount to treating them like wild animals. In truth, Kenya's progressive government was embarrassed by the half-dressed Maasai warriors. The latest stricture meant the Maasai couldn't earn money from tourists and thus deprived them of their only source of wildlife-related income. The resentment bubbled over when fresh rumors of a government takeover reached the Maasai. A warrior watering his cattle couldn't take any more and vented his fury on a tourist who snapped a shot of his cattle, then sped off in a plume of dust. Running after the vehicle, the herder hurled his spear through the rear window and skewered the tourist through the shoulder. News spread among the Maasai like wind through the grass, tempting other warriors to follow suit, if that's what it took to get attention.

Tourists were no less resentful of the Maasai intrusion into their pristine African wilderness. "We've paid good bucks to visit a national park, not a cattle ranch," they groused over drinks at the lodge bar after a day's game drive. By 1968 conflict saturated the game reserve like a leaky gas tank about to explode.

The germ of a new conservation plan came to me during an evening's walk. I had set out from the tent when the first weary lines of zebra and wildebeest began filing out of thickets onto the plains. The evening light slowly restored rich hues to the sun-scorched pastels, and deep shadows crept through the woodlands until only the upper branches of the trees caught the waning sun. On the plains the bleached grasses turned deep amber, and the eroded soils of Eremito Ridge warmed to a deep crimson.

The migrations are finally making sense, I told myself. During the rains the Maasai and wildlife range over an area five to ten times the size of their dry-season range, covering an ill-defined tract stretching around Amboseli like the penumbra of a waning moon. During the dry season the boundaries contract and sharpen as the migrants return to the basin, slake their thirst, and feed on the pastures within cruising range of the swamps.

"How can such enormous numbers of large game live in this extraordinary desert?" Joseph Thomson had wondered. The explanation lay in the seasonal migrations. Block off the herds migrating to the wet-season pastures, and their numbers would dwindle by half. Close off the swamps, and the entire ecosystem would die like a city denied water. Reduce the complexity of habitats to Tsavo's homogeneous bushland, and Amboseli would be as drab as the thorn scrub tourists thunder through on their way from Nairobi. I turned to watch a string of wildebeest thread its way through the scattered *mswaki* bushes, following a geometrical path precisely defined by the midpoint between the thickets. The burnished yellow of the fever trees had faded to gray as I headed back to camp. A year's work didn't amount to much, but enough to realize that what the national park conservationists had in mind would be as ecologically ruinous as tearing up a dollar bill. Dividing the Amboseli ecosystem in two was not the answer for the Maasai or wildlife.

The game reserve boundaries made no ecological sense either. The map of Kenya's parks gave the illusion of space and protection for Amboseli Game Reserve. In reality the western two-thirds of the reserve supported few animals and lay off the migratory routes which stretched to the north, far outside the existing boundary. Doubling the area of the reserve would add some protection, but not enough to secure the ecosystem. Such a huge expansion was inconceivable in any event. No independent African government in its right mind would entertain the political fallout of the mass deportations involved. The days when Ionides could move Africans like chess pawns to make way for elephants were gone. Every extra inch of conservation land came at the expense of an African family and created new enemies.

There had to be some better way to protect the entire ecosystem. Western preservationism behind the national parks movement stems from a legacy of extermination, stretching from the extinction of the mammoths to the passenger pigeon. Africa's far richer wildlife legacy rested on millennia of coexistence rather than segregation. So why not try coexistence?

Coexistence if not harmony was a fact of life, seen through Parashino's eyes. Any lion bold enough to attack his herd became sport for the warriors, reestablishing fear at the root of mutual tolerance between predators and African peoples. But what of the herbivores? His cattle outwardly grazed benignly alongside wildebeest, and zebra mixed freely with his donkeys. What lay behind the mutual tolerance? Such equanimity made no sense in the face of intense competition between wild and domestic herbivores during the dry season. Why, before the colonial laws and tourism turned the Maasai against wildlife, had the Maasai tolerated wild animals consuming half their pasture and spreading disease to livestock?

In Maasai mythology, recounted jokingly by men, wildlife belonged to the womenfolk, who attended them so poorly that the animals wandered out of the *boma* and into the bush. As a solitary voice opposing the rising clamor that the only way to conserve Amboseli lay in a national park, I needed a hard explanation.

Halfway back to camp, I glanced up at the dying acacia branches starkly silhouetted against the pink-tinged snows of Kilimanjaro. Soon the trees would be dead, exposing my fading yellow tent to the sun and minibuses. That's when the contradiction hit me. How could I have been so blind? Here in the wildlife sanctuary, where livestock were banned, the trees were either dead or dying. Around the Maasai settlements, trees flourished. Whatever else was killing the trees, it couldn't be the Maasai. The wildlife sanctuary was a natural experiment exonerating them.

Gathering the incontrovertible data needed to vindicate the Maasai would be easy enough. All I had to do was show that the condition of trees across the basin bore no relationship to the presence of Maasai encampments or livestock. When I eventually did so, the results were utterly compelling. The condition of the woodland trees was in fact inversely related to cattle activity; the healthiest trees were associated with the highest density of livestock.

Whatever the cause of woodland decline, it wasn't the Maasai, so there was no longer cause to evict them on the grounds of habitat destruction. If I were willing to be perverse, I could go as far as to say that, if anything, the Maasai preserved rather than destroyed the woodlands. At the time, that claim seemed so farfetched as to court ridicule; so I dropped it.

Try as I might, I couldn't get around the need for some protection of the swamps. If farmers turned the Amboseli swamps into *shambas* as they had in Kimana Swamp ten miles to the east, wildlife would disappear. The newly irrigated shambas and rows of thatch huts at Kimana had driven off the last of the rhinos and elephants and cordoned off the swamps, blocking wildlife access. So why not keep the protected area to an absolute minimum, just enough to secure the swamps and tourist game-viewing circuits? Coexistence rather than segregation could then prevail in the rest of the ecosystem.

Ideas of coexistence bolted through my mind like some Arcadian vision until checked by the reality of population growth and cultural disintegration destroying Maasai traditions. All the same, the Maasai would surely be better off with Amboseli than without it—and wildlife better off in their hands than anyone else's. Either the mutual tolerance of old would survive, or Amboseli would perish. I squatted excitedly in the dirt track and began roughing out a plan, using a stick to trace a rudimentary map in the dust of Kilimanjaro.

First I sketched out the protected area around the swamps and central surrounding woodlands. With the swamps safe from drought and settlement, wildlife would continue luring tourists. Why not call it a Maasai park, making the local community rather than government or county council the custodians of its wildlife? Under this scheme, tourism would provide money and jobs, diversifying the Maasai economy and preventing the pitfall of poverty and landlessness arising from their faltering subsistence lifestyle. The land outside the Maasai park could continue under pastoralism. Amounting to some three thousand square miles, or some 90 percent of the ecosystem, the land had no arable potential anyhow. Provided with additional water points, the dry-season range could be expanded to make up for the loss of pasture in the Maasai park. New incentives to conserve wildlife outside the protected area could also be explored, perhaps by giving the Maasai a percentage of hunting revenues. And there was no reason why tourism could not be expanded over the entire ecosystem, giving the Maasai additional revenue and reducing the visitor pressure in the park.

The light had faded, and the map sketched hastily in the dust was barely visible. Straightening up, I made for camp, anxious to write up the details while they were still fresh. Coexistence had all the right appeal. Not only did it explain the historical survival of wildlife on the continent, it also offered the only hope of perpetuating open ecosystems and large-scale migrations in modern Africa.

For over a century wildlife around the world had been preserved by government decree, by the establishment of game laws and national parks in the interests of society at large. Preservationism was a triumph of compassion over greed, a noble commitment to save endangered species and set aside the Yellowstones and Serengetis for the world and for posterity. But however well-intentioned, preservationism failed more often than it worked. Usurping rights to wildlife and land from its traditional owners and vesting them in the state didn't provide any assurance of preservation. All too often the well-heeled hunters, tourists, and preservationists won out over the rural poor—whether American Indian or Maasai. Disfranchising the people controlling the fate of wildlife was no recipe for its survival.

The time had come for a new approach, an approach resting on fairness and local involvement rather than on alienation and enforcement. Why should local communities not become the principal beneficiaries and ultimate custodians of wildlife, as they always had been, without sacrificing the larger interests of society?

The idea, however appealing, had a major flaw. Local participation challenged a century of governmental control and vested interest. There was sure to be resistance. Why should governments voluntarily give up their authority and commercial interest to tribal people who openly despised and threatened wildlife? What could the uneducated Maasai, who couldn't stop their own cattle from destroying the land, possibly know about conservation? How could they stop poaching and address their own population problem?

Persuading conservationists, the government, and the Maasai themselves was certain to be an uphill task, but I was undaunted: fairness and logic would prevail.

The tent loomed against the darkening sky as I made camp. The sound of wildebeest shuffling across the plain and a heavy hide scraping against an acacia tree reached out from close by. After savoring the night sounds and the cool breeze a few moments longer, I ducked under the canvas to jot down my thoughts.

The applause died down in the lecture hall after I concluded with a description of the new plan. The questions were unexpectedly sympathetic, even encouraging. Exonerating the Maasai of the woodland die-off had momentarily silenced the argument for a national park.

"I take your point about the reserve boundaries being all wrong, and about the need to conserve the entire migratory area," a voice spoke up from the rear. "But are you saying that we should only protect a small area, hand it over to the Maasai, and write off the rest? If so, you're advocating helping the Maasai at the expense of the animals."

I hedged, knowing that the mention of a Maasai park, indigenous rights, and social responsibility would smack of communism to the conservative white settlers in the audience. "What I'm trying to say," I continued cautiously, "is that we have to think about the entire ecosystem, not just the dry-season range. To conserve the ecosystem we must win Maasai support by accommodating their interests. We don't really have any alternative. Besides, we know that coexistence worked in the past, so why not now? My ideas are admittedly tentative, but there's reason to think the Maasai could be persuaded to preserve Amboseli if they got a share of the tourist revenues, social services, and jobs."

"Excellent, excellent." A short, balding man grasped my hand and pumped it enthusiastically as I left the hall elated by my unexpected success. "My name is Emil Rado, director of the Institute for Development Studies at the university. I was intrigued that you touched on the social issues. Do conservationists really think they can save animals and ignore people?"

We drifted outside with the crowd into the night. "Look," Rado continued, "how would you like to give a more detailed lecture on these ideas at IDS? You would have an enthusiastic group, I assure you."

Buoyed by the success of the lecture and the promise of an enthusiastic reception, I met Rado and his staff in downtown Nairobi shortly afterward. "Well, of course, I'm a sociologist," Rado began the introductions. "And this is Frank Mitchell, economist. Over there, Tim Aldington, livestock specialist. And Alan Jacobs, anthropologist. He worked on the Ilkisongo Maasai in Tanzania for his Ph.D., so you should have a lot in common." Rado continued around the table. "And finally, Dr. Leonard, a political scientist specializing in administration."

"I hope you don't expect too much," I responded. "Frankly, you're the people with the answers, not me. Amboseli is a tough problem, full of emotions. It needs the sort of social and economic approach you can bring to it. The professor of the Zoology Department told me I should think about a social science degree if I wanted to study humans. Seems I've come to the right place," I joked.

Mitchell, the economist, smiled and eyed me through steel-rimmed glasses. "The trouble with you biologists is that you never consider economic or social factors. You're a bunch of birdwatchers. That's why wildlife is in trouble. What I heard you say is different. Downright exciting in fact. We'd love to help with ideas."

Mitchell leaned forward, a lock of dark hair falling across his temple. "Seems to me that you need to state and quantify your arguments clearly. Tourism is the key to integration, right? So what do the visitor stats and income projections look like? Who benefits and who loses from wildlife?" The writing pad in front of him was filled with elaborate inked-in doodles around the margins. "Let me put it more simply. If you want to save wildlife you have to sustain the tourist industry and include the Maasai.

That means pumping money back into tourist management and covering the opportunity costs of wildlife to the Maasai . . . "

He caught my blank expression. "Sorry. By opportunity costs I mean the costs the Maasai incur through loss of grazing, disease, and so on from the wildlife migrating out of the park onto their land. You know, this laissez-faire approach to tourism is a damned disaster. It'll destroy Amboseli, but the conservationists just can't get it through their heads. The days when the colonial government could draw a line round Tsavo and kick out the Wakamba are over. We have to start dealing with the human problems or lose the parks."

Under Emil Rado, the institute had attracted an assortment of social scientists and economists from North America, Europe, and East Africa, most of them liberal, intellectual, and critical of the conventional economic models for transferring wealth from the developed to developing world. Few bodies anywhere in the late 1960s could have rivaled the institute's dedication to dismantling disciplinary barriers, challenging conventional modes of development, and trying out new ideas for incorporating the social and economic dimensions of change. The atmosphere in the institute fairly sizzled with ideas and acid humor about development schemes gone awry. All the institute lacked, in fact, was a focus for its rare collection of talent—and a touch of ecological reality. Amboseli provided both.

So began an association that over the next few months fleshed out details of the rudimentary plan sketched in the dust weeks before. Applying economic, social, and ecological models to Amboseli proved to be an innovative and exciting collaboration. We all sensed that we were breaking new ground, but none more than Frank Mitchell. He talked with great fervor about interdisciplinary studies, integrated conservation and development, and the social dimensions of change, but not even he anticipated that our team effort would help launch a new paradigm of integrated conservation and development in the 1980s.

Nine months after our collaboration began, I summarized our findings to an enthusiastic crowd in the institute's seminar room. This time the analysis focused on the economic and social implications of conserving Amboseli. Mitchell, who reveled in economic forecasts, had generated reams of figures on the opportunity cost of wildlife to the Maasai and the benefits they stood to gain from tourism and hunting. The analysis spoke overwhelmingly in favor of an integrated use of the land, rather than a separation of wildlife and livestock. Even under assumptions of heavy capital input, intensive management, and favorable markets, livestock would generate only some $600,000 if free to use the entire ecosystem. If, on the other hand, the entire ecosystem were turned over to wildlife use without any livestock present, income from tourism and hunting would amount to $8 million. The highest revenue of all came from combining both uses and excluding livestock only from the small protected area around the swamp. Under this scenario, revenues would rise higher still, avoiding the horrendous economic and social costs of evicting the Maasai from their traditional homelands.

Three conclusions came out of the collaboration. First, if the Maasai were cut in on Amboseli's wildlife proceeds, they would end up several times better off economically than if they relied solely on their herds. Wildlife, the livestock women had so inattentively let wander all over the countryside according to Maasai myth, had become more valuable than the men's herds! Second, the total number of wild animals and the ultimate volume of visitors would be far higher under ecological integration—a technical euphemism for coexistence—than under segregation. Third, the coexistence of wildlife and livestock would generate greater wealth for the Maasai than either option alone.

After the seminar, Mitchell walked me to my car. "You know, Jonah, you have a golden model here. You're onto something. Stick with it. Make sure you publicize it. Those crusty colonials who can only think of parks or nothing have their heads in the sand, and the wildlife biologists aren't much better. This is bigger than Amboseli. Make sure you pull out the general principles. I'll help you with the next stage, too, if you like."

Mitchell's admonition and help gave me a badly needed boost to push ahead with the plan. The next step was to win the approval of the Maasai, the county council, and, finally, the conservation community and government.

The details, it turned out, meant everything to Parashino. Mistrust flickered in his eyes the moment I laid out the plan. "What you are saying is that you want to turn Amboseli over to the animals and throw us out. Is that it? I thought you told me you were not Game Department? Well, are you on their side or ours?"

Parashino's anger caught me off guard. "No, no," I told him defensively. "Don't you see that Amboseli would be a Maasai park, not a government park? A Maasai park would not only prevent a government takeover, it would also make Amboseli's wildlife valuable to you. Wouldn't you want to preserve wildlife if you got money out of it?"

"You think you are helping the Maasai, don't you." he interjected. "Well, you're not. Wild animals are useless to us. Nothing but trouble. The British took our land in Serengeti and Tsavo, then in Mara and Samburu. Next it was the Kajiado County Council, which claimed our land in Amboseli. Now it's the Kikuyu government which wants it, and you're helping them.

"Listen to me," he went on, "to the way we Maasai see it. Wild animals are government cattle. We are told to look after them for the tourists. And even though we have, it's not enough. The government wants our land too. If we kill their animals because they eat our grass and kill our livestock, we are arrested. The Kikuyus want us to keep quiet while they steal everything. Why should they care about the Maasai or listen to you?"

I had never seen Parashino so angry. Far from winning his approval, I had betrayed his trust. "No matter what you say, Yonah," he added with finality, "a park means the Maasai lose."

I tried everything I knew to win his approval, or at least get a hearing, but he would have none of it. He perceptively saw that in vindicating the Maasai of the woodland destruction, I had spiked the argument for a national park. "So why do you still want a park if we are not to blame?" he demanded.

"Why?" I shot back angrily in frustration and defeat. "I'll tell you why. Aren't the Maasai already pushing government to scrap the reserve and turn it over to ranches? What then? Shambas like Kimana, then fences and houses? And after that? The wild-life will disappear, and you, the council, the government, and everyone else in Kenya will lose."

I was not going to let the plan get shot down without a fight. "Do you think the government will stand by and see Amboseli destroyed? Tourism is too important to Kenya for that to happen. And what of the Maasai in the future? Won't they need money, schools, and clinics? Won't you need jobs when your cattle can no longer feed your children? Surely it's better to make Amboseli your own park rather than let the government grab it."

Parashino's anger subsided as mine mounted, but frustration and distrust still showed in his eyes. I was looking ahead, to the dangers of population growth and a collapsing subsistence economy, he to the past and all the injustices the Maasai had suffered. We were talking at cross-purposes, I about threats and opportunities he barely grasped, he about memories and fears incomprehensible to an outsider. I had yet to grasp the full significance of space and mobility to the pastoral mind, or the significance of the swamps the Maasai would lose. Unwittingly, I interpreted all Parashino's fears in strictly ecological terms, as if he were herding wildebeest and zebra. What the ecological interpretation missed was psychology, the pathological fear of land loss and faltering Maasai power, which clouded everything else. Our mutual ignorance lay like a gulf between us, a gulf that only time, trust, and exposure to each other's experience would bridge.

Parashino's myopia and intransigence put me in a moral dilemma. Should I press ahead with the plans in the Maasai's long-term interests or accept their decision as paramount, whatever the consequences?

Sindiyo had no such qualms. The worldly Maasai had an obligation to persuade the more traditional. The greater moral crime lay in seeing the threats and walking away, leaving the Maasai to their fate. But then, Sindiyo was a Maasai—and they his people. I was an outsider and had no pretensions to being a Maasai.

It was Simon Salash who persuaded me to put conviction above paternalistic guilt, though he never knew it: I met him only once.

The day, June 22, 1979, was hot and windy. The long rains had been indifferent and the grasses had wilted prematurely, leaving the animals short of grazing. From the top of Kitirua Hill I sat watching small dust flurries billowing off the barren ground as a lone figure came tramping up the hill. He had the short-cropped hair, red-checked *shuka*, and *rungu* (knobkerrie) of a traditional elder and the battered raincoat, black patent-leather shoes, and holed socks of an urban Maasai. Shaking hands, he introduced himself as Simon Salash and said he was a farmer from Loitokitok who had cattle out this way. Our discussion quickly came round to Amboseli.

"The Maasai will never accept a park," he told me emphatically. "Why should they, when it stretches all the way to the Chyulus and Namanga? Where would the Maasai go?"

I laughed. "What do you mean? The park goes only from here to Kalunyet and up to Eremito, not to the Chyulus—only around the swamps and part of the woodlands."

He looked at me in disbelief. "Honest to God? But the Maasai here tell me Oloitiptip said it was two hundred miles long."

"Two hundred miles long? That's wrong. It's two hundred square miles, not two hundred miles long."

"What's the difference? Two hundred miles is two hundred miles, isn't it?"

I laughed again, unable to believe the damage done by a simple misapprehension. The local Maasai had adopted British measures and talked of distance in miles and area in acres. How could a mile possibly be square? I explained the distinction to Salash.

He laughed too. "Well, if it's as you say, then it's not such a big park, is it? But Amboseli will not survive even if the Maasai are given the park. They don't know what land titles mean. When they get a title deed they sell it for money and think they can still keep the land. Look at Kimana. The Kikuyus and Wakambas have already moved in. Why should Amboseli be any different? These Maasai don't see what's happening to them.

"And look at this place. Dry and dusty. The cattle are already showing ribs. How will the Maasai survive the coming drought?"

Salash's experience in the larger world gave him the foresight Parashino lacked. "They will have to change or lose everything," he had concluded. The words went round and round in my head for days and convinced me that Sindiyo's paternalism was morally the better course. Surely a touch of paternalism was better than letting the Maasai and wildlife go marching blindly up the path of mutual destruction.

Even if Salash's words had not made up my mind, an article in East Africa's *Standard* newspaper on July 4 certainly did. "The Money Locked Up in Amboseli" read the centerpiece spread. The article detailed the report I had prepared for the Institute for Development Studies and Mitchell's economic analysis. "So far Amboseli's potential as a money spinner has hardly begun to be realized," the article went on. "Given proper management as a wildlife area, Amboseli could look forward to a gross tourist revenue of between $8,000,000 and $14,000,000 a year by 1980."

The press coverage would have been welcome but for one omission: Maasai participation. Far from drawing attention to the need for Maasai involvement, the article mentioned only the economic profits at stake, giving the government a new excuse to step in to protect national interests. Sure enough, in Nairobi the promise of Amboseli's wealth glinted like a torch beam in the government's eyes. To make matters worse, conservationists promptly substituted national economic interests for the discredited dustbowl argument and pushed even harder for a national park. At a wildlife workshop, one conservationist accused me of suffering from Maasaiitis, as if it were a deadly disease.

"Some conservationist!" was how he put it, as if excommunicating me from the honorable fraternity. I was mortified at the slight but too young and timid to tell him that I cared more about Amboseli and wildlife than he ever would.

Frank Mitchell's hide was thicker than mine, and he relished the rebukes. "That makes it 460 so far," he bubbled, ticking off another bird on his Kenya list as we skirted Lake Amboseli on his first tourist survey. "Jonah, don't take it so hard. The old farts shouldn't get you down. There's more than a little hypocrisy and racism in their reaction and it's downright irresponsible of them to slam you for taking up the Maasai side. Fine, we all love to save elephants, but conservation won't work unless it benefits the guys who get saddled with the bill. Conservationists couldn't care a damn about disfranchising the Maasai."

Mitchell's caustic comments and encouragement always bolstered me, and at no time more than now. Sindiyo's response was just as emphatic when he read the *Stan-*

dard article. "We have to act immediately or lose Amboseli," he told the committee of Maasai elders. He had a particular idea in mind.

Royal Little arrived a month later. A lean, hard-driving American businessman who had built a multimillion-dollar business conglomerate, Little was a man in a hurry who let nothing stand in his way. He had become passionately concerned about wildlife on his many safaris to Africa and jumped into conservation with his legendary business zeal and acumen. He wanted the best for the wild, and if his famed guide and ex-hunter, Sid Downey, said Amboseli should become a national park, then Little would see to it.

Sindiyo and I met Little and his retinue in a small clapboard guesthouse at the back of the Kilimanjaro Safari Lodge, where elephants grazed on the well-tended lawn. Little wasted no time on formalities. "I hope my plan for the park and offer of money through the New York Zoological Society is still alive," he kicked off. He had earlier offered the government $90,000 to provide alternative water sources if the government removed the Maasai from two hundred square miles of central Amboseli and turned it into a national park. The informality of his khaki safari suit and languid appearance couldn't disguise his corporate impatience.

Sindiyo responded diplomatically, omitting Oloitiptip's acerbic comments about Little's plan and his insistence on a Maasai solution to Maasai problems. "David Western—Jonah—whom I introduced earlier, has an alternative plan we think will work, though. He'll explain it to you."

I was irked at Little's bombastic style and his assumption that anything he said went, even in Amboseli. "The plan you want to support will never work," I told him abrasively, "not for wildlife, not for the Maasai. The boundaries are wrong ecologically. Now that the Maasai have rejected your plan, we have to start from scratch." I went on to describe my own plan for conserving the entire ecosystem. "A small core park makes sense," I concluded, "but only to protect the swamps from agriculture."

Little stared at me coldly after the presentation. He did not take kindly to a twenty-four-year-old whippersnapper telling him his plan was no damn good. "Fine, if you think this plan of yours will work, I'm all for it," he growled. "I want to see it work for the Maasai too. The new ecological information makes sense. What matters is that we save Amboseli from going down the tubes."

He abruptly turned to Sindiyo. "This is your baby, Mr. Sindiyo. But if you want my money—and it's still available—you're gonna have to get approval from the Ministry of Tourism and Wildlife and New York Zoological. We'll only deal directly with government."

Much as I resented the put-down, Royal Little's offer could make all the difference to the viability of the new plan. Money, a lot of it, would be needed for Maasai water points outside the park. Sindiyo lost no time in taking advantage of Little's offer. Swallowing his pride, he called on Oloitiptip, who he knew would be the power broker in persuading both the Maasai elders and the Kajiado County Council. Once persuaded, Oloitiptip called a meeting of Maasai elders on August 2 to deliberate the threats and opportunities facing Amboseli. The member of parliament for Kajiado North, several county councilors, Sindiyo, and representative Maasai elders attended.

The elders, like Parashino, were decidedly cool, but Oloitiptip was nothing if not a master persuader. "You have to think about the future, not the past," Sindiyo later reported him as saying. "We must change or die. The park will be our bank. What will our children think of us if they look at the park and say it was their fathers who gave it away?"

No agreement was reached that day, but Oloitiptip—like Royal Little—was not a man to give up. "Don't forget what we thought of the British when they insisted we send some children to school for our own good, the good of our future," he argued when the meeting resumed the next day. "We resisted, didn't we? We thought they were wrong. But where would we be today without our educated Maasai to represent us, to fight for our interests? I should know. I was one of those children, and I am now fighting for your interests."

After two days of anguish, debate, and Oloitiptip's incessant haranguing, the elders adopted the plan to make Amboseli into a Maasai park. Everything had fallen neatly into place—a plan acceptable to the Maasai, a prospective donor who would provide money for the new wells, and the beginning of a new era in ecosystem conservation. The ecological surveys, time spent with the Maasai, the interdisciplinary work with the Institute for Development Studies, and my close relationship with Sindiyo had paid off. The rest was up to others.

6 — why conservation
in the tropics is failing

Tropical parks are failing in country after country because the institutions created to protect them are weak and ineffectual. Institutional weakness derives from many sources, but it arises ultimately from the low priority governments give to protection of parks. Much has been recognized since tropical parks began drawing the attention of the international conservation community. Conservation organizations have responded by providing assistance, but over time, as a result of frustration born of failure, the form of assistance has changed dramatically, and not necessarily for the better.

In the early 1970s, international conservation assistance took the form of donations of tangible assets such as vehicles, boats, motors, guard posts, uniforms, generators, and radios. Such assistance brought visible benefits, without which parks often could not function. By helping to put parks on an operational footing, the proffering of material goods directly addressed the challenges of protecting biodiversity. Manu National Park, for one, would have remained a paper park without direct material assistance.

But in the face of mounting pressures, tangible donations proved less and less effective. Lying behind the donations of equipment was the unstated assumption that improved transportation and communications would promote effective enforcement of park regulations. The model in the minds of donors was that of the National Park Service in the United States and its highly effective rangers. Unfortunately, all too often the model proved to be out of synch with the realities of the recipient country, and efforts to replicate it ended up being little more than an expression of the donor's cultural bias.

Having well-trained and well-equipped guards is an indispensable prerequisite to creating an operational park, but the presence of guards amounts to more show than substance if they cannot make arrests and if the police and courts do not provide the necessary backup. By default, guards who are not empowered occupy themselves with controlling tourists and scientists while closing their eyes to the more serious challenge of evicting squatters, loggers, and miners.

Conservation organizations have yet to devise a workable strategy for combating illegal activities in tropical parks. Law enforcement is not an area in which the participation of foreign organizations or their local surrogates is welcome. Law enforcement, to the extent it is carried out at all, is the cloistered province of police and military forces that are highly jealous of their authority and autonomy. In many tropical countries, civilian politicians have little or no ability to influence the uniformed services. A national parks agency with the best of intentions remains powerless without the backing of those who carry the guns.

Unable to influence the layers of society that hold all the cards, international conservation workers find themselves facing a gargantuan task in their efforts to oppose the forces that threaten parks. Awareness of this reality has gradually sunk into the consciousness of conservation professionals, who remain frustrated with their inability to exercise control over events on the ground. How can the integrity of parks be ensured when effective law enforcement barely exists in many countries?

In some circumstances, the only recourse may be to solicit intervention at the highest level. An anecdote will illustrate the point.

A colleague of mine received an urgent communication from an associate in Indonesia notifying him that a logging company had begun to harvest trees in his study area inside Sumatra's Gunung Leuser National Park. The matter was complicated by ties between the regional military commander and the logging company. Knowing this, the park's administrator was powerless to do anything.

By chance, my colleague happened to be well connected in Europe. He consulted with some acquaintances in the World Wide Fund for Nature, and it was decided that he should draft a letter to President Suharto of Indonesia, drawing his attention to the violation of the park and the damage that logging would do to an international scientific enterprise of long standing. The letter was transmitted to a prominent European prince, who sent it to Suharto through diplomatic channels under his own name. Shortly afterward, the logging abruptly ceased, and the company withdrew its equipment from the park. However, although this strategy proved effective in this particular instance, the use of international leverage to call for presidential intervention in a park enforcement crisis is a measure of last resort. It might prove effective the first time, but it would fail entirely as a general mechanism for combating violations.

Frustrated by its inability to grasp the stick of enforcement, the international conservation movement turned in the 1980s to the carrot of economic assistance. It was reasoned that local villagers might voluntarily respect park boundaries if they could raise their standards of living through means other than exploitation of a park's resources.

During the same period, the major international donors, led by the World Bank, were under pressure to adopt "greener" policies and lending practices. U.S. president George Bush promoted the greening of USAID, hoping to give credibility to his claim of being an "environmental president," even as he opposed most environmental reform at home. USAID's European counterparts were right in step.

The wispy notion of sustainable development provided the common ground for a joining of forces by the international banks and bilateral assistance agencies and the world's leading conservation organizations. The big donors knew little about sustainable development, but they wanted to look green. Conservation organizations, impeccably green but inexperienced in managing international development projects, wanted to expand their programs and their international reach. Through multimillion-dollar USAID projects, conservation groups could demonstrate impressive rates of financial growth to their boards of directors.

The self-interest of the two sets of organizations converged in the form of integrated conservation and (sustainable) development projects, called ICDPs. The stated purpose of many ICDPs is to reduce external threats to parks by promoting sustainable development in surrounding areas. Conservation organizations were enthusiastic about ICDPs because the title contains the word *conservation,* and bilateral aid agencies liked them because the title contains the word *development.* Each side could frame projects in its own image.

Frequently, but not always, the focal points for ICDPs were provided by biosphere reserves established under the auspices of the Man and the Biosphere Programme of the United Nations Educational, Scientific, and Cultural Organization (UNESCO). To qualify for UNESCO recognition as a biosphere reserve, a park must have regional significance as a repository of biodiversity, must possess an inviolate core, and must be surrounded by one or more multiple-use areas serving as buffer zones for the core.

Although ICDPs promote sustainable forms of development in the buffer zones, the projects frequently do not directly involve the park itself, on the ground that the park is the government's responsibility.

For USAID and its counterparts, ICDPs provided a green shield under which they could continue what they had been doing for decades, sponsoring rural development programs in developing countries. For the conservation organizations, ICDPs offered a path to rapid growth. In 1995, one leading U.S. conservation organization allocated more than 60 percent of its program budget to various activities under the rubric of "Conservation and Human Needs"—ICDPs by another name. Much of the funding came from USAID or other major donors.

Despite the gilded rhetoric presenting them as conservation endeavors, ICDPs represent little more than wishful thinking. Project objectives typically have little direct relevance to the protection of biodiversity.[1] To the contrary, project managers who successfully innovate and invigorate the local economy risk aggravating the very problem they are trying to solve. By stimulating the local economy, an ICDP attracts newcomers to a park's perimeter, thereby increasing the external pressure on the park's resources.

More fundamentally, the ICDP model itself is inappropriate. Whereas in principle, parks are intended to be permanent institutions, projects, by their very nature, are designed to be executed within a fixed term, usually three to five years. Money floods in at the beginning and then stops just as abruptly at the end. Activities supported by the money stop when the money stops. All too often, the conditions the project was intended to ameliorate revert to their former state when the project ends, with little or nothing accomplished.[2]

There are many other drawbacks to ICDPs as an approach to the conservation of biodiversity. Most basically, ICDPs shoot at the wrong target—local people instead of the park and its natural resources.

Rural development projects characteristically emphasize intensification of land use through agroforestry schemes, new crop varieties, enhanced methods of animal husbandry, improved land management practices, small-scale irrigation works, preliminary processing of products, and so forth. Rarely is it acknowledged that intensified methods and improvements in rural standards of living also stimulate increases in population density. A farmer whose income rises may well hire additional labor. Increased cash flow through a community will attract trickle-down businesses such as stores, transportation services, video parlors. The outcome? More people are drawn to the community at a time when there are already too many people living around park boundaries. That is the problem. Simply put, successful ICDPs are only likely to make population-related problems worse.

Another crucial problem with ICDPs, one that is rarely addressed, is land rights. Forestlands often belong to the state and are used on an informal basis by indigenous slash-and-burn agriculturists and recently arrived settlers alike. How different was the settlement of North America! Following cultural practices inherited from their English forebears, government agents sent surveyors into the wilderness to measure and map the land prior to its settlement. Settlers then bought or registered their land before investing in buildings, clearing, or making other so-called improvements.

Such a degree of forethought and organization is unimaginable in many tropical countries. Forestlands are rarely held under title, or, if so, the titles are held by wealthy absentee landlords or speculators, as in Brazil. The bureaucratic process of titling a parcel can be so arcane and labyrinthine as to be incomprehensible to a semiliterate peasant. Thus, in the absence of any legal alternative, an attitude of lawlessness toward the land has evolved. Lawlessness is honored in the breach by politicians unwilling to risk social unrest by depriving poor people of access to land.

Unlawful occupancy of land is simply a fact of life throughout Latin America, in both rural and urban settings. For example, much of the growth of the sprawling barrios and *favelas* of Latin megacities such as Mexico City, Caracas, Lima, and São Paulo has occurred through *invasiones*. Landless migrants to the city gather together, target a vacant plot, and, on an appointed night, rush in to erect makeshift shanties of cardboard and sheet metal before dawn. The next morning, the landowner is faced with a fait accompli. Appeals to the police are of no effect because the politicians have instructed them not to interfere. Politicians who are regarded as lenient toward land invaders can help themselves to the votes of the poor, and thus they view squatters as an easy way to expand their constituencies. And so the cycle continues.

In societies in which extralegal land occupancy is the norm among the poor, one cannot simply draw an invisible line around a tract of forest, declare it a park, and expect the line to be respected. By custom, unoccupied land is available for the taking. Such a long-standing practice cannot be overturned over the course of a three- or five-year rural development project. Moreover, land titling is a function reserved for the state and is thus beyond the practical scope of an international assistance project. These facts of life lie behind the failure of many ICDPs to strengthen park boundaries.

Yet another shortcoming of ICDPs is that they typically reflect a community's existing economy and infrastructure. But many developing countries are undergoing rapid change. Common project goals, such as establishment of agroforestry plantings, installation of microirrigation works, and other such facets of rural development, can be rendered irrelevant by suddenly changing economic conditions.

The most profound change to a rural community comes when the government builds a road connecting it to a major city. An entire spectrum of new development possibilities then arises: large-scale logging, intensification of agriculture, production of new cash crops, cattle ranching, and so forth. If the area has agricultural potential, land values can soar, and many of the original inhabitants will be bought out by expanding agribusiness. In short, the tacit assumptions that underlie a project's design and goals can go out the window overnight.

Parks are also affected by forces that lie entirely beyond the reach of ICDPs. Whereas village poachers and slash-and-burn agriculturists mainly nibble around the edges of park boundaries, doing minor damage, large logging and mining companies can inflict damage on a massive scale. Invasion of parks by big-time resource pirates is nearly always sanctioned (for a cut in the proceeds) by the local military commander or by influential power brokers in the capital city. People such as these are untouchable at the village level. They can be stopped only through appeals to the head of state, if they can be stopped at all.

For all these reasons, ICDPs, in my view, are an inappropriate response to the external forces that threaten parks. I see these projects as misguided efforts that mostly fail to advance conservation, regardless of any success that may be achieved on the development side. Moreover, I doubt that it will ever be possible to improve ICDPs to make them more effective as instruments of conservation. The basic concept is flawed. Meanwhile, millions of dollars are being poured into ICDPs in the name of conservation.

Let me be clear. I have no objection to ICDPs per se. My objection is to the illusion created by linking them to conservation. Instead of trying to promote economic growth around parks, it would be better to discourage people from settling in or near buffer zones, perhaps by persuading governments not to build roads in these areas. If there are to be ICDPs, they should be located at a distance from parks so that people might be drawn away from park perimeters rather than attracted to them.

Another misconception embodied in the ICDP concept is the conviction that social change can be brought about through bottom-up processes. The ICDP approach assumes that the destiny of parks lies in the hands of local people, an assumption that is only partly correct. What ICDPs do not take into account is that local people are only minor players in a much larger theater. The lives of village people are strongly influenced by decisions of the central government and conditions determined by it: construction of roads; availability of rural credit, subsidies, and tax incentives; inflation versus stability of the national currency; raising or lowering of trade barriers; laws governing labor practices; receptivity to foreign capital; and so forth. Against powerful forces such as these, ICDPs pale into utter insignificance.

Now we have come full circle. Unable to grasp the stick of enforcement, conservation organizations turned to the carrot of economic assistance, but they must now come to grips with the failure of that approach as well. Bottom-up processes initiated at the village level will not improve the security of parks because they rely 100 percent on voluntary compliance. The recent history of environmental legislation in the United States provides many examples of the failure of voluntary compliance to produce the desired results. There are cheaters in every society, and the only response to cheating is enforcement. There is no substitute for enforcement. Without it, all is lost.

The focus of conservation must therefore return to the make-it-or-break-it issue of actively protecting parks, a matter that hinges above all on the quality of enforcement. Active protection of parks requires a top-down approach because enforcement is invariably in the hands of police and other armed forces that respond only to orders from their commanders. When the commanders happen to be business partners of the local timber baron, the prospects for protecting nature are undeniably grim.

NOTES

1 M. Wells and K. Brandon, *People and Parks: Linking Protected Area Management with Local Communities* (Washington, DC: World Bank, 1992).
2 Ibid.

DAVID WESTERN AND JOHN TERBORGH

7 "trouble in paradise"
an exchange

To the Editors:

I am grateful to John Terborgh for his generally favorable review of *In the Dust of Kilimanjaro* [*NYR*, February 18]. However, the book covers far more than Amboseli, the theme he elaborates. It includes elephant conservation controversies, a half-century of change in East Africa, lives of the Maasai, and shifting views in science and conservation. Furthermore, in advancing his view that only heavily protected parks can save wildlife, Terborgh paints Amboseli as a romantic appeal to a past harmony and an isolated case with little broader relevance to conservation.

Far from being an appeal for harmony between people and wildlife fixed in a past era, the book calls for coexistence anchored in contemporary realities with all the problems that entails. As much as anything, the book is about the rising intolerance of wildlife in Africa and elsewhere due to the population growth, land shortage, and the spread of democracy after decades of colonial servitude and dictatorship. Ironically, I go to great lengths to dispel the notion so prevalent in the West (and in Terborgh's review title, "Trouble in Paradise") of East Africa as some romantic Eden.

Terborgh also draws a false line between conservation within parks and beyond, and between bottom-up (local) as opposed to top-down (government) approaches. I favor a pluralistic approach, based on what works. I proposed a park as the only bulwark against the agricultural encroachment threatening Amboseli's swamps and insisted on a strong government role. To that end I lobbied to replace the inept Wildlife Department with a strong Kenya Wildlife Service and later directed it for several years.

But also I saw the need to go beyond the park boundaries and military enforcement to prevent sanctuaries from becoming extinction traps and foreign playgrounds surrounded by resentful neighbors.

That view is no longer unique, as I showed in the appendix by directing readers to *Natural Connections: Perspectives in Community-Based Conservation,* which details case studies from around the world reflecting the new thinking. Even the veritable Yellowstone National Park, citing Amboseli, is attempting to provide the bison, elk, wolf, and grizzly access to the 13-million-acre ecosystem surrounding the 2.2-million-acre park. Clearly all is not well in America any more than Africa when it comes to insular federal conservation practices.

The chairman of the World Commission for Protected Areas (WCPA), representing 1,300 experts from around the world, also makes it clear that Amboseli is not exceptional. Thus, where once parks were planned against, WCPA now advocates that they be planned with local people. Where once the emphasis was on setting these places aside, now we look for the many connections which linked protected areas to the world around. Fifty years of experience has taught us that protected areas cannot survive and flourish in isolation.

Finally, the donors did not pull out of Kenya Wildlife Service due to the efforts beyond parks that I promoted, as Terborgh implies. To the contrary, they are in the process of expanding their support for local conservation initiatives.

—David Western
Nairobi, Kenya

John Terborgh replies:

The migrations of grazing animals that once took place in many of the world's great grasslands have become a vanishing phenomenon. In groping for ways to conserve one such migratory system in Kenya's Amboseli National Park, David Western champions the benign coexistence of humans and wildlife in a traditional pastoral setting. While our views may differ on tactics, the goal is not in dispute. It is to conserve Amboseli's wildlife, and, by extension, the wildlife of parks all over the world. What makes the issue difficult is that the goal itself is so in conflict with current global trends that it borders on the Quixotic.

That conservation can be achieved via the good will and active participation of local populations is a currently popular, but untestable, hypothesis. It is untestable because the world will not know for a hundred or a thousand years whether it is successful.

Western and I differ in our faith in reliance on bottom-up (local incentive, local control) vs. top-down (legally mandated, government-enforced) processes to create the stability of conditions on the ground that conservation requires. The challenge is clear, but it amounts to a defiance of social entropy: how to engender stability of land and resource use in the face of exponential economic and social change. Nobody knows how to do it, so different points of view have their legitimacy. My skepticism for the bottom-up approach derives from the historical facts of shifting land-use patterns and kaleidoscopically changing societal attitudes. When staring into an opaque crystal ball, all anyone can do is place bets, and no two conservationists are going to place bets on the same number. Meanwhile, the dialogue is refreshing and constructive.

Western has more faith than I do in the potential for conservation outside of parks. What I see is an economically driven trend toward intensified use of natural resources of all kinds. Whether in North America or in developing countries, markets encourage humans to overexploit natural resources, often to exhaustion. We overgraze grasslands, clear-cut forests, overharvest fisheries, and overdraw aquifers. Individuals, including corporations, driven by current aspirations rarely see an advantage in exercising restraint in the present for a vague promise of a more bountiful future. The future is too full of uncertainties, and its potential is diminished by the discount rate.

The battle over Pacific Northwest old-growth forests is a prime example of the clash between focused interests and society. If left to its own devices, the timber industry would liquidate all remaining old growth on national forests, as it has on privately owned timberlands. Conservation outside of protected areas will not happen by itself because individuals predictably strive to optimize current advantage. The incentives perceived by local people only rarely favor conservation, even in the short run. Over the long run, what is certain is that incentives will change with the inevitable ups and downs of the global economy. In practice, the imposition of restraint for the better good of society is a function of government. In matters of conservation, I would therefore rather bet on the strongest institutions at hand, those that emanate from higher authority, than on the good will of local people to preserve habitats and their wildlife.

Western correctly points out the difficulties we have here in the United States over two of the same issues that affect Amboseli—the tendency of large animals to ignore arbitrary boundaries and intolerance of the public for wildlife. Every winter, bison wander out of Yellowstone National Park onto adjoining private lands. The (bottom-up) political response has been to allay landowner fears of brucellosis (a disease of cattle carried by bison) by sending out teams of sharpshooters to slaughter hundreds of the animals, as much as 20 percent of the entire Yellowstone herd in one recent winter.

Clearly this politically expedient practice does not represent a good long-term policy toward Yellowstone's wandering bison. It would be much better to purchase the tracts most favored by bison and annex them to the park. That would be a long-term (and top-down) solution. Perhaps it is not too heretical to think along similar lines with regard to Amboseli.

8   zulu history

Magqubu could instantaneously penetrate a persona. He would give the individual an appropriate name, too. I have no doubt that he had summed me up within a few minutes of our first meeting in 1952. He further observed me in 1955, when I was recruiting game guards to expand our force in Mfolozi game reserve.

The Zulu have a way of knowing things you are going to do, sometimes long before you do them. They talk at great length about personalities. In 1955 I cannot recall any Zulu working in the game reserve who had a radio. Most of them were illiterate, so newspapers played no part in their lives. Game-guard families were allowed to visit but were not permitted to live in the park, so white rangers were a focus of gossip that led to intense discussions of character strengths and weaknesses. I once overheard the game guards talking around the fire. It was most revealing, a microscopic examination of character.

Magqubu had refused my offer of employment in 1955 because he wanted a rest after his long stint with the tsetse fly campaign in the department of agriculture. The men I recruited were his former colleagues, and they no doubt told him everything I was doing, so he had not only his own insight but also the views and observations of all the other guards and the laborers who were part of my workforce.

The Natal Parks Board at that time was severely limited financially. I disagreed with my immediate superiors over the spending of our allocated funds. I wanted more game guards, uniforms, firearms, and money for the building of outposts around the perimeter of the game reserve. These things did not come easily. I had to write memos and reports and lobby whoever would listen. Although the Zulu game guards were unaware of the details of my administrative difficulties, they saw the results because they benefited from new uniforms, improved quarters, and more pay. I knew they were the front-line men and had to be looked after if the game was to survive.

Using my military experience, I taught them squad drill, which they loved, and they almost drove me to distraction with their insatiable demands for more drilling. They took to it like the proverbial duck to water. We observed military rank and discipline, which fitted well with their Zulu warrior culture. They loved drilling so much that they would deliberately make mistakes, hoping that I would give them what we regarded as punishment squad drill. Vehicles and petrol were limited, so we did a lot of walking. It was the best way to learn the terrain.

The original proclaimed area of Mfolozi game reserve was the land between the two rivers, from their junction to the now nonexistent Mandhlakazi footpath in the west below the Mtunzini hills, but we were responsible too for the protection of game on the uninhabited crown lands, or buffer zones. So our patrols extended to the buffer-zone boundaries, which had no physical demarcation. This meant learning the names of hills, streams, and other natural features. I was constantly questioning the guards about the history of the areas. My curiosity, I am certain, was conveyed to Magqubu. Hugh Dent, a brilliant Zulu linguist who was in charge of the game reserve from 1956 to 1958, employed Magqubu in early 1956 and put him in command of the game-guard force. When Hugh left there was a farewell ceremony on the parade ground. The first question Magqubu asked was, "Who is taking over?" Hugh said, "Madolo—Ian Player." Magqubu grunted and said, "I know him."

Indeed he did. At some point before he joined the new game-guard force, Magqubu must have seen me as a potential recipient of his own vast knowledge. Game guards such as tall, light-skinned Hosias Mtetwa, or Mcetegi Mkwanazi, who unwillingly allowed me to take him to hospital to die, Madipa and Mtwebulu Sibiya, Mkono, and other guards would have told Magqubu my predilection for writing everything down in notebooks. Some unseen force, which the Zulu would say was the *amadhlozi*, made Magqubu pick me as a pupil.

My mind had drifted, but I was brought back to the present when Magqubu said emphatically, "All animals eat the berries of the *mpafa*. White rhino, black rhino, genet cat, aardwolf, guinea fowl, francolin, doves, zebra, wildebeest, impala, nyala, kudu, grey duiker, bushbuck, steenbok, wild pig, *nsamango* monkey, but it is not only the berry that is eaten.

Woza, look here," Magqubu said, beckoning me to an mpafa tree. He described how small antelope like the grey duiker and the steenbok eat the leaves on the lower branches. Slightly higher, the impala ate the leaves; nyala antelope browsed at the next level, but like the impala they too fed on the tender branch shoots. Next came the kudu. Magqubu put his hands up behind his head to show how the great kudu bull with its lyre-shaped horns came slowly to the tree, nibbled on leaves, and when the branch was bare put its head into the tree, twisted its huge neck, and broke the higher branches. Some fell to the eating height of the small grey duiker and the steenbok. He brushed dry grass aside, examined the earth, and pointed to the faint V imprint of a duiker's hoof.

"The kudu works here for the other animals, the duiker and the steenbok. But the warthog and the *ngulube* [wild pig], they cannot reach up high, so they feed on the fallen leaves."

He pointed to a big branch the kudu had broken that now lay stripped bare on the ground.

"The eland, it eats the branches and the leaves and again some fall onto the earth to help the other animals," he said. "Right at the top of the tree the giraffe eat the leaves, branches, and the thorns."

He made a sweeping movement with his head, opening his mouth and showing how the giraffe with its long neck could reach any part of the tree, slide its big lips or curl its tongue, and strip leaves, thorns, and the softer parts of the branch. "*Indwamithi*," Magqubu said. This is the Zulu word for the giraffe, "he who is taller than the trees."

Magqubu stalked forward, holding his torso upright, one hand behind his back brushing away flies like a tail, and he cantered a few yards, a perfect example of the horselike motion of this wonderful, strange beast of nature. The early Boer Voortrekkers called the giraffe a *kameelperd* (camel horse). They relied upon the Bible as their guide to all things, and this strange animal resembled the horse they knew and the camel in the Bible. Hunters would gallop up to it, being careful to avoid the long legs because one kick was death, then shoot the animal, and in most instances they took only the tail because it made an excellent fly switch. The rest was food for the jackal, the hyena, the vultures, and the maggots, leaving only the sun-dried skin on the veld.

Magqubu expanded on his giraffe story, showing how it would be feeding at the top of a tree while red-billed oxpeckers ran up its legs, under the belly, and to the anus, pecking at the blue bloated ticks. He made the churring call of the bird, lifted his head like the giraffe, and looked about. The birds warned of danger. He explained that the oxpeckers also helped to warn a man walking through dense bush. When they churred and flew off, you had to walk slowly because a black rhino or a buffalo could be waiting.

He returned to the mpafa tree and showed me how a black rhino had pushed and broken one of the two main stems of the tree. He stuck his chest out, snorting with sharp inhalations and exhalations, demonstrating the black rhino breaking the trunk and pushing it to the ground, then eating the branches, leaves, and thorns with its hooked, prehensile upper lip. He smacked his lips and chewed, making the stomach-rumbling and contented sounds of the black rhino.

"*Ubejane* [black rhino] helps the other animals, too. When the tree is flat on the ground the small animals—duiker, steenbok, warthog, wild pig, and the others—can reach and eat the leaves the rhino left behind. Do you know the porcupine?" he asked.

"Yes," I said.

"He helps the butterflies and the ants," Magqubu said.

He pointed Zulu fashion, with bent forefinger, at the lower trunk of the tree. The bark had been stripped and the teeth marks of the porcupine were clearly visible.

"The porcupine likes the bark, but when it strips it away from the tree the white sap oozes out and the ants and butterflies feed on it when the porcupine leaves. The mpafa and the *umGxamu [Schotia brachypetala]* and the *umThombothi* are the favorite trees of the porcupine."

I noticed that although the porcupine had fed on the bark, it had not ring-barked the tree. There were schotia and umThombothi trees nearby with bare patches where the porcupine had been feeding. None of these trees were ring-barked either.

The faintly red-colored dung of the porcupine lay in little clumps on a game path. Magqubu turned them over and said the red coloring came from the umThombothi. He scratched in the dung, which had a faint aromatic scent, the mixture of tubers and the bark of the three trees. But Magqubu looked until he found a seed of the mpafa. He picked it up, put it on the palm of his hand, and said, "Mpafa. *Imithi mpafa.*" The mpafa tree. Magqubu always ended his stories by naming what he had been talking about.

Once or twice in the middle of the city of Durban I saw men carrying twigs of the mpafa as they walked toward the crowded bus ranks where people departed for the rural areas. It brought back the special feeling of that first full May day when the red cyrtanthus blooms that I spent with Magqubu, listening to his long and involved description of the way human and animal moved in a circle around this tree. All over the lowveld of Zululand and the eastern Transvaal I was later to see the tree, and invariably the lower branches had been stripped bare. The sight always anchored me to the African earth. This was where we met with the ancestral spirits, the amadhlozi, and all the creatures of our special African landscape. I heard Magqubu's voice and saw him moving like the various animals. The scents of the afternoon would come back to me. The memories sustained me as though they were the berries, leaves, and soft branches. I kept my own notes and accumulated more observations about the tree, adding to the incredible exposition of Magqubu, but could never have acted out the story with the verve he displayed.

Many years later in London I visited a museum exhibition of an Egyptian tomb. My eyes were instantaneously drawn to a branch and berries under a glass bowl. It was the mpafa, in an Egyptian tomb. What a shock to see it on this cold grey day of a London winter. It was *Zizyphus,* all right but I was not sure of the species because the berries were twice the size of the ones we have in Zululand. Here it was, food for the journey into the next world. Had the ancient Egyptians observed the importance of this tree for the animals, birds, and insects, then made it sacred to their culture? I wondered if its use as the carrier of the spirit had originated in Egypt.

The story has another link. I had always been interested in the shroud of Turin. When the Catholic Church agreed to its being examined by scientists, one of them was a botanist. He found traces of pollen that proved to have come from the *Zizyphus* species. Scourging was a common punishment in Roman times, and the hooked and straight thorns would have torn exposed flesh. More importantly, there was the strong possibility that the crown of thorns could have been made from the mpafa. The traditional depiction in religious paintings of Christ's head circled by the crown of thorns shows the Mexican cactus thorn, which is not indigenous to Africa.

The mpafa is no ordinary tree.

It was four in the afternoon by the time Magqubu had finished the story of the mpafa tree. He shouldered his old army haversack, called out "*Asihambe*" (Let us go), and we climbed out of the depression of the Mpafa stream and followed the bank until we reached a well-worn rhino path heading in a southwesterly direction. Magqubu walked ahead, moving at a fast pace, his short, squat body powered by his extraordinarily strong legs. Had he wanted to he could have outdistanced me easily, but he listened to my breathing and stayed three to five paces ahead.

The path followed the contour through euclea scrub, dipping in old *dongas* and heading now toward the White Mfolozi River. We crested a rise, and I could see Nqolothi hill and the long afternoon shadows creeping down its slopes. I did not have to concentrate on any dangers with Magqubu ahead of me, neither now nor in the thousands of other kilometers I was to walk behind him. There were many administrative concerns, personality conflicts, and other worries on my mind. I was sorting through them as we walked, but gradually and almost imperceptibly the atmosphere of the land enveloped me.

It was a landscape that had been occupied by humans for hundreds of thousands of years: early hominids, Bushmen, and Nguni clans. Men had fought here with great savagery against one another. Dingiswayo the Mtetwa king was killed by the Ndwandwe people, and Shaka, the founder of the Zulu nation, had in turn chased the Ndwandwe people out and fought their chief, Zwide. I was partially aware of some of this history because in 1955 I had seen the broken maize-grinding stones littering the Mfulumkulu plain. The guards had told me it was Shaka and his warriors who were responsible, thus making sure the Ndwandwes would not return. The land had a feeling that in this fading May afternoon transported me into a realm of the mind and body much deeper than I had ever experienced. The chanting goshawk called from a dense patch of bush, and trumpeter hornbills flapped overhead with their characteristic one-two-three flight. A bushbuck barked in the distance, and a grey duiker bounded across in front of us, diving and weaving through the bush. Words could not describe the poetry of this ancient land. What I was connected to was the spirit of place, all life past and present intermingling at different levels and forming an intangible bond with the hard earth beneath my feet.

For a distance I floated rather than walked; then there would be a break in the terrain, or the sharp shriek of a monkey that had spotted us. This brought me back from my mind wanderings to the beaten rhino path and Magqubu walking at his steady pace. I became conscious of my body, the branches of trees touching me, sweat trickling down my forehead and dripping over my eyes or running down between my shoulder blades. I could feel the firmness of the compacted rhino-trodden earth through my *velskoene*. My socks rubbed against my heels and the burning start of a blister jabbed at me. Magqubu's head bobbed up and down above the top of his haversack, and I could hear his breathing, regular and without strain.

Then everything seemed to fade away, and it was only my mind moving high and above the path. For an indeterminate length of time I was like a bateleur eagle soaring above and gliding with wings hardly moving. I did not fight anything in myself, but I drifted into different states of mind, then into my body. It was a form of self-hypnosis in which one part of my mind was absolutely still and part of the landscape, unmoving and unchanged. The other part was very much aware, my senses so sharply acute that eyes, nose, and ears missed nothing: a blue waxbill feather being pulled by tiny black ants across the path; dry, caked mud clinging to an *mkia* tree where a rhino had rubbed off the mud from a wallow; a dead tick caught in the mud, the outer shell glinting in sunlight for a split second before my eye passed, focusing in short flashes on other things. A boulder dark at the base and white on the edge where warthogs and wild pigs had rubbed. A depression in the churned earth where they had braced themselves.

The sun dipped behind Nqolothi hill, and we walked in the shadows. I heard the sharp-pitched whistle of the mountain reedbuck that lived on the flat tops of Nqolothi, their calls noticeably shriller than the common reedbuck. We reached the thick *ndlovusiyashikana* bush at the base of Nqolothi hill.

Magqubu's pace slowed and his body movements changed. He exuded an air of caution. Every meter we walked deeper into the gloom of the bush heightened his awareness of possible danger. There were big pans here, some still holding a little water where trees had protected them from the sun. Others were dark mud, the consistency of thick porridge, and rhino and warthog had been wallowing. There were signs of them everywhere—dung, dropped mud, tracks, and scraping marks against trees. I was now no longer floating. My senses had become aware of Magqubu's vigilance expressed through his body actions. We were slowly enveloped by the bush and had to bend low to pass under overhanging thorn branches. The nocturnal rhythm was beginning, with white-browed scrub robins singing and toppies calling in concert as they do when they see a snake. It was a persistent kind of chatter but without the urgency of a warning. The guttural cries of crested francolin in front and behind startled some hah-de-dah ibises, who flapped and screamed out their piercing calls. This warned some rhino ahead of us, and they snorted loudly. Magqubu stopped, cocked his head slightly, and listened. The rhino snorted again and Magqubu relaxed, turned, smiled, and said, "*Mkombe*" (White rhino).

He had hardly spoken when there was a deep bellow followed by a growling sound like the beginning of a lion's roar. Then the bush erupted, and the din was frightening. The sound of breaking branches and loud scrapings as rhino rubbed against one another penetrated the still evening. The enclosed surroundings accentuated the noise, and I could feel my heart thumping against my chest. The ancient human response of flight or fight and the surge of adrenaline to assist either course flashed into my mind.

I watched Magqubu. He stood facing the sound, his head moving slightly, following the movement of the animals. He held up his hand, showing five fingers. How did he know there were five rhino when we could not see through the bush? Again it was an intuitive knowledge and the combination of all his senses. There was a sharp cry, like a cat mewing. Magqubu bent down, peering through the bush, then he indicated with his hand that the noise came from a calf. He held his hand up again, showing four fingers and the fifth bent over: four adults and one calf.

He jerked his head and we walked quietly away, taking another rhino path that led to the southern slopes of Nqolothi hill. We skirted round a big pan where there were many signs of rhino. Magqubu sniffed the air. I did the same and could smell rhino. I said, "Mkombe." He smiled and pointed to a path, then showed me five sets of tracks, one of which was of a calf. He patiently drew out each track, showing me the differences, but they were so slight that by the time he moved from one to the other I had forgotten the previous one.

We were now totally in shadow, and I knew it would be dark within an hour. I whispered that we should move, but I needed to know how he could identify the exact number of five rhino that we had heard. I asked him quietly, and he said he knew by the sound. He moved his body around, making the rasping noise of rhino rubbing against rhino then against trees and the calf's catlike sound and the suckling noise as it drank from its mother. My hearing is acute and has always been my most important sense, but this was phenomenal audible observation. He was able to differentiate between the tones, his mind taking in and eliminating unnecessary information and coming up with answers upon which our lives could have depended. I do not see color until the word is mentioned or I consciously think about it. It is like saying to myself, Look at the landscape, what colors do you see? Then they start to materialize. Sometimes they are so vivid that they force their way into my consciousness. It was only after I had stopped smoking that my sense of smell improved to allow me to be aware of subtle differences in scent. I had to concentrate, whereas Magqubu took everything in, filtering out what was not important but retaining it for further identification if needed. I can never recall a moment when he was not focused on his immediate surroundings.

The light in the sky was changing when we began the steep climb up Nqolothi hill. I was sweating and breathing heavily when we reached halfway. I called for a rest. Magqubu laughed and stopped. "Sinda" (Heavy), he said. It was a polite way of acknowledging my fatigue.

I turned and looked east while he pointed with bent forefinger and named the individual hills and the ranges lit up by the fading rays of the afternoon sun. A long line of dark green sycamore fig trees marked the course of the White Mfolozi River. Patches of damp sand glinted where warthog and wild pig had been digging for water near the reeds. The cliffs of Nqabaneni glowed a soft orange, and the themeda grass stretching from the Mantiana hills to Little Mpila and the Greater Mpila was a numinous red, emphasizing the origin of its Afrikaans and English names: *rooigras* and red oats grass. Walking through it on misty mornings with wet socks was hell because the seed burrowed into the damp wool and worked its way into your skin, causing itching and infection if you left it.

He pointed out other hills—Siyembeni, the junction of the Black and White Mfolozi Rivers and the scene of one of the greatest hunts in the history of the Zulu people. Shaka Zulu had a line of pits dug between the two rivers; then the game was chased into them by warriors. The carnage must have been immense because every local Zulu knew the story. Magqubu began to sing softly as he pointed at the junction. He sang the praise names of Shaka Zulu, how he had taken refuge with King Dingiswayo of the Mtetwa people, fought Zwide, and been a friend to the whites who had landed in ships at Port Natal. It was a spontaneous association with people and the land, a praise to Shaka's amalgamation of the Nguni clans. For Magqubu, Shaka's spirit was still here, moving across the brooding landscape.

Magqubu began to chant and dance. I stopped him and said we should move on because it would be dark by the time we got to the top of Nqolothi hill. For Magqubu this was an order that he obeyed without question, but I was to learn over many years that he would return to the story. It was a mark of respect for whomever he was praising and a subtle reminder to me that the amadhlozi were not to be treated lightly. It was a power Magqubu had, but at that time I had no inkling of it. I was still caught up with the arrogance of a white time scale and lack of sensitivity for any other culture when it impinged on what I was doing or wanted to do.

We climbed up the last slope of Nqolothi, reached the tabletop, and heard the mountain reedbuck whistle all around us. "*Nxwala*," Magqubu said, giving them their Zulu name. We looked back east again, and I asked Magqubu the name of one hill that was now prominently etched against the eastern skyline. "Dengezeni," he said, and began again to explain the origin of the name, how Shaka led the Mtetwa warriors against the Ndwandwe people. Shaka's men smashed all the clay pots and the grinding stones along the ridge of hills. Shaka ordered them to leave nothing alive.

I urged Magqubu on down the western slope of Nqolothi toward the caves below the Mhlopeni hills where we were going to spend the night. I did not know that before the year was out I would have an experience at Dengezeni that would smash through my own container of arrogant superiority. If the psyche can be likened to a clay container, a vessel of beliefs, customs, and attitudes, part of mine was going to be broken and recast.

It was dark when we followed the steep path down to where the Mhlologazane (a

Place of Little Suspicion) stream enters the White Mfolozi River, but the hills in the west were now lit up. Magqubu wanted to tell me the origins of their names, but I impatiently urged him on. I was tired and very thirsty and hungry. I suspect that Magqubu may have chuckled inwardly at the sharpness of my tone, but he showed no sign. He did stop and say that in the thickening scrub at the foot of the hill lived one of the few black rhino in Mfolozi at that time. As always he was right, and he had the last word, too.

We skirted the bush and walked over the flat rocks to the cave. I dropped my haversack and sat down, leaning wearily against rocks in the cave, still warm from the afternoon sun. Magqubu did not rest. He at once began gathering driftwood that still littered the banks from the big flood of 1957. He found a suitable cleft in the rocks, took a handful of dry reeds, and when the fire caught he blew and added small sticks. The flames blazed, their reflections dancing on the walls of the cave. A hyena whooped across the river from the direction of the Madhlozi camp, and Magqubu pronounced *mpisi* as though I had never heard one before. For him it was an acknowledgment of the present moment. I stretched out, enjoying the variety of scents of the wood smoke, the reeds burning, acacia, and a hardwood I guessed to be a combretum. I called out and asked Magqubu, "*Umuthi muni?*" "*Mbonde,*" he replied as he went off into the night to find another log. Mbonde is the combretum hardwood, and the coals stay hot for a long time.

Honor demanded that I do something. Magqubu was fifty-eight; I was thirty-one. I was already calling him "the old man." I got up, grunting, and I heard him ask, "*Uyapi?*" (Where are you going?)

"To get water," I said.

He disagreed and said he would do it as soon as he had enough heavy wood for the night, telling me I should rest because it had been a heavy day on my knee, having to climb Nqolothi, which was named for its steepness.

"You have to bend over as you walk up," said Magqubu.

I ignored his concern and made my way over the rocks to the river and scooped the billycan full. By the time I got back, Magqubu had gathered more logs and cut suitable sticks to hang the billy on. He was indefatigable. The main chores over before preparing food, he now went a few yards into the darkness, and I could hear him praying. His Shembe religion had a powerful grip on him, and he embraced it with obvious joy. It was no hardship to pray after a long walk. When he returned I asked what he had prayed about, and he said he had thanked God for bringing us safely through the day. It made me ponder my own religious state. I certainly believed in a god, some superior spirit. Whenever I had trouble I was quick to ask the help of God, yet I could not call myself a Christian. It was a long time since I had even been in a church to worship. The last time was when I attended the wedding of my friend Jim Feely, when he married Molly Kennedy in the little village of Kwambonambi in 1956. I sang the hymns and went through the ritual, but it did not move me. A change would be a long time in coming.

Magqubu filled his small three-legged pot with water. It was the one he told me he had bought for five shillings in 1925. He hung it next to my billy, and it shone in the firelight. He took a cloth bag from his haversack, waited until his pot boiled, then poured in *mielie* meal. He explained that it was meal that gave the Zulu people their strength, but he criticized the white man for refining it. This meal came from his own granary. It had been ground by his chief wife, Tabete. She visited Magqubu at his hut, which was separate from the game-guard barracks. She was the only person he would allow to cook for him. In his years of working for the early game conservators of Zululand—Vaughan Kirby, Roden Symons, and Captain H. B. Potter—as well as officials of the veterinary department in the *nagana* campaigns—R.H.T.P. Harris, Willie Foster, and Dr. Kluge—Magqubu had made many enemies. He was ruthless in enforcing discipline. Whatever law the white man laid down in the running of the game reserves, Magqubu made sure it was carried out. Laborers laid snares near their camps when they were working in the field. Game guards stole an extra round of ammunition so that they too could poach a buck when no one was around. Magqubu had informers. He would quietly investigate and catch the offenders, who would never forgive him, nor would their relatives. The easiest way to kill him would be to slip poison into his food. It was a traditional Zulu way, and impossible to detect.

One of the worst times for Magqubu was in the 1940s, during the last big nagana campaign. All animals within the Mfolozi game reserve and the surrounding buffer zones, except the white rhino, were killed. Hluhluwe game reserve, under Captain H. B. Potter's leadership, was spared. The veterinary department insisted that with rare exceptions the meat was not to be taken. Magqubu suffered badly in the enforcement of this instruction. Meat was prized food, and to see it left for the vultures, jackals, and hyenas caused resentment. The wholesale slaughter also went against the Zulu way of living with the animals. Hunting and killing took place, but not on this scale. The senselessness of it affected Magqubu psychically in much the same way that the North American Indians were affected by the extermination of the plains bison. When I said to Magqubu that Shaka's great hunt was a massacre, he replied that it was for food and sport with Shaka personally taking part in the hunt. "*Nyama*," he said firmly.

I told him that early explorers had written about the elephant hunts conducted by Shaka, Dingane, and Mpande, how the kings had sat on top of Nqolothi and directed the hunts.

"Yes," Magqubu said. "It was for the ivory that the *abelungu* [white people] wanted. The elephant were not killed for nothing."

I knew he was implying that we had killed for no proper reason. He was right, and the proof lay all around us. In early Nguni times there was game everywhere in what is now KwaZulu-Natal. The white man initiated the slaughter of animals and the transformation of the landscape. Now all that remained were the pocket handkerchief-sized witness areas we call game and nature reserves. We should be deeply ashamed.

Some of the statements of early hunters, such as Baldwin, Dunn, Drummond, and Cornwallis Harris, leave no doubt in one's mind that the killing of game was to satisfy the blood lust that lurks in the hearts of men. The nagana campaigns in later and supposedly enlightened years were no different. The purposeless killing of wild animals, birds, and wild people, to say nothing of ourselves in pointless wars, needs much more investigation by the depth psychologists. Yet, paradoxically, the modern hunter has contributed more to wildlife conservation than have many of the people who criticize hunting.

While we were eating his *sqamba* (hard maize-meal porridge) and drinking coffee, Magqubu began to tell me how he had been saved by the Zulu prophet Shembe, but I refused to listen. It did not stop him talking, but I persistently interrupted him, asking him about the old beliefs and the old times. Many years were to pass before I was to listen with rapt attention to his remarkable story of an internal journey of great psychic and religious importance.

After we had eaten, he carefully washed his little pot, tying the leftover sqamba in a piece of white maize sack. He never wasted food and was extremely careful of his diet. No butter or fat.

I lay on the hard rock, my head on my haversack and my body covered with an old World War II military overcoat. It would be a long time before we had the luxury of sleeping bags. Magqubu sat near the fire, singing a hymn quietly to himself. It was a beautiful night, and from the overhang I could see the clear sky with the blaze of southern constellations. The Mtunzini hills were outlined against the last light. Hyena called from the direction of Madhlozi camp, and I heard the faint drumming from the people who were invading the western buffer zone near the Hlungwana River. There was trouble coming, and the next few years of my life were to be spent fighting to get some of the buffer zones incorporated into Mfolozi game reserve.

We were also here to chart a trail for the people we intended bringing here on foot next year. I knew that if we could make individuals as passionate about this remnant of wild land as we were, there was a chance of saving it for posterity. Having the concept of a wilderness area accepted had been a bitter administrative struggle.

"*Nango ikanka*" (There, the jackals), Magqubu shouted. Their cries were ringing out from the bush-cleared zone. They disturbed crowned plovers, who flew up near us. The sound took my thoughts to my youth in the Transvaal, when I remembered hearing them for the first time on a moonlit night in an open field near our home in Lyndhurst. The Afrikaners called them *kiwietjies*.

Magqubu was singing a hymn. He had a good voice and sang with the fervor of a deeply religious man. I thought again about my own religious beliefs. As a child my maternal grandmother had taken me to Sunday school at the local hall. A banner strung across the room read, "God is Love." I didn't know what it meant. I listened obediently to the Bible stories but was not touched or moved.

My grandmother had strong religious faith, and I recall looking at her in amazement when she went through the Christian rituals. They meant nothing to me. It was something that you just did. Lying in the cave on this lovely African night in a land inhabited by wild animals with their own mysterious rhythms made me feel part of the universe. I could identify with the sounds of the night, the scents and the atmosphere. There was a tone and a rhythm that was beating in time with my soul. Some part of me had always been here, and everything that was happening around me evoked this sense of connectedness. There was a peace here, not in the general sense of the word, but in an alive way. One part of me remained quiet and calm while the other thrilled to all the wild sounds, each one arousing a different response. I wondered and worried if this made me an animist. Fear of Christian hell and damnation constantly lurked within me, threatening to erupt and put down anything that was opposed to it.

Walking through the Zululand landscape this day and hearing Magqubu talk about the life surrounding the mpafa tree, the audible contact with the rhino, feeling the spirits of the people—kings, *indunas*, warriors of Zulu and Nguni, and going further back to the little Bushmen—this had gripped me. Here was a drumbeat of the earth that permeated my entire psychic being. This was for me a religious experience. What I took to be Christianity was imposed upon this, a growth that the ancient part of me rejected. It was a paradox I was incapable of properly understanding, but a healing through a dream would come twenty years later.

The work that I had been involved in over the past three years had been painful. I had come up against some extremely unpleasant people. In many ways it had been a shattering experience. Some of the worst aspects of human behavior emerged when people went fishing, or when farmers' crops were threatened by wild animals.

The memory of some of the incidents made me sit up in anger, and I must have said something, because Magqubu rolled over and asked me what was wrong. There was no way of explaining my emotions and range of thoughts since we had eaten his sqamba around the fire. More than half a lifetime had passed. I tried to explain in my limited Zulu how important this particular patrol was for the future of the Mfolozi game reserve. I told him how next year we would be bringing people out here on foot, walking from the Mpila rest camp. He nodded as though this was to be expected. He had an ability to accept things, even though at the time they seemed outrageous.

Magqubu threw a handful of dry reeds onto the fire, and it flared up, lighting his strong face and the holes in his earlobes. He filled his three-legged pot with water from the billycan and put it on the fire. I passed him my tin of condensed milk and the packet of Five Roses tea. He made the tea and sucked the hot liquid from an old enamel mug, and stared into the fire.

By the light of a torch I wrote up my journal. I had kept a journal since 1946. It was invaluable in capturing the moment, the nuances of conversations, descriptions of country, animals encountered, sounds and feelings. I also used it to vent my frustrations. In 1954, when I was alone in Ndumu game reserve, I kept a detailed daily diary and had continued with this when I was transferred to Mfolozi. When I read it later I was bitterly ashamed of my prejudices.

Strange how one written line of a time long ago could trigger a whole host of detailed memories. Magqubu could talk nonstop, all of it fascinating information. I would have to keep halting him so I could take notes, but there were moments when the stories were so interesting and Magqubu was in full flood that I got caught up in the story, became totally involved, and wrote nothing. My limited knowledge of Zulu made no difference. Magqubu would repeat and continue to repeat the same story, telling it from innumerable angles, like turning a diamond around in the light to make the colors flash and fade. His expressions and elaborate acting made certain the essential part of the story was not missed. In the future I was able to tape-record his stories and descriptions of earlier times. Checking against diary notes it was incredible to see how, after twenty-five years, his memory was so clear.

I was keen to know more about the earlier conservators who had worked in the reserves. Magqubu had served them all and in typical Zulu fashion had seen through the personas. I decided to wait until the following morning because I knew that once he got going there would be no sleep for me. I finished my tea, said, "*Lala kahle*" (Sleep well), pulled my overcoat up, and with the night sounds echoing against the Mhlopeni cliffs went to sleep.

9 bruno manser
and the penan

The road Japan funded on Wong's timber concession cut right through Penan territory in the Limbang district and was clearly aimed across the border to the upper Tutoh, in the Baram. In the Tutoh area, at that time, was a small Swiss man, thirty-three years old, who had sought out the Penan and was living with them. He was perhaps the first European to learn the Penan language well and to live—not just visit or observe—their way of life. This is remarkable because the nomadic Penan, the "wild men of Borneo," had fascinated Europeans for over two hundred years. In many ways like nature itself, they were admired, overlooked, misunderstood, abused. About three hundred nomadic Penan are left. This is the story of Europeans, Malay, and Chinese coming to them and to their forest.

The rajah James Brooke and his friend Alfred Russel Wallace used to sit up evenings, in 1854 and after, at the palace in Kuching or at James's mountaintop retreat, a few hours away by canoe and foot. They took delight in arguing Wallace's new views on evolution, which he was developing concurrently with Darwin. James howled at the idea that his ancestors were orangutans.

Wallace had come to see the "little men." Just as the Galapagos and the voyage of the *Beagle* were inseparable from Darwin's intellectual growth, Borneo and the Malay archipelago shaped Wallace. Unlike Darwin, however, Wallace did not just sail through; he stayed eight years. He came to know the natives; and this, in turn, shaped his view of evolution and the descent of man.

In 1855, Kuching was lively. In the sixteen years since Brooke's arrival, the "very small town of brown huts and longhouses made of wood . . . sitting in brown squalor on the edge of mudflats," which he had described in 1839, had grown to include his attractive cottage-palace (The Grove) and several other British-style bungalows on the landscaped grounds of the compound. Wallace and the rajah looked out across the river to the thatch-roofed Malay houses and a growing Chinese bazaar with apartments above the shops. They could see hundreds of buildings through the tall jungle trees arched over the river, where birds hunted the mudflats and crocodiles lay in the sun. The casual, energetic, and fun-loving rajah set a good table and talked late into the night, often to visitors from Singapore. The rajah's unique kingdom and hospitable palace were favorite stopping places for British travelers on their way to various colonies. Wallace, two years in the archipelago, told James he wanted "to see the Orangutan, to study his habits and obtain good specimens."

The orangutan in Malay dialect is quite human (*orang utan* means "little man," as *orang tuan* is "headman" and *orang ulu* is "remote man," upriver, an aboriginal). But if the Malays spoke of the ape as a kind of human, Europeans were positively obsessed with the possibility. In his book on Borneo, Redmond O'Hanlon tells how in England, as early as 1792, Lord Monboddo "maintained that the orang-utan was a variety of *Homo sapiens* with a merely accidental speech impediment," and he "took his own pet ape out to supper parties dressed in a dinner-jacket to prove his point."

Wallace was fascinated with this leading candidate for a missing link; he shot seventeen. A few years later, in 1865–67, "the great Italian" as Tom Harrisson called him, Odoardo Beccari, came through Sarawak with his gun:

> Looking intently, I at last made out something like red hair amidst the dense foliage. There could no longer be any doubt—it was an orang recumbent on its nest. The creature was evidently aware that it had been discovered, and yet it showed no fear, nor did it attempt to fly. On the contrary, it got up and looked down at us, and then descended lower amidst the branches, as if it wished to get a better view of us, holding on to the ropes of a creeper which hung from a branch on which it was first squatting. When I moved to take aim with my gun, it hauled itself up again, pushing forward its head, to look at me as it held on to the branches above with its hand. It was in this position when I fired. . . . I caught sight of a second orang on another nest. Although I couldn't see it well, I fired. . . . I perceived something reddish moving on the top of a big tree. I fired at once almost at random. . . . As I was reloading, a second suddenly appeared, . . . [then] the huge beast turned, and it fell dead to a bullet in the chest. I should particularly have liked the skin, but I had to abandon both it and the skeleton and content myself with the head alone.

It was quite dark when we reached the camp, loaded with orangoutangs, drenched to the skin. . . . All told, I had got either the entire skeletons or portions of twenty-four individuals. Later, Azton brought to me several other heads from the same district. But with all this I came away without having been able to solve the doubts I had regarding the species or races of orang-outang.

"Hoorah for systematic collecting!" exclaimed Harrisson, quoting this passage in 1938. A few years later Harrisson returned during the Second World War, to direct the resistance from the Bario highlands. He stayed on as curator of the Sarawak museum.

The orangutan—an ape-man both theoretically valuable and physically expendable—wandered into European lore during the great romance of nature, 1750–1850, when Rousseau's "natural man" was a widespread ideal. Living rudely yet happily in a state of nature presumed the opposite of a state of civilization, the natural man was thought to be simple, innocent, direct, unspoiled. Holding to this fantasy, Europeans throughout the colonized world (on which the sun never set) overlooked the tribalism and complex socialization of natives, called them "primitives," and alternately envied them as free men and enslaved them as beasts.

Deep in the jungles of Borneo, which until the logging roads of the 1980s and 1990s was one of the wildest places on earth, lived—also—*Homo sapiens*: nomadic, thinly clad forest hunters with blowpipes. Given the drift of European thought, it is not surprising that the orangutans sometimes got confused with the Penan. Before he left England for Borneo, in 1838, James Brooke said he had heard of men "little better than monkeys, who live in trees, eat without cooking, are hunted by the other tribes, and would seem to exist in the lowest conceivable grade of humanity." And he wrote in Rousseauan manner that he "wished to see man in the rudest state of nature." By the late nineteenth century the desire to push orangutans forward toward men and nomadic men back, toward orangutans, in order to bridge the great man-nature gap imagined in Europe, had led to accounts of the "wild men in the interior of Borneo" living "absolutely in a state of nature, who neither cultivate the ground nor live in huts; who neither eat rice nor salt, and who do not associate with each other, but rove about some woods, like wild beasts; the sexes meet in the jungle, or the man carries away the woman."

The "singles bar" fantasy at the end is distinctly European, as is the notion of isolated individuals roaming alone. Even as recently as 1969, the "brown nomadic hunters, the Punan and Ukit" of Borneo, were identified with "the paleolithic virtues and vices of keen eyesight, alert observation, and incapacity for what neolithic man calls work."

Brooke's fantasies of a "natural man" live on to the present day. In November 1990, I was sitting at dinner with Chinese companions in Kuching, listening to one man tell of meeting (after flying into Mulu Park by company helicopter) a Penan man who could not tell how many children he had. This was interpreted not as a failure of communication or of numbers but as evidence of a social structure so "wild" that the Penan man had no idea who or how many were his children (horror to the Chinese man, and sheer nonsense). The entire incident was adduced as proof that their condition is so "degraded," so "barely human," that it is a favor to take the Penan out of the jungle or, more to the point, to take the jungle away from the Penan. The Chinese gentleman was trying to show me why logging benefits natives. Having taught Native American history, I felt the weight of centuries as I heard, yet again, a man justifying colonial exploitation by means of racist attacks on those born with the gold, the silver, the buffalo, the wood.

O'Hanlon, who wrote a book on Conrad and Darwin as well as *Into the Heart of Borneo,* so funny and humane it could be Irish, notes that Darwin, like my Chinese friend in Kuching, spent very little time upriver. O'Hanlon, lying on a Sarawak riverbank considering his Iban guide Leon and wondering how anyone could think these people stupid or insensitive, recalls that among the evolutionary thinkers, only Wallace spent time with native guides:

> Helped at every turn by Leon's ancestors and related peoples in his eight years of travel, often by native *prau,* from one island to another in the Malay Archipelago, he [Wallace] had come to conclude that "The more I see of uncivilised people, the better I think of human nature, and the essential differences between civilised and savage men disappear." He developed his concept of Latent Development—all the races of *Homo sapiens* had evolved a much bigger brain than they actually needed, at the same time. They just used different parts of its capacity in different ways.

Wallace found the interior natives beautiful, energetic, resourceful and clever, "lively, talkative . . . truthful and honest to a remarkable degree. . . . Crimes of violence (other than head-hunting) are almost unknown." James Brooke shared, and probably helped shape, this opinion.

So the natives in Borneo, and evening debates in Kuching, may have helped to give Europe its least racist theory of evolution, and Sarawak its least racist rajahs, for on one point Wallace and all Brookes agreed: the natives were extraordinarily fine human beings.

The origins of the Bornean natives are obscure. The oldest evidence of *Homo sapiens* in all of Asia is found in north Borneo, in the Niah caves and elsewhere: Stone Age remains forty thousand years old. Who these people were we do not know. The first Malay migration down from southwestern China was around ten thousand years ago, and the pockets of aboriginals *(orang-asli)* left on the mainland are probably descended from those people. They were supplanted, however, by "proto-Malays" about four thousand years ago, who were probably the ancestors of the Malays and natives of present-day Borneo. In the broadest terms, we can say that the people of Borneo—native, Malay, and Chinese—are one race, Mongolian, originally out of central Asia; that the natives and Malays are part of the great Malay migrations that repeatedly overran the peninsula, Java, and the islands thousands of years ago; and that the Chinese are much more recently arrived from the mainland. Across Southeast Asia, most of the people are Mongolian: pockets of Negroid natives remain in the Andaman-Nicobar Islands, Papua New Guinea, and Australia; and empires and emigrations have brought some Aryans and Dravidians from India to Malaysia and many Caucasians to Australia and New Zealand. Still, Malaysia and especially Borneo are thoroughly Asian. It can be hard to tell, at times, whether you are looking at a native of Borneo, a Malaysian, a Chinese, or an American Indian. Bornean native groups migrate and easily mix, merge, and split. "Malays" are those who became Muslim, and a ruling class, about five hundred years ago. Intermarriage between all groups has for centuries blurred the taxonomists' best attempts to keep men and women apart.

Languages have evolved to become substantially different and mutually unintelligible, so that language is one hard division; another is geography. The effective identity is by place, longhouse by longhouse, and by tongue. In the 1980 census, the Iban, that vigorous native group migrating north from Kalimantan over the last two centuries, could be seen to dominate Sarawak; the native groups up the Baram are minorities. Major native groups of Sarawak included the Iban (368,000), Bidayuh (104,000), Kenyah (15,600), Kayan (13,400), Kedayan (10,700), Murut (9,500), and Penan (5,600, probably undercounted). So the tribes represented up the Baram—the Kayans, Kenyahs, and Penan—all together amount to about one-seventh of the Iban. Clearly the issue of minority rights could arise, even within the context of a native-controlled government. The natives are about 45 percent of the Sarawak population, the Chinese 30 percent, and the Malay 20 percent.

The Penan, then, are a remnant of an ancient Asian invasion—the remnant that has stayed deep inside, away from the rivers, one of the last nomadic tribes on earth. Perhaps 300 of them (500 in 1989, 700 in 1987) still roam free in the jungles, eating fruit and sago palm and hunting animals with blowpipes, while 7,000 live in scattered settlements in upper stretches of Sarawak rivers, combining farming and hunting in

FIGURE 5. A page from Bruno Manser's journals. (Courtesy of William W. Bevis)

shrinking habitat. Most of the semisettled Penan have been forced into longhouses and rice-growing within the last twenty years. These are the people all the other natives know, with some awe and respect, as the ones at home in the forest. As nomads, they do not build longhouses. They were never headhunters. They are shy and secretive, coming out occasionally to remote longhouses to trade. They know you are inside the jungle, but you do not know they are present unless they choose to reveal themselves. Even among the other natives, who consider the Penan inferior socially and politically, who have sometimes treated them as property and slaves, the elusiveness of the no-mads creates a certain mystery. They move every few weeks or months, finding clean camps and fresh foraging and game. They are legendary: tough, sweet, kind, wild—and scarce.

These are the people—the wild men of the forest, the missing links, the "little men" and noble savages—that Bruno Manser, in 1984, left Switzerland to find. "And I can assure you," he said to us years later, in Tokyo, "that I have found these nomadic groups."

We had heard of Manser before leaving the United States but had little idea who or what he was. Then in August 1989, in Taman Negara Park in mainland Malaysia, a young woman wearing a white blouse and red skirt walked out of the jungle and into the river. She was blonde and blue-eyed. As her skirt billowed up, she sank to her neck with a sigh, closed her eyes, and let the current carry the heat away.

Hannah Olesan, twenty-two, from Denmark, was working on her master's degree on shifting agriculture in Borneo. She spoke quietly of primary forests, of forest farms and of forests gone, of wild pigs and orangutans in Kalimantan. Then she told of happening upon a native blockade of logging in Sarawak. She had been walking alone up the new dirt road. A logging truck stopped. As she climbed in, the driver said in English, "Do you know Bruno Manser?"

"That's what they always ask," she said to me with a smile and twinkling eyes. "They will ask you."

"Do you know him?"

"No. He is hiding with the Penan. They move him around in the jungle. I saw them at the logging blockade—five or ten natives behind wooden poles, holding blowpipes and knives. The police kept me away. Everyone said Bruno was somewhere near, in the jungle, watching. That's how the pictures got to the *Straits Times* in Singapore."

Bruno Manser was born in 1954 in Basel, Switzerland, one of six children in the German-speaking family of a gardener. At eighteen, after high school, he disappointed his parents by skipping the university and moving to a farming village. There, living alone, he worked as a shepherd and fisherman, grew his own food, and sewed his clothing. In his words, he "made practical apprenticeship in all fields of agriculture and handicraft, trying to get the base of economic self-sufficiency and independence, spending most of the time in the Swiss alps. Six years as cheesemaker with cows, six years with sheep." Small, wiry, impish—it is not hard to picture him beside his cows in Heidi's alpine meadows. By 1982, he was also interested in spelunking and spent much of his time in caves deep beneath the Alps.

His mountain retreat, however, was not enough. The next phase of his life he told vividly to Wade Davis, rain forest expert, ethnobotanist, and writer, when Manser won *Outside* magazine's Outsider of the Year award in 1991:

As a child, I collected leaves and feathers, and at night lay in my room imagining that it had become a jungle. I wanted to live with a people of nature, to discover their origins, to become aware of their religion and life, to know these things. In a library he came upon a single black-and-white photograph of a Penan hunter with a caption that read simply, "A hunter-gatherer in the forest of Borneo." The book offered no other information. Manser dug further, eventually discovering an obscure report that described the Penan's homeland: lush forest and soaring mountains, dissected by crystalline rivers and the world's most extensive network of caves.

Intrigued, Manser travelled to Malaysia in the winter of 1984, became conversant in Malay, and accepted an invitation to join a British caving expedition headed for Gunung Mulu, a national park that encompasses the heart of Penan territory in Sarawak [up the Tutoh]. . . . Manser and the British cavers traveled deep into the park, where they explored the caves for two weeks. The British then departed, but Manser had been told of a group of nomadic Penan living beyond the southern boundary of the park in a region called the Ubong, and so he pushed on, alone. For several days— most, Manser says, without food or water—he struggled through a dense jungle that seemed to mock everything he had learned in Switzerland about nature. On the ninth day, exhausted but reluctant to turn back, he climbed a tree and saw, across a valley, the white plume of a cooking fire.

It was nearly dark by the time he came upon the footprints in the mud by the river. "I knew they would be afraid," he says, "so I made camp. The next morning I let the sun come up. Then I heard two voices, a man and a woman's. For two minutes nothing happened. I held up my hand in greeting. The woman fled. But the man came to me. He spoke a few words of Malay. We touched hands and he drew his fingers back across his breast." Manser followed the Penan man up the slope to the encampment.

Without special provision, the tourist's entry visa for Sarawak is good for three weeks. By December 31, 1984, Bruno Manser had overstayed his visa. At first, this was of no great concern to the authorities and certainly not to him. He was in settlements or deep inside the forest, up the Tutoh a few days' travel above Long Bangan, near Long Seridan, stripped to his shorts, toughening his bare feet, learning the blowpipe and the Penan language, beginning his valuable journals of Penan vocabulary, customs, and drawings, most of which are still in the hands of the Malaysian police, who have refused to release them. Wade Davis writes:

> Fearful of the heat of the sun, ignorant of the seas, insulated by the branches of the canopy, the Penan live in a cognitive and spiritual world based entirely on the forest. Distance and time are measured not in hours or miles but in the quality of the experience itself. A hunting trip, if successful, is considered short, though a Westerner might measure it in weeks. An arduous journey is one that exposes a Penan to the sun.

Manser, as much as possible, became a Penan, and they accepted him. Pictures from the jungle years show him in his bowl haircut, in shorts, with Penan bracelets on

FIGURE 6. A page from Bruno Manser's journals. (Courtesy of William W. Bevis)

wrists and legs. Often he is seated on a tree limb, blowpipe nearby, Penan basket, notebook, and pet monkey in his lap. Sometimes, he is playing the flute. The puckish smile is actually Penan as well as Swiss; only the wire-rimmed glasses give him away.

In the 1980s, the Penan were distributed mainly across the upper Tutoh and upper Baram, and over the divide into the headwaters of the Rajang. A high percentage of the nomads were in the upper Tutoh, especially along the Magoh tributary (a few were also up the Silat and Tinjar, tributaries of the Baram). Like the grizzly bear in North America, the Penan had been driven to the most remote, inaccessible habitats.

The nomadic Penan move from base camps, which may last a year, to temporary camps near food sources and to travel camps—bivouacs—over a large territory. In all camps, nomadic Penan build light, thatched shelters of bamboo or softwood, one per family. Usually the huts are up on stilts, above the damp ground, above the leeches. The floors are split bamboo, well ventilated and springy, quite comfortable for sleeping. The roof is thatched leaves. Nomads do not build hardwood longhouses. A group of nomads might typically number thirty; those semisettled in longhouses, from fifty to two hundred or so.

The rhythm of Penan life is determined by the maturing of the wild sago palms, from which the Penan pound a starchy paste; by jungle fruits, which mature somewhat unpredictably because there are no seasons; and by animal migrations. Besides the sago palm, their staple food, they harvest *lekak,* an edible palm bud, and various fruits, ferns, vegetables, and roots. Wade Davis, who has studied twenty tribes of the Amazon and South America, says, "the knowledge of the forest by the Penan surpasses all of them. It's unbelievable. . . . They recognize more than a hundred fruiting trees and at least fifty medicinal plants."

Sago palms grow in clumps, several trunks springing from one mass of roots. "If there are many trunks," says a Penan,

> we will get one or two. We thin it out so it will thrive. If there is a lot of sago, we will harvest some, and will leave some. We don't like to kill it all off, in case one day there is nothing for us to eat. This is really our way of life. . . . If we harvest the [sago at] Ula Jek first and finish the *nangah* [mature sago] there, we *molong* [put a mark and preserve for future use] the *uvud* [young sago]. . . . After two or three years, mature sago will grow out of the young sago that we have preserved.

Scattered across the steep, intricate ridges and valleys of their district, many wild sago clumps will be known and claimed (marked) by a single group. They know when it is time, in two or three years, to return to a certain clump. And so with many other types of edible plants; in all of their fruit and vegetable harvesting, they are careful to preserve a sustained yield.

The other rhythm is hunting, which they love. The small, bearded pig of Borneo is their favorite food, and in virgin forest, pig supplies most of their protein. The pig is taken with the poison dart from a blowpipe (rarely), dogs and spears, or, increasingly, by shotgun. They also hunt, by blowpipe, deer, monkey, gibbon, civet, porcupine, squirrel, and just about anything else. The rhinos are gone, though fresh tracks were seen in the highlands in 1984. The pigs travel in bands, foraging for their favorite roots, fruits, and nuts. Fruiting can be unpredictable, but the Penan know exactly where the fruit trees are and live for the pig migrations to come their way. In one heartbreaking story of a few years ago, the small, clear tributary suddenly went brown, and the hunters jumped to their weapons—pigs must be crossing upstream, a lot of them. No, it turned out to be big and yellow. A bulldozer.

By all accounts, the Penan and the longhouses can live well in virgin forest. One ethnologist in Belaga in 1986 reported that Penan hunts lasted from sunup to early afternoon, covered six or eight miles, and had a 90 percent success rate. A century before, up the Rajang River in longhouses in 1865, Alfred Russel Wallace reported, "The people produce far more food than they consume, and exchange the surplus for gongs and brass cannon, ancient jars, and gold and silver ornaments, which constitute their wealth. On the whole, they appear very free from disease." Eric Hansen, who walked back and forth across the most remote Penan territories in 1982, says, "The only Penan I have seen who were not in superb physical condition were from Sungai Ubong on the ulu Tutoh. . . . Their traditional hunting grounds were squeezed between Mulu National Park and a huge timber concession." This is the Penan settlement the Chinese gentleman had visited by helicopter.

The Penan have for centuries traded with nearby longhouses, which in turn traded with Chinese boat peddlers working out of settlements downstream. From the forest they harvest camphor, wild rubber, *damar* (a resin), *gaharu* (the incense wood which boomed in the 1970s), bezoar stones (monkey gallstones valuable to Chinese medicine), and rattan, which they use to make the famous Penan baskets and mats, for their own use and for sale. They trade at longhouses for salt, cloth, tobacco, cooking utensils, radios, tape players, batteries.

Their personal style and the atmosphere in a camp are difficult to describe, and perhaps to believe. Mild and sweet in manner, curious and active, to us at least they are utterly charming. All food being shared, their governance democratic, their manner open, it is not surprising that generosity is a primary virtue. Davis reported of Manser that in six years "he never saw Penan quarrel. Only once did he see a hungry child neglect to share food." Manser said: "There was a boy in that first Penan group who caught seven fish. I remember watching the headman give three to each family and then carefully slice the remaining fish in two. That is the Penan. You will never find one with a full stomach and another who is hungry."

Readers from my own culture may feel that such a paradise must be lost. Alas, that is the story we are writing across the face of the earth. Bruno's first years with the Penan, 1984–85, were the years the logging moved up the Tutoh. In 1975, the annual cut in Sarawak had been 2.5 million cubic meters; by 1985 it was 12 million. By 1990, it was 18 million. In 1985, as Bruno was getting to know his new friends, who had probably been in the jungle for four thousand years, over an acre of forest was being cut each minute. The logging raced, very much like a wildfire, up from Marudi, up the Tutoh, past the park, into the district where Bruno was living. It happened so quickly.

An announcement in fine print would have appeared in the *Sarawak Gazette,* in Kuching, months, maybe years before. It would have given the natives six weeks to claim customary rights to tilled acres in a certain district. Nomads would have had no rights anyway, even if they had happened to see the newspaper (no mail service above Marudi), find someone who could read it, and compose a written reply within six weeks. The land now belonged to the government, and the government had seen fit to lease it out to a timber concession. Never mind that since the drifting apart of the continents, the rise of mammals, the first migrations from central Asia—that in all human history not a single government or its agents had ever set foot in most of this forest. Not the Malay sultans, the white rajahs, the Japanese in World War II, the British resistance (who chased the Japanese up one stream to Limbang), the colonial regime, or modern ministers of Malaysia and Sarawak. Government had never left the rivers and the park. Suddenly the forest was declared the property of those who had never seen it, who did not know it, who did not love it. But they were powerful people, and they intended to be rich.

For the Penan, the first warning was the sound of a helicopter, just before Manser arrived. "The Penan expected to talk about their situation. Instead, they were stunned as an anthropologist asked to measure their skulls." The "little men" were not amused. The government survey party did its work, said the land belonged to the state and would be logged.

After four attempts in the fall of 1985, a few Penan leaders were finally able to bring representatives of Tutoh nomadic bands and settlements together in a meeting. To the Penan, such a political gathering was not an accustomed activity; you might imagine the level of fear, frustration, misinformation, and ignorance. Manser, too, knew nothing. As secretary to the group, he helped send a petition to the government to protect five hundred square miles near the park as a nomadic homeland. "I was so naive," he recalled. "It was such a small area of land. You could walk across it in three or four days. I really expected the government to set it aside." The petition letter was never answered.

Still hoping for quick changes, he prepared in 1985 a report on Sarawak logging and sent it to twenty papers and magazines in Malaysia, Europe, and the United States. Nothing happened, though of course some seeds had been sown.

Other native tribes, settled tribes with more political savvy, had already blockaded some logging roads before Manser arrived in Sarawak. He urged the Penan, traditionally shy and nonviolent, to do the same.

In the spring of 1986, as told by Wade Davis:

> Manser and a group of 25 Penan stood in front of an oncoming bulldozer that was breaking ground for a bridge into the forest. The driver retreated, but the next morning 30 bulldozers appeared at the roadhead, backed by police and logging company officials. The Penan fled. Malaysian officials had trouble believing that the savages of the forest could devise such a strategy of resistance. They blamed instead a foreign agent of influence and ordered his arrest. Manser became a marked man.

From 1986, when the police took official notice of him, until 1990, the story could be heard essentially unchanged in any upriver cafe, any airport police office, the Sarawak state government offices in Kuching, the American Embassy in Kuala Lumpur, or in Friends of the Earth offices around the world: Bruno Manser, a Swiss, is hiding with the Penan, Malaysia has a price on his head, and he is organizing opposition to the timber trade.

It was a story Europeans wanted to hear, and also a story Malaysia wanted to tell, since it diverted attention from the new SAM [Sahabat Alam Malaysia, the Friends of the Earth organization in Malaysia] office in Marudi, staffed by Sarawak citizens, natives from the longhouses who thought the timber trade was rotten to the core. The Manser story focused all attention on the romance of a white savior.

After the spring of 1986, Manser could not safely leave the forest and come in to the settlements. The companies and government were said to offer $35,000 for his capture, and the nomadic Penan kept him for three years, moving about in the forest, passing him from band to band. The two hundred armed soldiers sent after him by Malaysia could not find the camps. Manser began to learn the meaning of the stick signs left by Penan for each other at every jungle trail or event: who was going where, why, when, what's up. Two pieces of wood across the completed sign meant that all people of the forest were of one heart. "In all my years among the Penan," Manser says, "I never saw a sign that did not bear this simple message." Thom Henley of Vancouver, Canada, tells of an old Penan placing one rock in the middle of a circle of rocks, threatening sticks outside the circle, to show how the Penan sheltered Manser from the police.

Manser was captured twice, and twice escaped. The first time, by chance, he ran into an off-duty policeman who recognized him; he ran away, shots whizzing over his head. A second time he was betrayed by a reporter who came to a Penan meeting by helicopter, left, and then the police arrived in the same helicopter. He was taken down the Tutoh by boat; on the way, he had time to review his situation, and in a rapids he jumped out. Shots again were fired; he swam to shore and disappeared into the jungle. That is how the police came to possess his notebooks. In both cases, he thinks they were probably not shooting to kill, but the doubt was sobering.

In April 1987, the Baram erupted with blockades and logging opposition. During the summer months, fifteen timber operations were shut down by various tribes at over twenty-three sites in the Baram and Limbang, and four bridges were burned. It was close to an undeclared war; the government passed new laws against obstructing timber operations, stepped up harassments and arrests, and went after Harrison Ngau and Bruno Manser. Manser was a rajah, they said, carried by the Penan on a bamboo throne; a Zionist (Malaysia is Muslim); a communist (armed communist insurgents were still operating at the Thai border on the mainland). The Sarawak newspapers loved it. The *Star*, April 30, 1987, reported:

I'M SECRETARY TO THE PENANS: MANSER

Kuching, Wed.—The *Star* has received a letter supposedly from Swiss fugitive Bruno Manser in which he says he is hiding in the Sarawak jungle to act as secretary to the Penans.

The writer says the land of the nomadic tribe is being destroyed by timber operators and that the State Government and logging companies are not looking into the Penans' demands.

He alleged that one timber company had already destroyed half of the forest area in Magoh where the Penans collected their rattan to make baskets, mats and other items. He says good quality rattan is hard to find in other parts of the State.

He adds that fruit trees, sago palms and tacem, from which the Penan get poison for their darts, are being felled by loggers. . . . Manser, 33, has stayed on illegally since December 1984. He is said to be carrying out a study on the Penans. . . .

The State Government has, however, said that it would not recognise the study because it was being carried out illegally.

A government spokesman said that even before Manser entered the jungle, several government agencies had conducted studies and research on the Penans and had drawn up plans to improve their standard of living.

He said the Penans have been accepting changes slowly and interference from foreigners like Manser had hindered the government's efforts.

For the past few weeks, the Penans have been blockading timber camps, bringing logging activities to a standstill. The State Government believes that the action was instigated by Manser.

By 1988 the international community was responding; the European Parliament passed a resolution to suspend Sarawak timber imports and debated banning them altogether; some Australian docks refused to unload Malaysian logs; criticism of the tropical timber trade mounted in Japan. Meanwhile, Manser, who had probably come to know the Penan better than any European since interest in "the wild man of Borneo" began, continued his unauthorized study. The government pointed out that he was not a trained anthropologist and therefore his findings were worthless. Manser, however, seems to have found a superior way of measuring heads: Henley recalls being in a longhouse, listening to a tape that was circulating among the settled Penan. "Bruno was singing, in Penan, songs he had made up about the government. The people were convulsed with laughter. One of them explained to me, 'He understands our language. He makes very good jokes.'"

The opposition continued. September 1989 saw the most massive blockades to date, with four thousand natives participating in twelve roadblocks. International attention had been gained. Yet, not only had the logging continued, moving up the Tutoh past Manser's home into the Magoh and up the middle Baram past Long San, it had increased. Day and night, the timber was coming out faster than ever, as if the companies and government were desperate. In five years, the annual cut had gone from 12 million to 18 million cubic meters. By 1990, it was clear that SAM and Manser and the natives scattered across the forest had succeeded in organizing themselves, had succeeded in staging protests and drawing international attention—and yet they were losing, losing badly. Only a few years were left for the Penan before a whole way of life would be gone; for the longhouses, a few more years, five to ten, remained. In the spring of 1990 Manser knew that what could be done from inside Sarawak had been done. Only world pressure, largely on Japan, could stop the cutting. He escaped from Sarawak—how, where, is a secret. But after five years of hiding deep inside, in March 1990, he came out. "I would have stayed," he said, "if the Penan could have been left alone."

On the afternoon of June 6, 1990, Bruno Manser was out of the rain forest, sitting on the eighteenth floor of a building in downtown Tokyo, staring out the window: across the street, a platform of five window-washers hung halfway down a wall of glass and steel. They looked like ants, a cliché that after six years in Borneo must have had a force for Bruno that we cannot imagine. To their left, painted on a fifty-foot-high billboard, was a huge, nearly naked Chinese woman with a semiautomatic assault rifle—a movie advertisement. Behind her were the blue Matsushita Electric building, the black Sony tower, and the department stores of the Ginza. "I went to Sarawak," he was saying in a soft and careful voice with a slight German accent, "to join the life of an indigenous people who still live independent, having their own economy, somehow in harmony with nature." He looked at his audience. "They have existed."

Bruno Manser seems small in baggy trousers and a rough cotton, open-necked shirt, about five feet nine inches tall and weighing 150 pounds, but pictures from the jungle show an adventurer's muscles on a lean frame trimmed by malaria. He wears rimless glasses and has an instantly engaging smile, at once witty, ironic, and compassionate—Ben Kingsley playing Gandhi. That afternoon, his gaze roamed the room and the wry smile was directed at the dark wall panels of tropical timber, as he spoke:

> The settlements are dirty. They will throw just anything out of the house. But when they are in the jungle, the dish is a leaf and they throw the leaf away, and when their hut will get greasy from the wild boar fat or black from the charcoal also they will just leave for a new place—they will be all new and clean—and that's how they can survive.

Hosted by Yoichi Kuroda of JATAN [Japan Tropical Forest Action Network] and the Friends of the Earth office in Tokyo, Manser was meeting Japanese government and industry leaders, holding vigils on the sidewalk in front of Mitsubishi, running off mimeos in the tiny JATAN office in crowded Shibuya, downtown Tokyo, trying to find his footing on the treacherous path of international environmentalism.

Bruno Manser, sui generis, Swiss shepherd, intellectual, spelunker, botanist, artist, is possibly the first man, and maybe the last, to stand with one foot in the stone age, or at least in a European Romantic's love of it, and the other foot in the offices of environmental science: a world of timber exports, hectares per minute logged, carbon dioxide emissions, German analyses of satellite photographs showing 4 percent of the Philippine forest left.

His new allies are hardly Penan: bright, young one-worlders in tiny, messy offices which in 1960 would have churned out civil rights mimeos and in 1970 anti-Vietnam or pro-consumer Xeroxes and now have the latest fax on whales. They and Bruno are friends, but they prefer law school to leeches. Yoichi Kuroda of JATAN and Thom Henley of Endangered Peoples Project are handsome and articulate, wear their suits comfortably, and answer stupid questions with courtesy, smart questions with facts. Henley is impressive in Washington and Tokyo and has visited Sarawak four times. Henley and Kuroda, however, would not prefer to remain with the Penan.

Strange that a man so independent, who wanted to get away to a life in nature, should wind up at the middle of so much. Some of Manser's activities would later be seen as competitive to SAM, while some of his popularity in Europe offends even activist Malaysians because it seems racist. Randy Hayes of Rainforest Action Network sums it up well:

> Bruno Manser's story evokes the notion of the Tarzan syndrome. No one cared about the Penan until a white man came to the scene; they were considered little brown men who needed guidance. While this is not Bruno Manser's fault, he plays into it unwittingly. It's a classic European fantasy—a Lawrence of Arabia. . . . Manser's impact lies in the fact that he brought attention to the issue. But there's a danger in letting the messenger steal the limelight.

Even opposition Sarawakians and Malaysians can easily tire of hearing about the rajah Brookes, and Manser. The white men, of course, were the ones who once thought the Penan were apes; who loved the orangutans to death; who brought the British land laws that now serve the government so well; who brought the helicopters, the bulldozers. And now, as international economies replace race as locations of power, the Japanese join the Europeans in the first world: these new Asian white men build the dozers, run the banks, buy and burn the logs. Being saved by someone else's Tarzan—that rankles.

There's another danger, besides the attention to the foreign adventurer: the Penan themselves, as nomads, play into the hands of European romanticism; also, as nomads, they divert attention from the issue of longhouse land rights, the overriding issue for most of the population and most of the territory. Therefore, the Penan issue is a double-edged sword: it attracts international attention but makes an easy target for government defenses of timber. Do you expect to keep them in a stone age forever? Just 700 . . . 500 . . . 300 of them left? Over and over, the Chinese in Kuching accused me of wanting to save the nomads in the forest; thus the conversation was kept away from the longhouses that wanted to gain control of their own modernization and industrialization. Over and over, I would have to say, "Forget the Penan, forget Manser, I don't care, pretend they don't exist," in order to talk issues.

No one blames Manser for these difficulties. He is single of purpose and pure of heart. There are tragedies enough in Sarawak, without setting one disaster against the other. Among the natives of various tribes, I found repeated and deep sympathy for the Penan; they are the ones who really know and love the jungle, they are the ones losing it all. Their numbers, many or few, make little difference. To Kayans and Kenyahs up the Baram, as well as to Europe, the Penan are symbols of a kind of purity and a kind of loss. An old Penan from the Magoh River said:

> We know that the dipterocarp seeds are pig food, we do not cut this tree anyhow. The river banks [roots] are what pigs eat, we don't pollute the rivers. Sago fruits, "tevanga" are what pigs eat, we make sure the pigs have their share of these sago products. There is a fruit tree called "tekalet" (acorn). That is pig food, we don't disturb the tree. But in Layun, Apho and Patah those trees are fast disappearing because they are cut down by timber companies. If the companies come here and cut all the trees in the Magoh, there will be nothing for pigs to eat. The pigs will not come here. They will go somewhere else, and we Penan will not have any food. That is what I fear if the companies come here. But as long as the Penan are left alone here, we will have enough food because we care for the forest, we look after it well to provide us our food, our life.

Since that statement appeared in the *Sarawak Museum Journal* of December 1989, the Magoh drainage has been cut. The "little men" have finally been brought into our world, on our terms. Hoorah for systematic collecting.

NOTE

For accurate information on current developments in the struggle to protect Malaysia's outback and surrounding areas, contact the Bruno Manser Foundation for its newsletter, *Tong Tana*: Bruno-Manser-Fonds, Heuberg 25, CH-4051 Basel, Switzerland; e-mail: bmf@bmfonds.links.ch.

10 roads where there have long been trails

In the rugged semitropical mountains of southern Mexico, in the northeastern corner of the state of Oaxaca, the Mazatec Indians grow corn, beans, and coffee. The Mazatecs are one of many discrete linguistic and ethnic groups in that diverse state. Due to their long isolation in the deeply folded terrain of the Sierra Madre Oriental, both the natural habitats and the cultural traditions have been able to remain somewhat more intact than in many more accessible areas.

Although traditions of healing with plants are rich and varied across much of Mexico, the Mazatecs are renowned for their facility with plant medicine and ritual healing. As a Zapotec man from another region of Oaxaca explained to me two years ago, when I was setting out on my ethnobotanical fieldwork in that area, "My people know many herbs; so do the Mixtec and the Mixe. But the Mazatecs know magic. They know how the plants talk." By looking at the way that the Mazatec people see nature and interact with it, both in the field and ritually, we can understand something of the indigenous Mesoamerican concept of natural order and of health and illness within that order. We can also get a glimmer of an enduring, multileveled worldview, which is rooted in the many species that dwell in their mountains and valleys and which resides deep in the animated landscape itself.

The rivers flow largely underground, through miles of cavernous tunnels. The world's greatest spelunkers are only now exploring the subterranean torrents of what is known as the Huautla Complex. During an all-night Mazatec healing ceremony with a *curandera*

FIGURE 7. The Sierra Mazateca, northeastern Oaxaca, Mexico. (© Kathleen Harrison)

or *curandero* (a female or male shaman who cures), there is heartfelt prayer, beautiful singing, and chanted invocation. In the penetrating silences that fall between these expressions, one can hear, or perhaps I should say *one can feel*, the river flowing close by underground. Each river, cave, spring, and the water itself has an individually named spirit, a *dueño*, that guards the water source and must be treated with exacting respect, or else, I am told, there will be dire personal consequences for the careless transgressor.

The curandero inhales the scent of his meter-long beeswax candle, which acts as the hourglass for the prayer session and tells us where the bees who made the wax came from and which flower pollen they were collecting. The pollinators, their blossoms, and the effort of making their hive are part of the offering we make to the deities we are invoking. He sings about the bees. He prays to a large, fresh *Nicotiana tabacum* (tobacco) leaf on the table, addressing it as two saints. "San Pedro," he murmurs, "San Pedro and San Pablo, please protect these people here and this work that we do tonight. Carry our prayers to God and help us communicate our gratitude and our needs." On the leaf lies a small mound of crumbled green tobaccos, *piciete*, two or sometimes three varieties, each grown nearby by a friend or relative or sought from healer-gardeners in distant villages. The shape and color of the flower—rose, creamy white, or the rarer purple—distinguish the variety visually, but it is the *espíritu* in the plant that makes it prayer medicine. Each variety has its particular being and qualities that differ from the next; each contributes a personality and a specific force to the act of diagnosis or protection that the healer is attempting. It is believed that together the spirits of two or three tobaccos, of two or three saints, listening and working on behalf of the one who needs help, will be better than one. During the ceremony, the tobacco saints will be rubbed briskly on the skin or held in a small quid in the cheek by the healer and perhaps by the patient. The participants will speak to these *santos,* who they feel sure are listening, and request that they urge the other spirits of life-forms, elements, rocks, sky, and ancestral time to engage in the ritual conversation too. The curandero will name every spirit he feels might help in his endeavor of the moment and will express gratitude to many more.

Over the past five hundred years, as the stories of the saints have been told, retold, embellished, and made locally relevant by neophyte converts to Catholicism, the saints' qualities meshed with the qualities that are particular to certain plant species and the primordial beings that have long resided in those plants, according to native recognition. The personification of plant species reflects a palpable perception of their intrinsic character, but it also provides a way to communicate with each species as a being, in a dialogue about the environment, the relationship with other species and with humans. Through a leaf, even without ingesting it, one can speak to the spirit of the species, give thanks, make requests for intervention or insight, and observe alliances. In fact, *the spirit is the medicine,* and it can be invoked without the plant material if necessary. The healers' divination and healing skills do not arise solely from the psychoactive chemistry of some of these plants, although they are powerful teachers. The practitioners know and assert that the spirit of some medicines can make one crazy, can leave one with mind-shadows, if one approaches without gratitude or without humility. Bodily purification, pure intentions, and direct verbal interspecies communication—prayer—are essential aspects of the medicine and the teachings.

During a late-night ceremony, the curandero and his patient have eaten the leaves of *Salvia divinorum,* which the Mazatecs call Shka Pastora, the Leaves of the Shepherdess. La Pastora is very shy, they tell me, timid like a deer. She will only come when we have eaten many pairs of the leaves and sit very quietly, perfectly still in the darkness, as in a glen in the forest in the moonlight. If someone moves or speaks suddenly, she will disappear in a moment. If we invite her and we are very clear and open to her, she will come; she will speak. She will whisper to us what we need to know and show us what she sees. She may help to heal us or bless us with good fortune. But we must pray, and we must listen. And we must pay her our full attention in the still darkness of the hut perched on the steep mountainside—amid the maize patches, the savory leaves of *Piper sanctum*, and the night-scented blossoms of the rosy *Brugmansias*.

We are on a rock mountain, beside a clean spring, above a narrow path. One wall of the hut in which the healers live and do their work is solid, swirled, vertical rock. It is El Cerro de Curación, they tell me, the Hill of Healing. Four of us sit facing the rock wall with its suggestive patterns as we pray. "That is why we came here, to gaze upon the rock, to speak to the rock, because we can heal here, and no one will bother us," smiles the elder. Recycled planks, black tar paper, and battered tin make up the other walls and roof of the two-room house. The floor is swept earth. An old table set against the rock wall is the altar, with flowers, single leaves, seedpods, candles, and paper images of the saints arranged along it.

The Virgin of Guadalupe, the patron saint of Mexico, the spiritual heart and soul of its native people, is there too. She speaks through some of the plants that are used in ceremony. A Mazatec lay anthropologist has told me that the same goddess spoke through these plants in preconquest times. She just had a different name then, but always the same compassion, the same *personaje*. The Seeds of the Virgin, from two species of morning glory, *Ipomoea violacea* and *Rivea corymbosa*, are ingested to seek vision and to help in difficult childbirth. The leaves of Santa Maria, another name for La Pastora, help with prayer and insight. But no matter what, she is always there to speak with—the compassionate emissary who will bring solace and carry prayers on to Dios. She has God's ear. Flowers, tears, and beautiful words, *copal* incense, candle-light, and absolute honesty are offered to La Guadalupe. She is not jealous of the other saints or of the spirits of the plants and the deities of the earth that are called together in these ceremonies. Together, they are a team of spirit-beings who can be invoked in times of need if the intentions are good and the proper offerings are made.

The healers know that at this level of awareness there are no absolute cultural boundaries: Catholic and chthonic, cave and book, ancestors and mushrooms, indigenous and international—all are working in a vibrating tapestry of *la medicina*. Not everyone knows how to ask for medicine or how to receive it, they tell me, but there is no one in the world who does not need medicine in his life.

The Leaves of the Shepherdess, Shka Pastora, grow in small hidden glades in the upland moist forest. The plant is rarely known to set seed, propagating itself vegetatively from the fallen nodes, usually with the help of those few humans who know where it grows. It is speculated that through centuries of human tending, it has lost the

FIGURE 8. A farmer with his digging stick, on the steep Oaxacan slopes where he grows coffee, corn, and beans. (© Kathleen Harrison)

ability to set seed effectively. Or perhaps it is so rare and sensitive in nature, confined to a small region and very specific conditions, that had it not been for its beautiful medicine and human alliance, it would have died out long ago as a species. We hike higher into the mountains to visit a hidden patch, which I am told has been the curandero's family patch "forever." No one else knows of it, nor would any honorable person harvest leaves from these plants even if he stumbled upon them, for the Shepherdess is known to have a delicate relationship with the man or woman who tends her in the forest, and she would not work for another who took her illicitly.

We were up on a mountain that was known and named for its pines, the *ocotes*, yet I saw only twenty or so of these pines on the mountain, up above us on a precipitous ridge. The spring is also named for the ocote, and the ocote is the namesake of the ancient, stone-stepped trail on which we ascended. When I asked why there were so few pines, my friend told me that all the others had been taken, to build with, in the past fifteen years. These few were preserved only because they were too hard to take down. We were silent for a while, eating bananas that we had picked nearby and appreciating the vista of folded hills, worn stone-lined trails, cornfields, forest remnants, and distant dwellings. Above us, at the very end of the pine trail, was a small extended-family settlement of three houses, with a donkey and a goat pegged in the swept yard. My friend gestured across the landscape and said, "From up here one can see all the *cerros*, also the distant higher mountains, and it is not too hot to work in the *milpa* [the cornfield]." He nodded at the several wattle-and-daub huts with tin roofs across the lush ravine from us. "These people live a good life up here, quiet, growing their food," he mused. The tiny grandmother raised her hand in greeting from their door. Two young women looked up from a bench in the shade where they sat embroidering flowers on white dresses. A brilliant yellow rectangle of corn was raked out to dry in the sun next to them. "And besides," he continued, "up here they get great television."

One day as I was walking on a muddy path high up above the town of Huautla, the now-bustling center of Mazatec country, looking for interesting plants and the occasional wandering herbalist to question, I saw a remarkable "worm" in a wet wheel rut. It was several inches long, thick and greasy-looking, a rather transparent gray, with incipient organs and dark eyes visible through its oily surface. It seemed to have no means of mobility, and as I gently turned it over with a twig, I saw the beginnings of six tiny legs trying to poke through its fat sides like thorns. I am intrigued by unusual natural phenomena, but something about the murkiness of this creature repulsed me. It was probably an insect larva of some sort, I thought, that had perhaps fallen onto the road from an overhanging tree. Two weeks later, on another hot, wet afternoon, when my Mazatec parabiologist friend and I were exploring the high trails, I spied another such entity lying in a mud puddle.[1] Excited, I asked my friend what it was. He said that he had seen them from time to time and that during the rainy season, it was normal to see them in the red mud of the roads. I asked him if it was indeed the larva of an insect and if he knew what kind of insect it would become. Surprised at my assumption, he asserted, "It is not an insect. It is the seed of a small tree." Unconvinced, I questioned him again, and he then described the tree it would become. I felt the cognitive ground shift beneath us and reminded myself that diversity comes in remarkable packages.

Another time, I visited a family in a small town in the lowlands, at the end of one of the roads that radiate out over the steep countryside. The forty-year-old husband has teaching credentials and instructs twelve- and thirteen-year-old students in both Mazatec and Spanish. He is curious about the world and enjoys discussing many contemporary issues, although he has not traveled far and laments the shortage of interesting visitors. The teenage daughter and three younger sons all prize education and hope to study further at the university in the neighboring state of Puebla. They have a bookshelf, a rarity, in their two-room, stuccoed, tin-roofed house on the hill above town. Like everyone else, they draw water from a well, wash their dishes in a plastic tub on stones outside, and cook over a fire on a pounded-earth table. Loofah sponges hang like green cucumbers from a vine on their arbor.

From dusk on, the scent of Queen of the Night, *huele de noche (Cestrum nocturnum)*, fills the air, and her leaves are cooked in chili and vinegar to accompany meals. The youngest child in the family, a boy of seven, asked me if I would like to taste his favorite food. I said yes, wondering what was up as he ran off into the trees. Soon he was clambering up a huge leguminous tree and came running back with several fifteen-centimeter-long caterpillars, thick as your thumb, brilliantly patterned in yellow, lime green, and black. He grabbed a twig off the ground and thrust it lengthwise through one of the caterpillars, forcing out its innards. He quickly slipped the elastic skin off the stick, turning it inside out, and offered me the pearly tube that remained. "They're best fried," he explained. His mother told me that in midsummer, when certain trees are covered with the larvae, they eat platters of these crispy caterpillars. They leave many behind, she assured me.

The next time I visited the family, a regional election was taking place. We discussed their political views and their dissatisfaction with the hopelessly self-obsessed ruling party. After the heat of the day had passed, they offered to walk me up to a viewpoint above the town. As we ascended a rough trail through the trees, past rocky hollows known by the children for their individual snake inhabitants, under the ripening edible fruits of a vast tree, they stopped to point out the exquisite blossoming epiphytes higher up. When we reached the rocky peak, they noted how the trees had grown and the path had shifted and that someone had planted tiny plots of corn in the sunny spots. We stepped out onto the rocky promontory together and examined the town far below us. They told me the history of the streets and the school, of the church and its decay and revival now under the guidance of an Indian priest. "He is a good liberal," they said. "He respects us all, and he knows the plants!" In the basement of the church, young women make tinctures and salves from the local native plants and sell them for only a peso or two, with advice, to anyone who needs medicine. "The state has forgotten about our people except when they want votes—then they build a few more miles of road. But we are remembering how to take care of ourselves. It is so important that our children understand that La Naturaleza [Mother Nature] can sustain us, if we pay attention." The schoolteacher stopped talking, and we all looked out over the valley and the village. One of the children I know there wants to add English to his Mazatec and Spanish and become a translator. His cousin wants to grow food and gather from the wild, like his grandfather. Everyone wants to eat tomorrow and to grow up to have their own families.

We scanned the trail that wound up the mountainside immediately across from where we were. Steeper and higher, it felt as though we could reach out and touch it. I was told that the spirit of that hill is a woman, very tall and very fat, who wears a beautiful dress, almost too beautiful to look at. She is a spirit of abundance. Sometimes the curanderos of the village are blessed with a vision of this guardian woman.

Because the landscape that the Mazatecs live in is so vertical, with so little horizontal space and so many interwoven hillsides, they long ago developed a whistling language to augment their spoken one. Like yodeling, the whistle-speech can project across chasms and along mountainsides. This versatile language has a great variety of tone and meaning. Not everyone knows it anymore, but I often heard the young men whistling to each other instead of using words as we traveled in the backs of trucks through the small towns that dot the ridges and valleys of the Sierra or when we walked the trails through hamlets without roads. Many Mazatecs are monolingual, and most of the older people who live outside of the larger towns speak only their native tongue. Many of the women in their forties and older do not know, nor do they seem to need, Spanish. Much of the negotiation in the marketplaces and almost all private conversations occur in Mazatec. Despite five hundred years of colonization and intentional cultural disruption by Europeans in a country next door to the United States, there are large populations for whom the colonizer's tongue is neither primary nor even widely known. Their tenacious nurturing of their own pragmatic and poetic languages reflects the degree of living diversity of the culture, the endurance of their ritual traditions and vibrant mythology, and their interactive encyclopedia of natural phenomena.

Since I was there to study plants, cures, and plant lore, I often asked people for the names of things. Most often I was told that there was no corresponding Spanish name and that the Mazatec name for one thing often combined the names of other things or qualities in nature, so that the name of each species reflects its metaphorical or literal association with other species or natural processes. Nothing exists by itself. A bird can be named after a flower and thunder, a flower named for the ear of an animal, or a wind for the scent that it carries. It occurred to me: if a pollinator were decimated by a virus or an herbicide, and the blossoms could not fruit, and then the next year the flowers did not scent the air, what would we call the wind? If the diversity of the natural world is intact and the human world is able to note and appreciate that diversity, then it all rolls along as a self-aware system of interdependence. The Mazatec wise people maintain that all participants in that system communicate with one another in dynamic relationships, using languages that call on all the heightened senses. From the very multiplicity of life-forms a unified world is created. To recognize a deity in each place and thing is not contradictory to the unity of all things. Rather, in this biodiverse worldview, it is a requirement.

After I had been in the Sierra Mazateca a while, collecting medicinal plants, photographing, cleaning beans, interviewing those who live on the trails, watching a new concrete house being built on the roadside, listening to conversations, carrying water, and playing with the children, I began to notice a certain dissonance in the biotic mapping. My friends had mentioned characteristics of the deer in their description of plant qualities, and yet considering the scarcity of animal protein in the local diet, I wondered why they hadn't mentioned deer as an animal they hunted for food.

One evening, the elder and his grandson, armed with a shotgun, invited me along on a hunt for armadillo, hoping for a rare meal of meat. As we watched in the deepening dusk from under a huge mango tree, having seen no armadillos, I was relieved to sense that we were about to give up. I asked about the deer. "There are no more deer here," confirmed my young friend. "We killed them all for food or scared them away. But we still speak of them in our songs. A few live up very high in the mountains," he announced with a matter-of-fact resignation that was neither guilty nor tragic. But when I told him in Spanish that many deer graze each evening in my wild northern California garden, does and fawns and even the occasional buck, he was deeply impressed. He quickly translated this into Mazatec for his grandfather, the *curandero*. This presence of deer in my life became one of my best credentials for learning about shamanic work. It compensated somewhat for the almost unbelievable fact that I did not know how to make tortillas.

The psychoactive mushrooms that grow in the area have many folk names that describe who they are and how they grow. The little ones that spring forth. The little holy children. The landslide. One species is called San Isidro, the patron saint of laborers, whose aid is solicited in beginning a new endeavor. A beloved species of *Psilocybe* is called *los pajaritos*, the little birds. As a midwife-curandera sorted through a banana-leaf packet of mushrooms that a trusted collector had brought to her, she held up one small, brown, elf-capped mushroom and said, "*Es un pajaro* [It is a bird]." Since they are always eaten in pairs to reflect the balance of the feminine and the masculine, she carefully matched it with a smaller one. "*Un pajarito* [a little bird]," she chirped. "Together, the little birds sing."

According to my naturalist-assistant Carlito, he and his father sometimes go high up and far away, on a pilgrimage, to collect with their own hands the particular species of mushroom they need. But it is a long trek, and sometimes they have to hunt or camp for days waiting for the mushrooms to appear after rain in the misty weather. The alternative is to "order" them from someone, a particularly reverent and discreet man who collects the mushrooms only from distant, wild places that are very "clean." He knows La Naturaleza and picks the mushrooms in the right way—with prayer and attention to other entities or possible magical disturbances in the surroundings. The collector's intentions will be absorbed by the mushrooms, so it is crucial that he be a good soul. This year it was hot and dry during the height of the rainy season, so there were almost no mushrooms, and only one healing session had occurred in three weeks. When there are mushrooms and all is well, two healing or blessing ceremonies might occur each week in this household. This is possible several months of the year when there has been normal rainfall.

At other times of the year, the leaves and seeds of other species are the medicines. My friends became increasingly worried about the shift in weather, the blazing heat, the absence of medicine, and the man in a nearby town who had received only the first of two sessions necessary to cure him from *hecheceria*, a bad spell that had been put on him. They were concerned about the health of the seventy-year-old curandero himself, whom they call "the chief of the wise ones." He seems strong today, but he is now beginning to sing about his vulnerability. Only in the recent ceremony did they acknowledge aloud that someday he would be gone, like the deer, like the jaguar they have not seen in years. During the mushroom ceremony, he sang to us that his son, his wife, his grandson, and even I, his friend, must learn fast—before it is too late to learn.

For years the family has lived in the sky blue *casita*, tucked high in the forest and milpas, camouflaged by lilies and coffee trees, above a little-traveled trail. Privacy is essential, they tell me, for doing medicine and for staying out of harm's way as *doctores*. But now they are building a concrete-block house down by the road, much more spacious, with concrete rather than dirt floors. Their younger son left his own family, moved to Mexico City where he works in an office, and married a second wife who is urban Mixe and very modern. He returns for a weekend every month or two to help with construction and to bring money for building. During my stay we moved, bit by bit, down into the road house. They assured me that the curandero would continue to hold his diagnostic consultations and that ceremonial work would continue in the old hut on the hill. But in the meantime, contemplative time was being interrupted frequently by the foot traffic on the road, the curious acquaintances who stopped by, and the distraction of the occasional passing truck.

The road has passed through this valley only for the past seven years, and still very few people own vehicles. The ubiquitous Coca-Cola truck, the battery dealer, and the pickups that ferry passengers, animals, and supplies make up the two or three vehicles that pass each hour. The old curandero pantomimed to me that the people of the road, himself included, are now like monkeys because they all rise to their feet at the sound of an approaching engine to stand in a row and stare at the road. No conversation is more important than who is passing, he said to his grandson, mocking himself. He plans to sell sodas and *aguardiente,* cane-liquor, from the bedroom window, since so many people do like to ask him for advice anyway, and he figures he can make enough money to paint his new house that way. After all, he conceded, it was getting harder for him to climb the mountain and work in the steeply inclined patches of coffee, beans, and corn with his digging stick. He'd rather plant lower down in the valley and buy some of his food from others.

One day Carlito and I walked and hitched ten kilometers beyond the town, down a road that was only three months old. It was a wide, raw cut in the landscape, a few men still cracking the most obstinate rocks with hammers. Children stood in front of each of the few houses along the way, watching us pass. When a beer truck dropped us at the end of the new road, we found that it abruptly narrowed again into a footpath, an ancient *camino*, with shaded resting places, large stones set flat to use as the occasional bench, and trees generously hung with edible pods along the way.

Returning up the road, we stopped to visit an herbalist and his wife and six children. They all had an illness they had never heard of and didn't know how to treat. I was sure that it was mumps, and we agreed to use some of their plants for fever and discomfort while I assured them that they would get well. I asked how they liked living on a road after years of living on only a path. "Well, we like it so far because we can sell more plants, and sodas of course, and maybe the peanuts and ginger that we have planted up the mountain." The herbalist informed me that the ginger he had planted came all the way from India and that it was both good medicine and good food. "Not many people have it here," he explained, "and the peanuts make a valuable protein for us because we don't have much meat. We can make a better living with the road going past us," he proclaimed optimistically. His green coffee was spread out in the sun to dry an arm's length from the road's edge, *Aristolochia* vines were hung to age in the shade for tea against stomachaches, and I counted seven species of butterflies flitting around the dung of their single pig. The whole family, with swollen necks, wanly posed for a photo—at their request because this was an opportunity to preserve a memory.

A couple of months later, while I was recovering from hepatitis A, which I had contracted while I was in the Sierra, I thought about the road and what it opens up, what it lets in, and what it lets out. More disease enters, for one thing, and news of the world, and theft and trade and gossip and allies and enemies. Education, politics, influence, and change. Some Mazatecs leave, looking for work. Outsiders like me come in, for better and for worse. The sixteenth-century reports of Bernardino de Sahagún convey that the old native people, observing the increased use of the early roads for trade and for carrying tribute to their conquerors, gave the name *coatl*, or serpent, to the road:

> Thus they said: "Can it be that it is a little danger, a little serpent of our Lord?" Or they said: "How hast thou come? Can it be that it is the serpent, the road of stumbling?" They named the road "serpent" because it is long and winding. And they called the road *tequatoc,* since there is stumbling, there is the running of thorns into the feet.[2]

In this deeply metaphorical world, the serpent winds its way into the known and changes it as he goes. The Indians saw that the serpent-road causes change and that he consumes what he needs as he goes. As consolation, I try to remember that there are things of value that we each bring, that we leave behind, that we are given, and that we take with us. Is there a way, I wonder, as the past melds into the future, that we can contribute by spiritual and cultural means to nurture the diversity of life-forms?

These people were able to maintain or creatively adapt their language, much of their culture, and their spiritual traditions in the face of their defeat and colonization by Spanish systems of commerce and forced labor. Diseases introduced by the colonizers in the sixteenth century decimated the native population, and with the promulgation of Catholicism, the folk religions were suppressed, their sacraments banned. The geographical isolation and the scarcity of resources for generating change have long worked to the advantage of the Mazatec people and their territory. With the developments of recent decades—roads, services, dams, communication—they already live much more in the world of the outside. The roads opened the doors, and the outside has come in.

But there are still learned healers, the plants continue to be known and collected for singing powerful prayers, and offerings are still left where water wells up from rock. Daylong pilgrimages are made by townspeople, collecting armloads of scented leaves as they ascend, to offer to the beings who dwell on mountaintops and who have the power to bestow good luck on the pilgrims. Cause and effect are documented in the natural-mythical world because, I am told, no species can live without its spiritual alliances. It just won't work. These alliances are what make the world hold together, *the real world* that is seen in the visions. Thankfully, there are contemporary *indigenas* (Indians) and *mestizos* (of mixed Spanish and Indian heritage) in all regions of the diverse state of Oaxaca who are involved in cultural-revitalization movements. They photograph and record rituals, interview the old ones who will talk, and hold multiethnic meetings to discuss their successes and frustrations. But all three of the healers with whom I have worked these past two summers did not want any such documentation. Nor did they welcome the intrusion of outsiders unless they had come for healing, and then only after a course of recommendations and intuitive prediagnostic interviews.

"When we are singing with *la medicina*, if you turned on the machine with the little red light," said the elder curandero, "the spirits simply would not stay with us. They would run back into the darkness, and then what would be the point of it all?" So, instead, we are given stories to share, and we are taught that profound attention is our best instrument.

NOTES

1   Some anthropologists might call my friend an informant, but I prefer the term *parabiologist,* which I feel is more accurate and more respectful of his bountiful knowledge.

2   Bernardino de Sahagún, *Florentine Codex: General History of the Things of New Spain,* trans. Arthur J.O. Anderson and Charles E. Dibble (Santa Fe, N.Mex.: School of American Research; and Salt Lake City: University of Utah Press, 1963), p. 269.

11   volcano dreams

Sitting in an airport lounge in Newark, New Jersey, I am thinking of brimstone and fire. A television above flashes images from *Volcano*, a film that posits the near-destruction of Los Angeles by a pyroclastic mass nestled beneath the La Brea tar pits. "The coast is toast!" exult the ads. The film's producers must have been bankrolled on the assumption that a movie-going public sated by the shopworn repertoire of Southern California images—looters carrying pillowy packages of Pampers, homeowners dampening their roofs with green water hoses as a brushfire beckons—would warm to the novelty of computer-generated lava coursing down Wilshire Boulevard. LA is the country's newest major city, but it has long been its oldest joke, and we ring in destruction not just as reactionary wish-fulfillment but as another humorous endurance test for Angelenos. On television, a scientist explains his role in ensuring the accuracy of *Volcano*, but a flurry of departure announcements drowns out what he is saying.

Much later that evening, I am watching the television news in the largest city in the world. The evening before, the volcano Popocatépetl, located thirty-nine miles from the outskirts of Mexico City, issued a series of "exhalations." Remote links from Puebla show a veil of volcanic ash descending on the city; illuminated by the white light of the news cameras, it looks like snow. In *Volcano*, the eerie gray precipitate is a brief prelude to fragmentary explosions and incandescent fury, but Popocatépetl—or Popo, as it is widely known—has been exhaling sporadically since 1994, when an "ash-gas eruptive event" blanketed the valley of Puebla with some eighty-two hundred tons of ash. Its output has become like the mild tremors of LA, a glimmer of apocalypse that nervously bands together the city: an ensuing media vigil, an alert status ("yellow"), instructions on what to do in the event of an eruption (the same banal mixture of service and salvation that smiling, oxygen-mask-wearing flight attendants deliver), a joke printed in the newspaper on all the hopelessly bureaucratic measures the corruption-plagued government will take if Popo blows ("designate an intermediary official"). Reports would later show that ash, carried east by the winds, which during the other half of the year blow toward Mexico City, fell as far away as the Gulf of Mexico port city of Veracruz.

Villa Rica de la Vera Cruz is where Spanish navigator Hernán Cortés and his crew landed on Good Friday, 1519. By November 1, they had quit Cholula, having on October 18 massacred nearly ten thousand inhabitants. Bound for Tenochtitlán, a thousand Tlaxcalan allies had joined their march. Hovering over all their diplomacy and bloodshed was Popocatépetl, which *conquista* chronicler Bernal Diaz would later note dryly "was throwing out more fire than usual." Hoping to avoid the Mexica warriors, Cortés plotted a path between Popocatépetl and its smaller companion to the north, Iztaccíhuatl. In a letter to Carlos V, he noted that "from the highest of the two by day and by night a great column of smoke comes forth and rises up into the clouds as straight as a staff, with such force that although a very violent wind blows over the mountain range, yet it cannot change the direction of the column." Nevertheless, Cortés assigned a band of ten men, led by Diego de Ordaz, to scale the volcano and discover the "secret of the smoke." In his *Pleasant Historie of New India,* Francisco Lopez de Gomara wrote that the expedition "reached very near the top, so near in fact that being there when the smoke began to rush out, they reported it did so with such noise and violence that the whole mountain seemed to fall down."

Ordaz, for his trouble, was allowed to add a smoking mountain to his coat of arms. He gained something else: his view from Popo was a stare into a five-hundred-year history about to be overwritten, a palimpsest buried like so many composite layers of the stratovolcano on which he stood. In his memoirs of the conquest, Francisco Aguilar recounted that upon returning Ordaz had said that "he had seen another new world of great cities of towers and a sea, and in the middle of it a very great city had been built and in truth it appeared to have caused him fear and astonishment." As a prelude to entering the great Mexica capital of Tenochtitlán, the climb of Popo must have emboldened the conquistadores, who with New World bravado overcame what William Prescott called the Indian's "puerile superstition" to regard the volcanoes as gods.

Although written evidence shows that Indians entered Popo's crater, Spanish accounts consistently claim that they were afraid to climb higher than the religious sites they had erected on Popo's flanks. Having unlocked the secret, the Spaniards, laying siege to Tenochtitlán, returned to Popo to collect sulfur to replenish their dwindling gunpowder supply. Before thousands of spectators, five men climbed to the summit of Popo, where Francisco de Montana, a lieutenant from Ciudad Real, was chosen to be lowered some four hundred feet by a thin, Indian-woven cord into a noxious, seething cauldron. In his bid to conquer the city first viewed from Popo, Cortés used the people's very gods against them.

The next morning, I meet with Lucio Cardenas, a researcher at the Institute of Geophysics at the National Autonomous University of Mexico (UNAM), who would that day be monitoring gas emissions from Popocatépetl. Joined by his assistant, we head east on Autopista Mexico in a Nissan van owned by CENAPRED, the country's disaster-prevention agency, and an hour later we stop for breakfast at a truck stop called Que Chula es Puebla. Cardenas advises me to eat as much as I can, saying, "It's going to be a long day," and I really have no idea how long indeed. I can't even see the volcano yet, but the restaurant features placemats that describe what it is like "to live under the volcano," including a sidebar of Popo stats: height, 5,452 meters above sea level; crater depth, 300 meters; estimated population affected by an eruption, 800,000.

Back on the highway, we twist our way upward through the Sierra Nevada, and looking back, I see a thick band of gray that blots out the city. It has simply disappeared. Ahead, Popocatépetl surges into view, its glistening peak hanging on the morning mist. A thin plume stretches up from its crater. Cardenas explains that the volcano is burning off a basinful of the previous night's rain. The clouds, always clustered near Popo, are even denser this time of year, so as we rattle for miles around the volcano that morning and afternoon, our view of the volcano drifts between clarity and a gauzy opacity. At times it appears faintly like an etching on the far horizon, its peak gently marbled by veins that are actually deep ridges; at others, it thrusts forward as the focal point of a band of clouds arranged in a peacock plume thrown up from the depths of Popo.

As the clouds congeal in the late afternoon, my plume-spotting efforts begin to flag. The nimbus and the snow line begin to blend, and as I constantly scan for Popo, I begin to wonder if there isn't some telluric equivalent of the condition known as calenture—a delirium that affects sailors, who, thinking they see land, leap into the ocean. In *Under the Volcano*, Malcolm Lowry—whose "Mexico of the mind" (as William Gass called it) casts its insolent shadow at every turn in this region and which is in itself a form of delirium—compared the timberline of Popo to "a gigantic surfacing whale."

For the Consul in *Under the Volcano* (a thin disguise for Lowry himself), "the volcano had taken on a sinister aspect: like a sort of Moby Dick, it had the air of beckoning them on as it swung from one side of the horizon to the other, to some disaster, unique and immedicable."

Here, on this bright day, the only disaster conceivable is the volcano itself, but it too is quiet. By now, Cardenas and his companion have unveiled their equipment: a Barringer Correlation Spectrometer, an oblong gray box with a periscopelike device that juts out a side window. Known as COSPEC monitoring, the process involves collecting ultraviolet rays and determining the sulfur dioxide content in the air. As we drive through the plume, or at least that invisible part of the plume that has been blown eastward, the needle on a recording device begins to tremble back and forth. It all seems rather nebulous—pulling data from the innocent sky as we pass a small shack where I see a grotesque line of dead chickens dangling out of a window. But there is a laboratory precision to it: we make four more passes through the plume to correlate an average result. When the subject of inquiry is a volcano that straddles four Mexican states and whose crater is five times larger than a soccer stadium, these measurements consume the entire day. Cardenas tells me that the Barringer device, now so vital to volcanology, was invented to help monitor sulfur emissions at factories.

"Factory of volcanoes" was what Mexican poet Carlos Pelliceres aptly called the Valley of Mexico in a sonnet he wrote upon giving a friend a painting by the artist Gerardo Murillo, better known as Dr. Atl. For Diego Rivera, Dr. Atl was "everything less than a satisfied and static bourgeois." Stern-looking with a flowing white beard, Atl painted, wrote poetry, conceived of utopian cities, supported the Mexican Revolution, and then later turned his admiration toward Germany and fascism. His greatest obsession, however, was Mexico's volcanoes, and Dr. Atl was a volcanologist before such a field had academic accreditation, motivated by beauty (the "symphonies of Popocatépetl," he termed its activity) before science, but ultimately uniting the two. The painter-volcanologist brought sketchpad and charcoals to the shadow of two of Mexico's great volcanoes, Popocatépetl and Paricutín, a volcano that ruptured out of a Michoacán farmer's field in the 1940s. Atl lived and—quite literally—breathed volcanoes, so much so that Paricutín's gases brought on a degenerative cardiovascular disorder and eventually gangrene in his leg. That pain resonates in his work, which captures unlike any other his subjects' tantamount intensity. To fashion works like *Popocatépetl* he created a special set of "atlcolors"—terrifically febrile earth tones, glowering grays, and ominous purples that depict the volcanoes as the dynamic creatures they are, agents of their own renewal and destruction.

The two volcanoes Popocatépetl and Iztaccíhuatl, which Prescott described as "two colossal sentinels to guard the entrance to the enchanted region," are stock figures in the national iconography, worthy of a place in the heart and on the diez nuevo pesos note. In Rivera's *Civilizacion Huasteca,* they bask above a group of women making tortillas, while in Juan O'Gorman's *Ciudad de Mexico,* a 1949 work that gazes on the city from atop the then-under-construction Monument to the Revolution, they arise clearly from an arid plain. Nothing in that painting but the prelapsarian pair of volcanoes is constant in today's Mexico City. That they are no longer readily visible from the capital has done nothing to diminish their standing, for they are part of the national mythology: anyone can tell you the famous story of how Popocatépetl, prince of the Chichimecs (literally "dog people"), fell in love with Iztaccíhuatl, princess of the noble Toltecs. The princess's father forbade the romance, but swayed by her sorrow, he agreed to give the Chichimec prince a set of honor-proving tests. She died before he could complete them, however, and in homage the prince built a fire for her and watched for her return. An empathetic Quetzalcóatl turned them both into volcanoes—she dormant, but his torch glowing in perpetual vigil.

Popocatépetl has been in activity well over a dozen times since its earliest recorded eruption in 1347. The last and most serious eruption was in 1921. Until 1994 it was dormant, its flanks ceded to weekend picnickers and its summit the choice of moderate-level climbers. "People forgot it was a volcano" is how Hugo Delgado Granados, a leading UNAM volcanologist, describes to me the late-twentieth-century evolution of Popo. Dr. Hugo, as he is known, is, like most volcanologists, a mountain climber first: shaggy hair, down vest, an ice ax balanced on his desk. "I met Popo when I was fifteen years old," he tells me one afternoon, recalling his first ascent. Now he feels as if "an old friend is sick," although he admits there's nothing he can do to remedy it. Instead, Popo is on a kind of life support, with concerned specialists monitoring it and trying to decide the best way to break any bad news to the immediate family. In activity, it has moved from mythology to celebrity: its picture adorns the front pages of newspapers, "Popo watch" columns track its slightest moves, people in line at the cinema drop its name.

There are no plurals in Nahuatl, the indigenous language spoken by most of the residents closest to Popocatépetl. A number is simply added before the subject. There are two exceptions, however: stars and mountains. The logic of this etymology becomes clear as one moves closer to the volcano. Along single-lane roads one can see white-hatted campesinos hunched over in the fields or guiding mule-driven wagons, and looming over the neat furrows is Popocatépetl ("smoking mountain" in Nahuatl), its size suggesting something not quite of this world, as unknowable and ethereal as the constellations. It is said that the Spanish would not allow the buildings of a town to eclipse the height of its cathedral. But next to Popo even the most resplendently polychromatic church or the tallest pyramid seems insignificant. When there is nothing for miles except repetitive fields and hardscrabble villages, when the only clouds on an otherwise brilliant day hover near the volcano's summit, when an icy peak crowns a crater whose temperature can exceed 600 degrees, Popocatépetl is a phenomenon that is deserving of a special relationship.

And that it has. In the villages that lie along the perimeter of Popocatépetl, there are cults who view the volcano not just as a volcano but as a living spirit who comes to certain chosen villagers in dreams. The volcano spirit comes to sleepers in the form of a person named Don Gregorio Chino Popocatépetl. Shortened, it is Gregorio, after the saint; shortened further, it is Goyo. Led by *tempieros,* seers who claim to speak with Goyo, villagers have always—in a tradition that survived the conquest—climbed to the small shrines on the sides of Popocatépetl. Offerings of food, clothing, pulque, and even accordions are placed in the snowy nether reaches in the hope of bringing rain and other good fortune. Once Popo becomes active, the offerings take on a tint of appeasement. There are endless variations on the myths: one says that the rain god Tlaloc lives inside Popo's crater; another that Popo and Iztaccíhuatl once walked the earth. Magdalena, a woman I met in an ice cream shop in Cholula, told me of a small Popo-esque hill in a local neighborhood called La Libertad that is said to be the head of Popocatépetl itself, severed in a battle with Pico de Orizaba, Mexico's tallest volcano, over the affections of Iztaccíhuatl. She also told me of a common rumor that Carlos Salinas had sold Popo to the Japanese.

Volcanoes, reservoirs of apocalyptic wrath, are tempting additions to any cosmology, a fact that no doubt impressed the Spanish. In 1824, in a mining company prospectus thinly disguised as a history of Mexico, Nicholas Mill wrote of the 1759 eruption of Xorullo, a volcano in the state of Guanajuato. "The belief among the more rude Indians," he wrote, "is that the convulsion was a miracle wrought by some Capuchin friars, who had preached, but without effect, to their tribes; that, being thus rejected, they poured forth imprecations, and declared that the plantation should first be destroyed by earthquakes and volcanoes." The monks, he asserted, were so zealous in their conversion efforts that "they seldom fail to avail themselves of any natural occurrence that can be made subservient to their views." In a book on Mt. Pelée, the volcano whose eruption in 1902 killed thousands and launched modern volcanology, J. Martin Miller flatly asserts that "the priests of not a few religions have cast victims with great pomp into the gaping hollows of their immense furnaces." The missionaries in America, he wrote, "recognized in the burning mountains of the New World not the work of a god, but that of the devil, and went in procession to the edge of the craters to exorcise them." One legend has it that a group of monks climbed Nicaragua's Motombo "in order to quiet it by their conjurations, but they never returned; the monster swallowed them up."

In a wildly apocryphal tale from a 1940s travel account, a planeload of sightseeing Europeans eager to learn the "mysteries of a smoldering volcano" flew too close: "Popo had sucked the plane and all its sensation-seeking passengers into its brimstone maw." In 1994, a group of Mexican climbers were killed as they descended from the summit of Popocatépetl; a long autopsy eventually concluded that they had died from the heat and gases of a volcanic explosion.

Several days later, I take a Volcanes bus to Amecameca, a village where Cortés and his officers once stayed and the model for Lowry's Parian, where the Consul meets his "dismal way to die." It is a bucolic town, still dominated by what Lowry called "the inevitable public square with its little public garden," the middle of which is marked by a hauntingly familiar sign that begins, "¿Le gusta esta jardín? (Do you like this garden?)" Its cluttered streets look unchanged from turn-of-the-century photographs, although behind one battered and studded wooden door throbs an aerobics session. The square is flanked by a massive granary and a red and white stone church, and to the east towers the white crest of Iztaccíhuatl. Sitting over the cilantro-strewn counter at an outdoor *taqueria*, I talk about Popo with the proprietor. Like most residents of Amecameca, which sits in Zone 2 (medium danger) on the Geophysics Institute map drawn up to show the risks of Popo, he regards the volcano as a contingency. Warnings are treated with the same urgency that the old Emergency Broadcast Network television signal aroused in Americans.

But the danger of Popo is real. Its most immediate effect seems to be on tourism. A small white trailer on the square marked "Tourist Information" is empty, its windows tacked over with announcements for local music performances. "¿Quieres ir al volcan? (Do you want to go to the volcano?)" my hotelier asks one morning, returning with a visibly desperate taxi driver. We agree on a price and an hour later are at the Paso del Cortes, the road that was the Spaniards' aperture into the heart of the Aztec empire,

FIGURE 9. Photo by Tom Vanderbilt.

now closed by the government because of volcanic activity. We are now in Zone 1 of volcanic risk, and I half expect a palpable mood shift. But at the Paso, food vendors are doing brisk business with television crews and curiosity seekers, and two *policia* lie stretched diagonally, asleep in the front of their car. Popo is lost behind the clouds. Here the road changes from two-lane pavement to a narrow, curving, deeply pock-marked dirt track, and the driver struggles to steer as he holds a current-providing screwdriver into the ignition block. Continuing east, we pass several country-estate-style resort hotels, all closed. And farther on, we enter farm country, the thick ever-green forests yielding to stubbly fields of maize and frijoles, interrupted only by trash-strewn barrancas and rocks painted with signs in favor of one of the three main parties competing in the upcoming congressional elections.

A short time later, we arrive in Santiago Xalizintla, the community of some three thousand that lies closest—eleven kilometers—to the volcano's crater. This is the heart of Zone 1, but as we pull in, the village appears like any other small Mexican pueblo in the middle of a weekday. The square is empty, save for a few wandering dogs and some Indian women who are doing scant business as they sit and talk over their wares. The dirt streets are also mostly empty. A woman runs by, stooped over and carrying an immense bundle of cilantro. Houses are fashioned out of cinder block, most of them adorned with a propane tank and bands of skeletal iron rising from the roof. As in most poor Mexican villages, they look neither old nor new, merely temporary.

I climb the steps of an anodyne concrete building, emerge onto a large patio, and find Pedro Silvestre Augustin, the village's *commandante*. He has lived his entire life here. Our conversation is a testament to how far indeed the art of spin has traveled. When I quote him a figure from the newsweekly *Proceso* that the village's population has dropped from six thousand to twenty-seven hundred in the last two years, he quickly asserts that the population was only three thousand to begin with. He picks up a fistful of ash that has been swept into a corner—fine and silvery like fingerprint powder—and says, "Yes, we have had some ash and heard some sounds," but then he gives me a rather forced, public-relations-officer smile and adds, "Aqui no pasó nada (Nothing is happening here)." He says that volcano or no, he will remain here until the last person leaves, which in itself is rather moot since most people have nowhere to go. As he explains the town's volcano warning system, the sum total of which is a small bell atop the municipal building and large whitewash arrows splashed onto rough walls around the village, I hear the unlikely strains of Spandau Ballet coming from a tape vendor downstairs. On the roof, a university geologist sweeps samples of ash into a small plastic bag.

Soon after, I meet Nestor Torres, a teacher from Tlaxcala who presides over the local grammar school. He motions to me and several photojournalists and says, "I see we are internationalizing ourselves here." "Today is the Dia de Maestros," he announces, embracing me heartily. I later learn that in the capital, teachers are marching and in some cases fighting police in the streets. The volcano is a secular matter to him, as a well-educated outsider, but he shows the careful respect of an anthropologist when he discusses the local customs. When I ask him if there is fear, he senses condescension (or is just weary of answering pained questions about life under the volcano) and states sharply, "To have fear is to be human."

The presence of the journalists and an armored personnel carrier manned by teen-age-looking troops imposes an expectant air on the village, but in geologic time there is little precision in the photo opportunity: Popo's 1921 activity came after more than a century of dormancy. On a side street, I meet a *viejo*, his wrinkled face backing his claim to be ninety-seven years old, who tells me that, as someone who remembers the revolution, the latest bout of activity is no cause for alarm. "It comes and goes, like the revolution came and went and like the rain comes and goes." The local volcanic sooth-sayer is nowhere to be found, although I virtually expected klieg lights and a CNN feed. The first house where I stop, however, I meet Luz Augustin, who sells *pan de feria* at festivals in Tlaxcala and elsewhere. Standing in his dirt-floored front yard, which runs, like the chickens, uninterrupted into the house, he extinguishes my illusions of an entire town under the volcano in mystic thrall to an archaic and whimsical god. "It is a volcano and nothing more," he tells me. "If Popo's activity steps up considerably," Augustin adds nonchalantly, he will go to live with friends in Ozumba or even Mexico City.

The town of Santiago Xalizintla, which sits wedged between the Huiloac barranca and the Anexcac River, has two phone lines and must itself pay to call the civil defense in Puebla for information on Popo—a substantial expense for a town of campesinos. The mayor has been promised a cellular phone, but it has yet to arrive. Like most of the villages that ring Popo, there are few cars (one estimate for the region was 1,816 vehicles for 54,459 inhabitants, meaning that 36,758 would have to find other means or go on foot if the volcano were to blow), and the roads are poorly constructed and connected. Although the volcano has been active since 1994, only now has a comprehensive evacuation plan emerged.

A phrase in a newspaper sticks in my mind: "There does not exist a culture of civil protection in Mexico." What little these residents have, they cling to tenaciously: after an evacuation in 1994, residents of several villages came back to find much of their livestock dead, their houses robbed. Torres tells me that while the cult of Goyo is still strong, residents are beginning to acknowledge the scientific and logistic risks that Popo poses. But this does not preclude conceiving the volcano as a living being, nor did it prevent them from partially ascending Popo several weeks before—on the day of Saint Gregory—to leave offerings of clothing and other objects. When I ask Torres what religion allows the villagers to sit in the town's Catholic church on Sunday and bring offerings to a volcano several days later, he tells me flatly, "Es un poco de todo (It's a little bit of everything)."

The closer one gets to the volcano, the less information one has on its activity. From my apartment in New York City I can browse a Popo Web site and learn that "on September 20th, 1996, there were several small tectono-volcanic earthquakes at the Popocatépetl volcano." I can find out the height of the lava dome, the date of the last "ash-gas eruptive event." But here, Popo announces *itself*, it exceeds information. It is bigger than the government, more immediate than the media. The roads that volcanologists and camera crews take to get there do not pass through suburban subdivisions or any other products of modernity; they are modernity itself, an abrupt gaze into a life quite dissonant to that which passes it. Subsistence agriculture crowds to the edge of the road, cattle graze in the loops of uncompleted freeway exchanges, and women dip buckets into wells and wash clothes in streams as we drive by in a van equipped with the latest in volcano monitoring equipment.

Popocatépetl is a volcano, but it is also an agent of history. Its activity changes the arc of people's lives; indeed, several volcanologists have claimed that an eruption in A.D. 800 caused the downfall of the important religious site of Cholula. As Popo heaved, pumice fell and volcanic mudflows reached the base of the town's great pyramid (upon which the wrathful Spaniards would later build a church), leaving the town a muddy wasteland. The sulfate record from the Greenland ice sheet, the volcanologists point out, shows a massive eruption somewhere in the world around that time: it may be a geographic cenotaph to Popo. "A major catastrophic Plinian eruption in the future cannot be ruled out," they conclude.

In the spring of 1848, the capture of Mexico City marked the end of the Mexican-American War. For the United States, the campaign had been a first brush of imperial expansion, an action true to the national spirit. For the U.S. soldiers, Mexico was an enchanted land, the paths they trod, those of the conquistadores before them. "Mexico! Land of romance and boyhood's waking dreams," wrote a soldier in one of the numerous collections of letters eventually published from the war. In April, Ulysses S. Grant, then a captain, decided with a group of officers to scale Popo, motivated by "national pride and a spirit of emulation" toward Cortés's effort. Along with soldiers such as Lieutenant Richard Anderson and Simon Bolivar Buckner, who wrote that "the Mexican War was our romance," Grant made it to the summit of Popo. His group promptly planted a U.S. flag where, in the words of one climber, "it would receive the sun's first rays as it rose from the Atlantic and its last beams as it sunk into the Pacific."

By the late nineteenth century, Popo was becoming an object for Victorian dissection: science, exploration, and extraction. Writing in 1895, one observer noted that "of late the ascent of Popocatépetl has become almost a fad of the foreign traveler." As a warm-up for the Himalayas, the occultist and mountaineer Aleister Crowley climbed Popo and Iztaccíhuatl, where he claimed to have been the first to use "claws" on the ice. Crowley lauded the crater of Popo as a "joy to glissade." A geologist from Chicago's Field Columbian Museum went so far as to wonder whether "the greater number of ascents as compared with the few of earlier years, indicates that an improvement has taken place in the condition of the race, or whether the failures of earlier travelers were due largely to imagined fears."

At the turn of the century, as foreign capital flowed into the country under the welcoming eye of President Porfirio Diaz, a Manhattan-based concern called the

Popocatépetl Company conceived of a plan to purchase the volcano, which it called "the largest and purest sulfur deposit in the world." Working with Mexican war hero General Gaspar Sanchez Ochoa, who had been mining sulfur in small amounts from Popo—using Indians who would carry twenty-five-pound sacks from the crater and then toboggan down Popo's icy slopes to a waiting mule—the company would build a funicular railway to the top. The sulfur would go via rail to Veracruz and then by ship to New York, undercutting the price of Sicilian sulfur by nearly half. With tourism beginning to flourish, the concern also envisioned Popo Park, a health resort that would be "a second Manhattan Beach," a rival to Saratoga Springs, an "ideal retreat for consumptives." The Sanborns, prominent Mexican pharmacists, believed that it would "furnish a remedy to counteract the ravages of what is the most terrible scourge of modern times." But before any of this could begin in earnest, the revolution erupted, led in this area by Emiliano Zapata of the nearby town of Cuatla, and the sale of volcanoes to foreign capital had to be postponed.

By 1918, though, a local outfit had resumed small-scale mining of Popocatépetl. Hoping to plumb new channels of sulfur, it dynamited the crater. A ravaging snowstorm blew in shortly after, and the two dozen *vulcaneros* (who, as an American writer euphemistically phrased it, "are a hardy class of Indians, and, if well supplied with *mescal* and *aguardiente*, endure their hardships wonderfully well") were trapped in the crater where they had been living and working. As the snow accumulated, the walls became icier, the food dwindled, and one by one the miners died, until there was one, Jose Mendoza. After nine days, the storm broke, and rescuers from Amecameca were able to reach the lone survivor. A year later, Popocatépetl woke from hundreds of years of dormancy. Dr. Atl speculated that the mindless dynamiting of the crater had roused the volcano into activity.

The observers at the central command post of Mexico's Center for the Prevention of Disasters resemble a cadre of doctors watching the volcano in a state of restless sleep. In a white-paneled room that overlooks a highway, giving it the false semblance of an air-traffic-control tower, Dr. Roberto Quaas, exuding technocratic efficiency, says, "We have not had much sleep around here lately." One wall of the room is filled with slowly rotating drums on which needle-thin pens trace signals from the Center's sixteen "autonomous recording stations," small huts scattered around Popo inside of which triaxial broadband seismometers were driven into the ground. As the small red needle begins a hummingbirdlike fluttering on one drum, Quaas tells me that it is probably a helicopter. A page from a 1994 eruptive event is nearly solid black with frantic etchings.

Nearby, a phosphorescent band sweeps around Popo on a radar screen, and a video camera records a fixed image of Popo, now cloud-covered. Three years of Popo tapes sit on a shelf. It is in this room where the decision is made to change to a "red alert" status; a call to civil defense authorities in Puebla would ensue. On the wall are several photos of Popocatépetl's crater: it looks like a surging lunar crater, with taut lines stretching from the mouth to the base—wrinkles on an anguished face—the smoke and ash as convulsively dramatic as a Bikini Islands mushroom cloud.

Popo is a fully wired patient, with a battery of tests at the ready. Visual surveillance tracks the obvious stirrings: emanations of smoke, ash, or gas. Seismic monitoring helps locate the energy that is driving the activity. Geodesic monitoring—inclinometry, gravimetry, and other arcane pursuits—charts deformation of the volcanic structure due to pressure from within. Geochemical monitoring tests the gases, ashes, and contamination of nearby spring water, as well as temperature and pH balance. And assistants circle Popo by van and by airplane. Authorities claim that it is the most closely watched volcano in Latin America, while another report says that after the earthquakes in Iran, it is the second-highest priority for natural disaster authorities. Despite an increase in the number of volcanologists worldwide and stepped-up monitoring efforts, as well as the erosion of mysticism by science and civil defense, there have been more deaths from volcanism since 1981 than there were in the previous eighty years.

What is it about volcanoes that summons such fascination? The volcanic brimstone and fire that rained upon Sodom and Gomorrah were seen as divine retribution; to budding nineteenth-century geology, volcanic activity was mysterious "earth motions"; and by the turn of the twentieth century it could still be written that "the eruptions of ashes and incandescent matter have not revealed the mysteries of their formation." Volcanoes are a channel to the earth's inner world, outlets for destruction, but in themselves graceful cones and rugged peaks. They are both producer and destroyer, heaving out of the earth on the same material with which they bury cities. Herman Melville, in his tales of the "Encantadas," the chain of volcanic islands that looked like the world after a "penal conflagration," described a hermit as resembling "a volcanic creature thrown up by the very convulsion which exploded into sight the isle." In dormancy, Popocatépetl once produced sulfur and ice for the Mexican economy; now it generates tourist revenue. In activity, it is an emergency that tests the competence of the beleaguered government—and indeed, according to popular opinion, Popo's rebirth in 1994 coincided with the devaluation of the peso.

Unlike hurricanes or blizzards, volcanoes have no season. Unlike earthquakes, they are always visible. But there are exceptions: in Mexico in 1943, Paricutín rose from a fissure in a farmer's field and just kept growing, pouring out a million tons of lava and covering the nearby town of Parangaricutiro up to its church tower; and in 1982, El Chichonal, in the south of Mexico, surprised the nation as it burst into activity, blanketing the area with a billion tons of ash. A year later, a cloud of Chichonal material had circled the earth. There is an impulse to assign volcanoes human characteristics: they lie dormant or at rest, they "exhale," they are born, or they die. In *The Volcano Lover*, Susan Sontag wrote, "It's the mouth of a volcano. Yes, mouth; and lava tongue. A body, a monstrous living body, both male and female. It emits, ejects. It is also an interior, an abyss." They are the earth's leviathans, and the residents living on their flanks are their subjects—a mass of bodies connected, as in Hobbes's famous woodcut, to the king himself.

I return to Mexico City, where *flow* vaguely describes the Gordian traffic tie-ups and every day the contaminant-sodden sky is an "ash-gas eruptive event." On my last morning in the capital, I notice upon leaving the hotel a hundred-strong troop of police behind riot shields, guarding the entrance to the social security building. It is the second day of a demonstration by the country's teachers, roughly sixty thousand of whom have taken to the streets to demand a 100-percent increase in their salary, which amounts to U.S. $300 a month. Grouped by state, they chant slogans and carry banners, many bearing the visage of Che Guevara, as they march down the Paseo de la Reforma into the heart of the Zona Rosa, past pinstriped, cell-phoned executives checking their watches and wondering how they might traverse the human snarl and get to lunch. An overflowing truckful of soldiers rumbles past, yet another reminder of why "militarization" of the country has been on the minds of editorial columnists. The military, it is said, is the one institution in which President Ernesto Zedillo has faith.

Kilometers away, out of sight, Popocatépetl hisses through its fumaroles, and scientists try to divine what the years have wrought inside its secret chamber. Subdued, the volcano did not even make the pages of today's *Reforma*. The ground is warm and gently vibrates with human activity.

12   recycled
rain forest myths

The creation of protected areas has been one of the principal strategies adopted for the conservation of nature, in particular in the countries of the Third World. The establishment of these areas increased substantially in the 1970s and 1980s, when 2,098 protected areas were created around the world, encompassing more than 3.1 million square kilometers. According to a 1996 report of the World Conservation Center, today about 5 percent of the earth's surface is legally protected under twenty thousand different categories, not only at federal levels but also at provincial, state, and municipal levels, covering an area the size of Canada and spread throughout 130 countries.

In 1990, Brazil had 34 national parks, 23 biological reserves, 21 ecological stations, 38 national forests, 14 environmentally protected areas, and 4 extractive reserves, totaling 31,294,911 hectares, or almost 4 percent of the territory. Ninety percent of this area is located in the Amazon region. The increased interest in creating protected areas in Brazil could be explained by a combination of factors: the rapid devastation of the Amazonian rain forests and the Mata Atlântica (Atlantic rain forest); the loss of biodiversity; the availability of international funding for conservation efforts; the possibility of revenue generation from tourism in the parks; and, above all, the pressure on the World Bank to create new protected areas to counterbalance the development projects it is funding in fragile areas such as the Amazon. The establishment of protected areas is also a powerful political weapon for the dominant elite of many countries of the Third World, who continue to obtain external financing for large projects that have an impact on fragile ecosystems.

FIGURE 10. Martin Johnson Heade, *South American River*, 1868. (Courtesy, Museum of Fine Arts, Boston. Reproduced with permission. © 2000 Museum of Fine Arts, Boston. All Rights Reserved)

Already, there is more protected area in Brazil than in many European countries. If the proposal of the U.N. Environment Programme (UNEP) is achieved, in which approximately 10 percent of national territory would be put under some form of protection, around eight hundred thousand square kilometers of Brazilian territory will become parks and reserves, a surface area equivalent to France and Germany combined. Apparently, most environmental agencies maintain that the greater the area that is put under some form of protection, the better it is for conservation. Today, about 18 percent of the Amazonian region is protected. UNEP's goal has in fact already been achieved in seven countries in Asia, fourteen countries in Africa, and six countries in Latin America. But in the United States, one of the proponents of this idea, less than 2 percent of the protected territory is designated as national parks, and in Europe, it is less than 7 percent. Judging from this, it would seem that UNEP deems the idea of national parks to be more appropriate for the Third World than for industrialized countries—and this in spite of the fact that many Third World countries are experiencing food shortage crises, which are in part due to insufficient agricultural land and inequitable land distribution.

A North American model of conservationism, which dichotomizes "people" and "parks," has spread rapidly throughout the world. Because this approach has been adopted rather uncritically by the countries of the Third World, its effects have been devastating for the traditional populations—extractivists, fisherfolk, and indigenous peoples. This model was transposed from industrialized countries with temperate climates to the Third World, whose remaining forests have been, and continue to be, inhabited by traditional populations.

The United Nations has estimated indigenous populations at three hundred million in seventy countries and throughout various ecosystems, ranging from savannas and forests to polar regions. According to Jeffrey McNeely, the people known as tribals, natives, traditionals, and other cultural minorities occupy about 19 percent of the land surface, living in isolated regions with fragile ecosystems.[1] It is most often these ecosystems that are labeled as "natural" and transformed into protected areas from which the residents are expelled. With this authoritarian action, the state contributes to the loss of a wide range of ethnoknowledge and ethnoscience—of ingenious systems for managing natural resources—and of cultural diversity itself. The expulsion of inhabitants has contributed to even more degradation of park areas because, due to insufficient monitoring—despite the fact that the majority of the budget for these protected areas is allocated for monitoring and enforcement—they are invaded by logging industries and miners who illegally exploit the natural resources. Inhabitants also illegally extract their means of subsistence from these protected areas.

Governments rarely assess the environmental and social impact that the creation of parks will have on the local inhabitants, whose land-use practices often have preserved these natural areas over the years. They are transferred from regions where their ancestors lived to regions that are ecologically and culturally different. The hunters, fisherfolk, and other resource users who have developed a symbiosis with the forests, rivers, and coastal areas have great difficulty surviving, once relocated to other areas, due to the accompanying prohibition of their traditional activities.

These populations have difficulty comprehending how their traditional activities could be considered detrimental to nature when hotels and tourism infrastructures are created for the use of people from outside the area. Very little of the budget for protected areas is allocated for improving the living conditions of the traditional people, who, if encouraged, could make a positive contribution. When they have organized and become vocal about defending their historical right to remain on ancestral land, they are accused of being against conservation. In most cases, these are people who are illiterate, lack political power or legal ownership of the land, and are therefore not compensated when their land is expropriated. But, as has occurred in the Mata Atlântica in Brazil, when land is expropriated from the large landowners, who often have obtained their land by usurping the rights of the traditional residents, they are royally compensated because they can prove legal ownership.

The authorities who are responsible for the preserved areas perceive the traditional inhabitants as destroyers of wildlife, which eliminates any real opportunity for their inclusion in the conservation project. In many cases, and especially in the Amazon, the so-called participation of traditional populations in the establishment of parks and reserves does not go beyond well-intentioned words that are offered to assuage international demands from such large institutions as the World Bank, the International Union for the Conservation of Nature, and the World Wide Fund for Nature.

This model of preserving wilderness has been criticized both inside and outside the United States, and part of this opposition has come from the American "pure preservationists." John Rodman holds that the idea of parks subscribes to an anthropocentric view, that the creation of parks principally values the aesthetic, religious, and cultural motivations of humans, demonstrating that it isn't wilderness in and of itself that is considered valuable and worthy of being protected. Yet Rodman considers this mode of preservation, based on the model of parks and natural reserves, to be unjustly selective because it privileges natural areas that appeal to a Western aesthetic—such as forests, large rivers, and canyons—and discriminates against natural areas that are considered less noble—swamps, bogs, and marshes.[2] Arturo Gomez-Pompa and Andrea Kaus have also criticized this notion of a "natural world" that privileges an urban perspective:

> The concept of wilderness as untouched or domesticated is fundamentally an urban perception, a view of people who live far from the natural environment on which they depend for raw material. The inhabitants of rural areas have different perceptions of the areas that the urbanites designate as wilderness, and base their use of the land on alternate views.[3]

More recently, a socio-environmental focus has been adopted in the critique of "the Yellowstone model." This new approach to conservation arose out of the collaboration between the social movements that fight for the continued access of peasants, fisherfolk, and forest people to land and natural resources and the Third World environmentalists who see the environmental crisis in their countries as being linked to the existing model of development. This movement, which Eduardo Viola and Hector Leis have called "peasant ecology,"[4] critiques the imported environmentalism for its lack of consideration of the traditional communities that depend on the forests for their livelihood.

In North America, the myth of "wilderness" as an uninhabited space has fueled the move to create protected restricted-use areas. By the end of the nineteenth century, after the conquest and widespread massacre of the native peoples and the westward expansion of the frontier by European settlers, the land was perceived to be uninhabited. With the movement of human settlements to the West, the mid-nineteenth century saw natural areas being degraded by mining and forestry companies. This raised protests from the nature lovers who had been influenced by the ideas of Henry David Thoreau and George Perkins Marsh. In 1864, in his widely read book *Man and Nature,* Marsh argued that the preservation of virgin areas was justified as much for artistic and poetic reasons as it was for economic reasons, and he held that the destruction of the natural world threatened the very existence of humans on earth.

In the early nineteenth century, artist George Catlin traveled throughout the American West. He cautioned that the Indians as well as the bison were threatened with extinction and suggested that the native peoples, the bison, and the virgin areas could be equally protected if the government were to establish a national park that incorporated humans and animals "in all their primitive and natural beauty."[5] This idea was not implemented, however, and the notion of wilderness as a virgin, uninhabited area prevailed. On March 1, 1872, when the decision was made to create Yellowstone National Park, the U.S. Congress decided that the region could not be colonized, occupied, or sold, but would be separated as a public park or recreation area for the benefit and enjoyment of the people. Any person who occupied any part of this park would be breaking the law and would be removed.

In the 1960s, after much of the "wilderness" had been "tamed" and even destroyed in most of the northern countries, environmental preservationists, in search of this lost, untouched nature, turned their attention to the vast rain forests and savannas in tropical countries, particularly in Africa and South America. In Brazil, the Amazonian rain forest became the focus for the construction of a new myth. Called the "lungs of the earth," this tropical forest was considered to be "empty space," only sparsely inhabited by the remaining indigenous tribes—although it is now estimated that at the beginning of the sixteenth century, five to seven million Amerindians were living in the region, largely concentrated in the river floodplains *(várzeas)*, an even higher density than today.

The Brazilian military group in power in the 1960s and 1970s exploited this neo-myth in order to occupy the region, which led to the rapid transformation of vast rain forest areas into large cattle-raising and agricultural farms. It is no coincidence that most of the protected areas also began to be established during this period in order to counterbalance the widespread forest destruction. Neither the preservationists nor the military acknowledged the presence of the people living in those areas. Indians were confined in special reserves, and non-Indian local inhabitants were resettled outside the borders of the newly created national parks and other strictly protected reserves.

Due mainly to a lack of support for this type of conservation within southern countries—particularly among the communities that live inside and adjacent to protected areas—there have been frequent failures in the implementation of protected areas. Consequently, nature-conservation practices and the underlying ideas that have guided the creation of protected areas are changing in many countries around the world, including Brazil. There is a growing awareness that the reason for this lack of social support is the unsuitability of this conservation model to local realities rather than, as some preservationists argue, the lack of appreciation for the importance of protected areas. National parks and other strictly protected areas cannot simply be considered "islands" created to conserve biodiversity, since biological diversity also lies beyond the parks.

In southern countries, environmental movements are emerging that are different from those in northern countries in that they are attempting to harmonize nature conservation with the need to improve the living conditions of the inhabitants of national parks and adjacent regions. These new socio-environmental movements recognize the importance of the knowledge and management practices of traditional populations. In many of these countries, the process of decolonization and democratization has also led to the challenging of the imported model of nature conservation. People living inside protected areas have mounted spontaneous and increasingly organized resistance against resettlement.

There are basically two representations of nature—and particularly of forests and woodlands—that coexist in modern mythology. By "mythology" I mean the symbolic representations of the natural world that are a cultural and historical product of the various forms and moments of the relations between diverse societies and their physical surroundings.

On the one hand is the naturalist myth of an untouched nature or wilderness in a "pure" state, prior to the appearance of humans. This myth presupposes the incompatibility between the actions of any human group and the conservation of nature. Regardless of their culture, humans are, in this equation, destroyers of the natural world. The idea of a "paradise lost" informed the creation of the first North American national parks in the second half of the nineteenth century, where portions of territories that were considered "untouched" were closed off to human habitation. These "wild" areas were created for the benefit of urban North Americans who could visit them and appreciate their "natural beauty." This "modern" model of conservation and its underlying ideology have spread to the rest of the world in cultural contexts distinct from those in which it was created, generating serious consequences.

On the other hand is the representation of forests as a natural resource to be traded. According to this view, nature has value only when it is transformed into commodities for human use. The ideal would be to transform the tropical forest, with its great variety of tree species, into a homogeneous forest, like those of the temperate climates, which would be more easily managed (cut) and used industrially. This view has fueled the extensive transformation of the rich Atlantic forest of Brazil into plantations of pines and eucalyptus through the fiscal incentives that the Instituto Brasileiro de Desenvolvimento Florestal (Brazilian Institute of Forestry Development) has granted to the timber companies since the 1960s.

Paradoxically, both of these approaches see the forest as uninhabited, negating the existence of innumerable societies who live in the forest and make use of it within a sociocultural framework very different from urban-industrial societies. The human communities that live in the forests would at most be identified as a "species of fauna" or "threatened species"—one more component of the natural world—the local culture and its myths and complex relationships with nature deemed "savage" and "uncivilized."

In their re-creation of the myth of a "wild" nature, preservationists from North America and other countries ignored the myths that guided and interpreted the relations between the North American indigenous populations and nature. For these peoples, the world referred to as "wild" by whites did not exist. But these myths—which Edgar Morin has called "bio-anthropomorphic"—are not exclusive to the indigenous populations in North America. They also exist among populations of hunters, extractivists, fisherfolk, and peasants in the Third World, who still live somewhat apart from the market economy of the urban-industrial world.

In many traditional societies, "wilderness" and the "natural world" are understood contextually in terms of myths in which humans might assume natural features and plants and animals might present humanized characteristics and behavior. According to Morin, in this mythological universe, the fundamental features of animate beings are encountered in inanimate things. This unity/duality of humans is also reflected in the ways that reality is perceived. One is empirical, technical, and rational, by which complex botanical, zoological, ecological, and technological knowledge is accumulated (today the subject of ethnoscience); the other is symbolic, mythological, and magical.[6] However, these forms of knowledge, although quite distinct, do not live in two separate universes; they are practiced in the same (although dual) universe. According to Mircea Eliade, in this dual universe, space and time are both the same and different—mythical time, the time past, is also always present, returning in regenerative ceremonies.[7]

This symbolic representation of the cycles in which all of creation is born, dies, and is reborn is strong among the indigenous societies of Brazil, but it is also present in the communities of peasants, fisherfolk, and gatherers that continue to live according to nature's cycles and a complex agricultural or fishing calendar. There is a time for *coivara* (burning of vegetation that has grown after the first burning), to prepare the land, to sow, to weed, and to harvest; and there is also a time to wait for species of migratory fish, such as mullet (*tainha*). Upon completing one cycle, the next cycle is begun. These activities are often ordered by signs—such as a particular phase of the moon, the appearance of rain, and so on—that are celebrated in festivities that mark the planting or harvesting of a specific crop.

According to Morin, contemporary history, while dissolving old mythologies, creates others, regenerating symbolic/mythological thought in a modern form. He holds not only that mythological thought persists in remote rural regions, but that there is also a resurgence of myths in the urban world. And Eliade suggests that myths related to nature endure and resist the incursions of science, surviving as "pseudo-religions" or "degraded mythologies." He goes on to say that in modern societies that declare themselves atheist, religion and myths are buried in the unconscious, periodically returning to the surface as new mythologies. P. Thuillier states that in hundreds of texts inspired by ecological concerns, the old myths reappear with an almost religious enthusiasm and apocalyptic vigor.[8]

In Brazil, the first inspiration for the creation of national parks came from the abolitionist André Rebouças in 1876 and was based on the model of North American parks. In defending the creation of the National Park of Itatiaia, the geographer Hubmayer, as early as 1911, stated that this national park was

> without equal in the world[;] it will be at the doorstep of our beautiful Capital [at that time Rio de Janeiro] offering scientists and researchers immeasurable potential for the most diverse research, as well as offering the ideal retreat for physical and psychological renewal after the exhausting work in the cities. Also, it will provide a source of satisfaction for travellers and visitors interested in the attractions of nature in the area.[9]

The first national park was created in Itatiaia in 1937, upon an initial proposal by the botanist Alfredo Loftgren in 1913, with the objective of encouraging scientific research and offering leisure to urban populations. Little thought was given to the indigenous populations and the fishing and gathering populations that were already there.

The concern for traditional populations that live in conservation areas is relatively recent in Brazil, and until a short time ago (and still today for classical preservationists), this was considered "a police matter," since they were to be expelled from their traditional lands to make way for the creation of parks and reserves. The positions of the environmental movements in Brazil vary regarding the presence of traditional communities in conservation areas. The "preservationists" dominate the older and classical conservation groups—such as the FBCN (Brazilian Foundation for the Conservation of Nature), created in 1958, and the more recent ones, such as the Fundação Biodiversitas, Funatura, and Pronatura, which are more linked to international preservation organizations. Their influence continues to prevail in many of the institutions that have been responsible for the creation and administration of parks, such as IBAMA (Brazilian Institute for the Environment) and the Forest Institute of São Paulo. These groups have generally been formed by professionals in the natural sciences who consider any human interference in nature to be negative. Ideologically, they were, and continue to be, influenced by the U.S. preservationist view: they consider wild nature to be untouched and untouchable.

Working in difficult circumstances, these preservationists very often have dedicated their lives to protecting endangered flora and fauna, and probably, without their devotion, many unique habitats and species would have disappeared. In some cases, the protected areas they helped to create prevented the expulsion and resettlement of the traditional populations by outside logging and tourist industries. However, despite their accomplishments and goodwill, their approach to conservation has led to conflicts with local populations, and they have contributed less and less to finding a real solution to existing problems. Many of these preservationists are still very influential in Brazilian government conservation institutions, and they resist any attempt to change their imported model of environmental protection. Rather than attributing the failure of this model to its inappropriateness, they have usually blamed its failure on inadequate funding and enforcement.

Beginning in the 1970s, an "ecologism" of denunciation emerged in Brazil, represented by AGAPAN (Gaúcha Association for the Protection of the Natural Environment), Ecological Resistance, Catarinian Association for the Preservation of Nature, and APPN (São Paulo Association for the Protection of Nature). The military regime in power at that time was more tolerant of nonleftist movements, such as environmental nongovernmental organizations (NGOs), and repressed social protest movements. The 1970s was a time of rapid growth for the Brazilian economy, particularly through megaprojects that resulted in serious impacts on nature. Most of these, such as chemical and petrochemical plants, were established or expanded in coastal zones, the most populous areas of the country, and brought levels of degradation never before seen in Brazil. At the same time, the agricultural industry was growing considerably, resulting in a massive increase in the use of biocides and insecticides. Millions of rural workers were forced to move to the cities, which led to the growth of *favelas* (slums).

This extensive environmental degradation and social pauperization was masked by the ideology of the so-called economic miracle, in which the Brazilian government's objective was to attract industries of the industrialized countries. It is in this context that the *Brazilian Ecological Manifesto: The End of the Future* emerged in 1976, headed by ecologist José Lutzemberger and representing ten ecological organizations. Written at the height of the repressive military regime, the document was indeed a courageous act. The manifesto advocated the human-nature relations of traditional societies—the indigenous people and small-scale subsistence farmers—as an alternative to the predatory use of natural resources. The *Ecological Manifesto* played an important role in the ecological struggles of the 1970s and 1980s, denouncing environmental degradation, construction of nuclear power plants, and militarism.

In the mid-1980s, another type of environmentalism, more linked to social questions, began to emerge. This new movement developed along with the beginnings of redemocratization after decades of military dictatorship and constituted a critique of the model of economic development whose inequitable concentration of wealth and destruction of nature had had its apogee during that period. The widespread destruction of the Amazon and Atlantic forests led to the beginning of what has been called "social ecologism," a movement that struggles to maintain access to territories with natural resources and places a high value on systems of production that are based on traditional technologies. The National Council of Rubber-Tappers, the Movement of People Affected by Dams, the Movement of Artisanal Fishermen, and the Indigenous Movement are all part of this movement, which reached one of its highest points in 1989 in Altamira, with the Meeting of the Indigenous People of Xingu. These movements acknowledge the necessity to rethink the role of national parks and reserves as well as the role of the traditional inhabitants within the parks. The final declaration of the Altamira meeting counseled: "Do not destroy the forests, the rivers, that are our brothers, since these territories are sacred sites of our people, Home of the Creator, that cannot be violated."[10]

Some of the local movements, which have no direct links to national movements, fight against the curtailment of their traditional activities in conservation areas. Other local organizations have pressured park administrations to begin negotiating alternative uses of natural resources. But they are incipient and fragile and are still subordinate to the local movements that are under state control. More spontaneous local resistance movements—the small-scale local extractivist producers defending their traditional territory against outsiders—are struggling to gain control over access to natural resources. For example, in response to their reduced access to local fishing sites because of fences that were erected by large landowners and to the threat posed by incoming commercial fishers who use predatory fishing equipment, one such action was the "closing of the lakes" in the Amazon region and the establishment of lake reserves by many vargeiros (riverine communities) of Amazonia, who themselves assumed control over the territories they have traditionally occupied.

The traditional populations that lived in the areas that were made into parks have been ignored by the state authorities for decades. When the State Park of Ilha do Cardoso was created in 1962 on the land along the south coast of São Paulo, a sophisticated and detailed management plan was developed for the flora and fauna and for support structures for tourism and research. This top-down plan, developed by the Forest Institute with the assistance of two "specialists" from the Food and Agriculture Organization (FAO), did not even mention the existence of the hundreds of families who lived there. Fortunately, the plan was shelved. Nevertheless, many of the families left their birthplace because of persecution by the park wardens.

Some local movements in isolated regions—such as the Movement of the Riverine

Population of Mamirauá, Amazonas—are supported by NGOs and research institutes, although they are not linked to any major social movement at the national level. The incorporation of traditional populations in restricted conservation areas is a project of the Mamirauá Ecological Station (EEM), administered by the Mamirauá Civil Society and supported by several international environmental NGOs, among them the World Wide Fund for Nature. The EEM was created to protect a large part of the floodplain between the Japurá and Solimões Rivers. Forty-five hundred vargeiros live in this huge area, spread over fifty small communities, with an average of fourteen households in each. They live from fishing and from hunting and gathering forest products. However, logging takes place along with these traditional activities, and the wood is sold to the sawmills in the cities. Rather than expelling the vargeiros, as was legislatively mandated, the project administrators decided to allow them to remain in the territory.

During the floods, water covers millions of hectares, making law enforcement, carried out exclusively by government officials, an impossible task. The management team, belonging to a local NGO, believed that the biodiversity and culture of the region could be protected only through community participation. This type of management, which differs substantially from the management plans established and imposed by scientists and bureaucrats, takes longer to develop since it depends on constant dialogue and consultation with local populations, the inclusion of social research teams, and more flexibility in planning. It places more value on the process of decision making than on the establishment of rigid conservation objectives. This project demonstrated that once a decision is made by the local population, it has a much greater chance of being followed. In the consensus that was reached by the local population regarding the conservation and sustainable use of lakes—which was extremely important, both biologically and socioeconomically—the communities decided to define six categories of lakes. These included lakes for reproduction of fish (untouchable, with the shoreline included in the area of total preservation); "subsistence lakes" (for exclusive use of the community for subsistence fishing); "market-oriented lakes" (for exclusive use of the community, with the fish to be sold); and "lakes for use of the nearby urban centres" (where fishing is permitted to satisfy the needs of municipalities).

The rubber-tappers' extractive reserves are one of the outcomes of the rubber-tappers' movement, which was created in the 1970s during the height of the conflict over land in Acre. This movement organized the first *empate* (blockade), in which the organized rubber-tappers confronted the machines that were cutting down the forest and threatening their way of life. In 1975, when the first rural union was created in Basiléia in Acre—an area with a high density of rubber trees—the reaction of the landowners was violent, and in many cases the houses of the rubber-tappers were burned and the leaders were assassinated.

The National Council of Rubber-Tappers, established in 1985, pursued the creation of "extractive reserves." The extractive reserves gained international notoriety in 1988 when the rubber-tappers' leader, Chico Mendes, was assassinated. The first official extractive reserve was created in 1988, and in 1990 the extractive reserves became part of the protected areas system. The extractive reserves are administered communally. Although not allocated in individual lots, families have the right to exploit the resources along their traditional extractivist *colocações* (tapping routes). The land cannot be sold or transformed into nonforest uses, except for small areas that are allowed to be cleared for subsistence agriculture (approximately 1 to 2 percent of the area of the reserve).

Despite the organized opposition through the UDR (Democratic Rural Union) of large landowners, the rubber-tappers' movement expanded not only into Acre, where already by 1980 around 60 percent of the municipalities had rubber-tappers' organizations, but also into other states, such as Amapá, Rondônia, and Amazonas, which include ten extractivist settlements and four extractivist reserves, covering 3,052,527 hectares and benefiting about nine thousand families. In 1992, IBAMA created the National Council of Traditional Populations (CNPT) to lend technical support for the reserves in Amazonia and to disseminate the idea to other regions of the country. There are also extractivist reserves outside of the region, based on *babassu* found in the *cerrado* (savanna vegetation in semiarid areas) and on fishing resources in the state of Santa Catarina.

The movement to establish extractivist reserves is an effort to defend, reinforce, and re-create threatened ways of life. Furthermore, in Amazonia it is an alternative that can enable a sustainable use of natural resources that respects both biological diversity and traditional ways of life. Official and public recognition of these reserves was made possible only through the collaboration and solidarity that grew between the strong social movement and the National Council of Rubber-Tappers. Together they seek national as well as international legitimacy, especially in their struggle against other forms of ownership, particularly large landholdings. The frequent meetings of the leaders of the National Council with the rubber-tappers in many regions of Amazonia have helped them to organize additional associations that will propose new reserves.

One of the preservationists' arguments against the existence of traditional populations in "restrictive" protected natural areas is the assumed incompatibility between their presence and the protection of biodiversity. The establishment of protected areas for the preservation of biodiversity is, however, a relatively recent objective, promoted by international environmental organizations in response to the disappearance of species and ecosystems. The earlier parks were created primarily for environmental education, research, and the recreation and enchantment of urbanites.

Recent studies have shown that the maintenance and even the enhancement of biological diversity in tropical forests is intimately related to the shifting agriculture practiced by traditional communities. The use of small areas of land for agriculture and their abandonment after the decline of agricultural production (shifting agriculture) has an effect similar to that produced by the occasional destruction of the forests by natural causes. Shifting agriculture has been a natural means of using the regenerative properties of the rain forest for the benefit of humans. Arturo Gomez-Pompa suggests that tropical ecologists have recognized that "a large part of the primary vegetation of many zones, seen as virgin, actually contain vestiges of human disturbances, and there is more and more difficulty in finding zones that are totally virgin."[11] Many dominant species of the primary forests of Mexico and Central America were actually protected by humans in the past, and their current abundance is related to this fact. In the case of tropical forests, it is very difficult to distinguish "virgin" forests from "disturbed" forests, especially in areas where itinerant agriculture is practiced. The establishment of protected natural areas that respect these traditional practices can contribute to sociocultural diversity as well as to conservation of the natural world, whether it be "virgin" or already altered by traditional populations.

Protected areas, especially those with very restricted use, are more than a government strategy of conservation; they are emblematic of a particular relation between humans and nature. The spread of the mid-nineteenth-century U.S. idea of uninhabited national parks is based, first, on the myth of an untouched natural paradise, an image of Eden from which Adam and Eve were expelled, and, second, on what Serge Moscovici has called "reactive conservationism." This reactive conservationism of the nineteenth century, in which the natural world is attributed all the virtues and society all the vices, was a reaction to culturalism, which sees in nature the infirmity of man, a threat of return to savagery to which culture must be opposed.[12]

Even when urban-industrial society and the advance of science has desacralized the world and weakened the power of myths, the image of national parks and other protected areas as a paradise in which "virgin nature" is expressed in all its beauty—transformed into an object of reverence by urban humanity—confirms the idea that mythologies continue and can be reborn under the shadow of rationality. This myth of an untouched and untouchable nature not only reshapes old creeds but also incorporates elements of modern science—such as the notion of biodiversity and ecosystem function—in a symbiosis expressed by the alliance between particular currents of natural science and preservationist ecology. The persistence of the idea of a wild and untouched natural world has considerable force, especially with urban and industrial populations that no longer have daily contact with the rural environment. This occurs despite growing scientific evidence that for thousands of years, humans have, in one way or another, interfered with many terrestrial ecosystems, so that today very little untouched virgin nature remains.

In tropical countries, the historical realization of the myth of an untouched nature in the creation of national parks and reserves continues unabated. The conflict between the views of the so-called traditional populations and the preservationist and state conservationist institutions cannot be analyzed simply in terms of the oppositions between different mythologies and symbolisms. The conflict also revolves around a political ecology to the extent that the state imposes new spaces that are "modern and public" upon territories where traditional populations live—the parks and reserves from which, by law, inhabitants must be expelled. To those with power, these social actors are invisible. The acknowledgment of their existence and their importance to the conservation and maintenance of biological diversity is a recent phenomenon—the result of the socio-environmental ecologism that has developed in Third World countries.

This new ecologism has been translated into social movements that propose a new alliance between humans and nature, the need for democratic participation in nature conservation, and a respect for cultural diversity as the basis for the maintenance of biological diversity. Park inhabitants became more visible as a result of the conflicts that arose when landless populations occupied park areas that were not effectively administered by the government. Traditional populations and newcomers have recently begun to organize against the enforcement actions of the state, which, in most cases, impede the social and cultural reproduction of these human communities.

In Brazil, at the federal level as well as in some NGOs, the question of the presence of traditional inhabitants in national parks and other conservation areas has been dealt with from a conservative point of view, one that is still influenced by urban perceptions of the natural world and wilderness. In underdeveloped countries, conservation could be better achieved through the real integration and participation of the traditional populations, which to a great extent have been responsible for maintaining the biological diversity that today we are trying to rescue.

However, there is also a need to guard against a simplistic view of the "ecologically noble savage."[13] Not all inhabitants are "born conservationists," but among them there exist traditional people with a vast store of empirical knowledge of the workings of the natural world in which they live. We need to better understand the relations between the maintenance of biological diversity and the conservation of cultural diversity. An interdisciplinary view is urgently needed, whereby biologists, forestry engineers, sociologists, anthropologists, and political scientists, among others, work in an integrated way in cooperation with traditional populations. As Gomez-Pompa and Kaus have said, we are discussing and establishing policies on a subject that we know little about; and traditional populations, who know their environment better than we do, rarely participate in debates and decisions about conservation management.

NOTES

1   Jeffrey McNeely, "Afterword to People and Protected Areas: Partners in Prosperity," in E. Kemf, ed., *The Law of the Mother: Protecting Indigenous Peoples in Protected Areas* (San Francisco: Sierra Club Books, 1993), p. 90.

2   John Rodman, "What Is Living and What Is Dead in the Political Philosophy of T. H. Green," *Western Political Quarterly* 26 (1973): 566–86.

3   Arturo Gomez-Pompa and Andrea Kaus, "Taming the Wilderness Myth," *Bioscience* 42/4 (1992): 273.

4   Eduardo Viola and Hector Leis, "Desordem global da biosfera e a nova ordem internacional: O papel das organizações do ecologismo," in H. Leis, ed., *Ecologia e política mundial* (Rio de Janeiro: Vozes/Fase, 1991).

5   J. McCormick, *Rumo ao paraíso* (Rio de Janeiro: Ed. Relume-Dumará, 1992).

6   Edgar Morin, *La Méthode 4. Les idées, leur habitat, leur vie, leurs moeurs, leur organization* (Paris: Seuil, 1991).

7   Mircea Eliade, *Imagens e símbolos* (São Paulo: Martins Fontes, 1991).

8   P. Thuillier, "Les mythes de l'éau," *La Recherche*, special issue (May 1990): 221.

9   In Maria Pádua and Adelmar F. C. Filho, *Os parques nacionais do Brasil* (São Paulo: Edit. José Olympio, 1979), p. 122.

10 M. Waldman, *Ecologia e lutas sociais no Brasil* (São Paulo: Contexto, 1992), p. 90.

11 Arturo Gomez-Pompa, C. Vasquez-Yanes, and C. Guevara, "The Tropical Rainforest: A Non-Renewable Resource," *Science* 177/4051 (1972): 762–65.

12 Serge Moscovici, *Hommes domestiques, hommes sauvages* (Paris: Unión Géneralle d'Editions, 1974).

13 K. Redford, "The Ecologically Noble Savage," *Orion* 9/3 (1990): 25–29.

13 the park of ten thousand waterfalls

Each time my small family and I have made the seven-thousand-mile journey to south-ern Chile to visit my father-in-law, Doug Tompkins, and his wife, Kris, I have been drawn into an epic struggle to preserve a wilderness. Both former California residents, they now live amid the world's largest remaining temperate rain forest, six hundred miles south of Santiago, where it rains twenty feet per year. I always return from these austral journeys grappling with some of life's monumental questions: What are our ultimate responsibilities as humans? And are we defending the world's wild remnants as selflessly as we ought to be?

Sparsely inhabited and reachable only by boat or small plane, the Chiloé Continen-tal region truly feels like the end of the earth. To the west are fjords and the Pacific Ocean. Just twelve miles inland tower the snow-capped peaks and volcanoes of the Andean Cordillera. In between, about all you can see are forests, rivers, and waterfalls. Sometimes stormy for weeks on end, the expansive sky dramatically crowns the land-scape. Ironically, it was in escaping to this wilderness that the Tompkinses—and Doug in particular—became public figures, embroiled in a national struggle between Chile's pro-development interests and an emerging environmental movement.

In 1991, disillusioned from competing for two decades to establish a globally recog-nized fashion company, Doug sold his shares in Esprit (the company he had cofounded in 1969), donated his San Francisco house and art collection to his newly formed envi-ronmental organization, left family, friends, and colleagues behind, and moved to a country where he'd been mountaineering, kayaking, and flying since the early 1960s.

At forty-nine years old, he was starting over, inspired by a philosophy known as "deep ecology" and with philanthropy rather than international entrepreneurship as his life's focus.

At first glance, Doug doesn't appear to be the formidable opponent who has become Chile's fierce champion of the wilderness. Of medium height with silvery gray hair, he still has the slight yet sinewy build of the mountain climber he's been since his teenage years. Although he didn't realize it when he bought his first property in Chile—a thirty-seven-hundred-acre cattle ranch that includes three lakes, three rivers, and part of the flat-topped cone of snow-clad Michimahuida volcano—he just happened to stumble upon an eighty-kilometer section of Chile where the land's sole north-south highway is interrupted. Without access to development, the forests had remained intact, harboring some of the world's oldest and tallest living trees, the *alerces* (and a concentration of biomass three to ten times more per acre than in the Amazonian tropical rain forests). "It just seemed like a good deal at the time," Doug said. "All that land for the price of a house or even a condominium in San Francisco."

Once he had acclimated to Reñihue's rainy microclimate, the surrounding wilderness took root in his imagination. He acquired a few adjoining parcels from absentee landowners who were anxious to liquidate their large tracts of land, which, without any road or infrastructure, yielded no profit and seemed to have no potential value. "One guy sold me two thousand hectares to pay off a gambling debt," he gave as an example.

Not long after, the idea of creating a national park began to gel. Four years and quite a few million dollars later, he had assembled twenty-two contiguous tracts totaling nearly eight hundred thousand acres—roughly the size of Yosemite National Park in central California. But when Doug's intention to donate this privately acquired land for a Chilean park became public early in 1994, a group of politicians and government officials vehemently objected. The Chilean landmass is pinched to a slender thirty miles wide at this point, and the proposed park would span the width of the country and share a high-altitude fifty-plus-mile border with Argentina. How had a foreigner managed to purchase such strategic property? What of the potential for economic development in the area? What of the need to have settlers established in these areas for security reasons? What about the highway, which remains unconnected?

Back in the capital, Santiago, and the congressional seat, Valparaiso, outrageous rumors began to circulate: Tompkins was building a nuclear waste dump up in the snowy wilds; he was establishing an ecoreligious sect in the area; he'd discovered oil; he was replacing Chilean cows with U.S. buffalo. In a matter of weeks, stories appeared in dozens of the country's newspapers, caricaturing Tompkins as "the man who cut Chile in two parts," stripping him of his anonymity. He could no longer go anywhere without being recognized.

Emotions were running high. Chile had become South America's economic miracle, primarily by exploiting its forest, fishing, mining, and agricultural resources. Government officials were jockeying for Chile to become the first South American country to join the North American Free Trade Agreement (NAFTA). Yet the environmental consequences of Chile's development were also surfacing.

I distinctly remember a visit to Puerto Montt, the capital of the 10th Region and a busy shipping port. On the waterfront of this rapidly sprawling and modernizing town of one hundred thousand, not far from an open market of stalls where hand-knit sweaters, carved wooden bowls, and various tourist knickknacks were being sold, stood a mountain of wood chips. A bare-chested worker standing atop this cedar-red mass looked about the size of a house cat. In just a few days, Pacific-bound freighters had reduced the pile to wharf level. A week later, it had become a mountain again.

As the most visible opponent to this accelerated development, and as a millionaire gringo who could fund his own activism, Doug became a favorite target of the conservative right and the pro-development Christian Democrat center. Ironically, if Weyerhaeuser, Champion, Mitsubishi, or any other foreign timber company had purchased the land with the intention of clear-cutting the ancient alerce forests, Chile's leaders probably would have welcomed the land acquisition as progress. The government summoned Doug to testify before senate subcommittees. Then the Catholic University of Valparaiso, which owned Huinay, a critical thirty-thousand-acre property that could have completed the park from north to south, refused to sell. University bishops—responding to stories spun by his political opponents—accused Doug of being an abortionist, after learning that his San Francisco–based Foundation for Deep Ecology funded groups advocating family planning. A communications specialist would later confirm that the Tompkinses' phone and fax lines in Puerto Montt had been tapped. "It seemed clear to us that our political opponents would have preferred we left the country," Kris said of this period in their lives. A petite, fit woman with shoulder-length hair and a youthful smile, Kris has shared the peaks and valleys of the wilderness battle for many years. She and Doug were married in San Francisco in 1994.

With the land legally purchased, he and Kris dug in their heels. Between 1994 and 1997, half of their energies would be spent defending their dream of creating a park and preserving it for future generations of Chileans.

In spring 1998, the Catholic University of Valparaiso sold its thirty-thousand-hect-

FIGURE 11. Reñihue, Chile. (© Sharon Risedorph)

are Huinay property, which divides the land from north to south, to the energy corporation Endesa. In return for the establishment of a national park, Doug had agreed not to purchase any property of over seven thousand contiguous hectares in the southern region of Chile for one year, effectively thwarting any negotiations on this key property. The Huinay deal was completed during this period.

Endesa, responsible for constructing a massive hydroelectric dam on the Bío Bío River farther north, has pledged to create the first sustainable development project in South America at Huinay. No specifics have been released. This recent turn of events illuminates the irony, not just in this situation, but in cases all over the world where the forces of conservation and development are colliding.

Early one January morning, during our 1997 visit, Doug took me flying in his Husky bush plane to traverse the wilderness area tentatively called Parque Pumalin. Forested mountains rose three thousand feet straight out of the ocean, forming ridges and valleys that climb in just a dozen miles to the granite bowls and jagged spires of the Andes. We flew over valley after U-shaped valley of forests so dense that probably no human feet had ever explored them. As we dipped down to scout a meandering ribbon of green water, Doug said, "Now that river would be good kayaking, but see here, it just disappears." And it did, concealed for a half-mile or more by the forest canopy. "It could take days to hack your way through that with a machete to meet up with the river again. But it's beautiful to be swallowed up in all that vegetation."

We skimmed a valley of pure alerce, the tips of the trees—some of which could be more than two thousand years old—pointing up thick and luminous. These mountains, their domes, and their glacial valleys seemed animated, their shapes like fangs and camel humps, sleeping mammoths and elephants. The tree-clad forms appeared to be the joints, sockets, and bones of the earth. Seen from above, the granite and lava beneath the forest were clearly still part of a fluid process.

Inside a sheer-wall canyon, a huge granite bowl carved into a mountainside—thick forest on one side, exposed rock on the other, from which a waterfall pitched out— Doug began a slow spiraling descent, the way an osprey might corkscrew for a fish. By the end of this dive we had fallen a thousand feet and exited the canyon, banked past another mountain face, and spun out over a mile-long lake. At one end it became a river, which coursed through steeply sloped woods and finally emptied into Cahuelmo, the fjord "Where Dolphins Play," as the Mapuche Indians named it. This area, reachable only by boat and now part of the park project, is equipped with simple facilities for campers and hot-spring visitors.

"I'm thinking about renaming this the Park of Ten Thousand Waterfalls," Doug said, rather than Parque Pumalin, a name inspired by the 120-pound pumas (mountain lions) that roam the forests, hunting the *pudu,* a short-legged deer, among other animals. If there is one thing that becomes impressed in one's memory about this part of Chile, it is the sheer volume of water and its many manifestations—the glacial and gemlike shimmering rivers and lakes and the cascades that plunge dramatically toward the sea. From the air, fish and seals and dolphins were often visible hundreds of feet below, swimming in the shallows.

Most of the people who live in the area have settled where the valleys meet the sea. These *colonos,* or settlers, were drawn to the area by the prospects of gaining title to land after a legal period of homesteading. Farther south, in areas accessible from the road, the damage caused by extractive corporations has been far more extensive, with clear-cuts and burned hillsides a common sight. Because of the extreme climate of Chiloé Continental, and because of the effects of the global economy on the beef, lamb, and fish markets, *colonos* have cut and burned deeper into the forest in their attempt to survive.

Smoke swirled above two mounds covered with sod, grass-side down. It was January 1997 (austral summer), and Doug and Kris were hosting a *curanto,* or seafood bake, to celebrate their third annual folk festival. Musicians and dancers living within a fifty-mile radius had been bused and boated to the ranch at Reñihue: children as young as five to adult groups who'd been performing in their villages for years. As the chefs peeled back the earthen barbecue lids, a group of about fifteen musicians sang enthusiastically to the accompaniment of classical guitars, accordions, a skin drum, jaw bone, and hand clapping.

In a wooden barn, a simple platform stage and bleachers had been erected for the two-day festival. Acts ranged from the small guitar and vocal duets to twenty-piece bands, all unamplified. The women and girls wore scoop-necked, lacy dresses, and the men and boys donned the traditional flat-brimmed hats, woolen ponchos, boots, and spurs of the Chilean cowboy, or *huaso.* Songs described the colono life, romanticizing their local mountains, valleys, and rivers or dramatizing courtship. The courtship songs fueled the *cueca,* a blend of flamenco and square dance in which both partners flourish a handkerchief and pantomime, among other things, a rooster cornering a hen. With fast stomping steps and angular movements of the elbows, hands, and shoulders, the dancers shuffle sideways, making brisk turns and spins, females pinching their hoop dresses out to one side. Even the youngsters performed the cueca's complex steps, stern looks of concentration on their faces. Some of the acts parodied the culture itself—dancing the cueca with marionette-like movements and dirty handkerchiefs and performing impromptu skits about the ups and downs of the life of an itinerant worker.

One after the other, the groups acknowledged Doug and Kris for the tremendous effort involved in coordinating their transportation, food, and housing, but most importantly for having provided this unique forum for their music. In a closing ceremony, past midnight, Doug and Kris presented each group with a certificate. Despite an aversion to public speaking, Doug addressed the group in Spanish. "It's becoming very rare that agrarian customs like this are valued in an ever-encroaching global monoculture. I have come from California, a place where the individual is the most important, and I am so happy to be living in this region where there is a vital culture, and I thank you very much for coming and for helping to keep this music alive." Various impromptu jam sessions kept the music going on long into the night.

After the folk festival, we traveled for a week by boat with our fairly seaworthy two-year-old son, through the fjords south of Reñihue, down to Marin Balmaceda, then on to Isla Refugio, through landscapes few people will ever see, with dolphins zipping from port to starboard beneath the boat for miles. In the occasional coves up and down the coast, people were gathering seaweed. Some were colonos. Others lived on anchored boats, homemade wooden crafts with yellow-painted bottoms and a woodstove in the cabin.

We walked on shoals of solid mussels, interrupted only by lava flows, where fishermen and their families homesteaded along the margins of huge mountains. Colonos occasionally invited us into their Spartan homes, shared their homemade bread and jam, passed around silver pots of bitter matté. "When it's not raining, it's raining," one man told us. He wanted to move his family north again.

It was summertime, and usually people would be fishing, but there were few fish that year. "Overfishing," Doug said. Instead, the gathering of seaweed had continued. We passed mounds of the black fiber on our beach excursions, strewn across the volcanic sand like long dark wool, smelling pungently green and fishy at the same time. One morning I watched a woman gather *alga marina*, holding an empty sack with one hand, shoveling the seaweed in with the other, and then hauling it up the beach to a pile she was making to dry it. Drying is critical but difficult because there is so much rain. Since fresh water makes the seaweed rot, a few sunny days are necessary to successfully pack it up. That season it fetched about 70¢ per kilo, so the seaweed collectors could earn thousands of dollars in the short two-month season, enough to subsist for some time. The price had nearly doubled because of a failure, I heard, of a genetically engineered product.

When I visited Reñihue in December 1993, not long after Doug had bought the ranch, he was living in a refurbished complex of smokehouses he called The Hobbits. They were three tiny buildings—eight by ten feet at most, with a kitchen and two bedrooms— connected by a slatted wooden walkway that led to an outhouse and woodshed. During that time, Doug, designer Marci Rudolph, and Chilote architect Eduardo Rojas were developing the architectural vocabulary for the many subsequent buildings that would in four years become a small village. Doug and Kris now live in a two-story, four-bedroom, shingled house. During my visit in 1997, four families were residing permanently on the farm, in smaller versions of Doug and Kris's house. The children attend a school at the ranch (rather than being boarded on outlying islands), and the families eat food grown in a communal organic garden, which, through intensive methods and heated greenhouses, greatly augments the typical diet—even during the rainy winters.

It is clearly Doug's village. All the buildings share the same architectural vision— the shingled roofs and exteriors, dark green trim around doors and windows, tiled kitchen floors, and steeply pitched stairs. In addition to a schoolhouse, bunkroom, dairy barn, sheep barn, and airplane hangar, there are greenhouses, woodsheds, garden sheds, chicken houses, and compost sheds. The car-free compound is connected by a series of wooden slatted walkways, gravel roads, and bridges, and a four-story water tower provides gravity-fed water to the houses.

Guests ebb and flow at Reñihue, journeying from all parts of the country and the world. One rainy evening, an Englishwoman from Vancouver arrived at Reñihue. Mary was sixty-three years old, a botanical watercolor artist whose father had traveled in Chile in the 1920s and brought back plant specimens and tales of exploration to England. Later I volunteered to show her around the farm as she searched for specimens of flora to paint. One day we headed for the Reñihue River on a fairly level trail through dense forest. It wasn't raining, but the leaves were wet and huge ferns and other foliage had grown over nearly the entire trail, so we were soaked almost as soon as we started. Mud sucked at our boots. In a clearing, we came upon a skeleton, moss covering the bones' soft surface, white fur scattered in the mud almost in a perfect circle, like a woolly halo. Puma country. Mary and I were on one of their highways. The farm at Reñihue had become one of their favorite dining areas in the last two years, where they had killed more than sixty sheep.

Many of the colonos who live in the area could be considered unintentional Luddites—there being no electric power grid. Doug is one by choice. Light aircraft and tractors, you might say, are his major exceptions. The electricity doesn't come on in the house until after eight o'clock, when the generator, which may soon be superseded by local hydropower, kicks on. Since he has never learned to use a computer, Doug pens out correspondence in longhand.

I was particularly struck by the power of this rustic, media-free aesthetic when, after two rainy weeks of immersion in the handcrafted farm environments of Reñihue, we stopped at a small airstrip on the nearby island of Chiloé. It was funky by American standards: a smoky room with a billiard table, posters of "babes" in bikinis slugging on beer bottles, a television broadcasting a violent urban-American-drug-dealers-versus-cops movie with Spanish subtitles, a few pilots hanging around sipping Nescafé. Our return to the towns and civilization, the billboards, media, architecture, and road systems mounted a pornographic assault on my temporarily soothed senses.

Doug came to this part of Chile in 1961, an eighteen-year-old mountaineer with dreams of racing in the 1968 Olympics as a downhill skier. A few years later, he started The

North Face, a popular outdoor-gear store in San Francisco. Throughout the 1960s he was one of the United States' most accomplished rock climbers, along with friends Yvon Chouinard and Royal Robbins. By 1969, he'd sold The North Face and returned to South America to make a documentary film of an ascent on Fitzroy in Argentine Patagonia. In 1970, he flew a small plane, with his then-wife, Susie, and two young children, from San Francisco to Tierra del Fuego and back, camping every night. During his subsequent journeys, which included kayaking and mountaineering expeditions throughout the world, he became drawn to the southern Chilean landscape and culture.

Ten years ago, at the height of Esprit's exponential growth—it had reached $800 million in worldwide sales by the late 1980s—you might have seen him intensely engaged in discussions of product licensing, architectural expansion, or the acquisition of a painting by Francis Bacon or Fernando Botero. But by 1990, he had sold his interest in the U.S. Esprit company, exiting with a swan-song catalog that introduced the concepts of deep ecology and encouraged customers to practice responsible consumption, "buying only what they needed, whether from Esprit or any other company." With over $100 million from the sale, he started a number of environmental foundations, including the Foundation for Deep Ecology in San Francisco and El Bosque Pumalin in Puerto Montt, Chile—and headed south.

Perhaps his association with deep ecology has been a strike against him because of its reputation for being somewhat elitist or even fundamentalist. This would be ironic, given that deep ecology is a loosely organized and intentionally inclusive philosophical platform—a broad ideology that insists that humans are just one of a huge array of interrelated creatures and that in determining a livelihood, we must be responsible for maintaining the great diversity and integrity of life. Such an endeavor involves the ongoing process of asking ever-deeper questions, finding the roots of the environmental crisis we face today, and adjusting individual behavior accordingly.

I was in Chile in 1993, not long after Doug had come across a dead sea lion, a bullet through its head, on the shore near his ranch. He told the local *salmoneros* (salmon has been introduced to Chile in the form of huge commercial farms) that he would offer a reward of more than one year's salary to anyone with information about the illegal poaching of sea lions. The incident definitely sparked the mobilization of local political forces against Doug's nascent park project.

I was also there four years later when Kris walked in having just learned from the foundation headquarters in Puerto Montt via radio—their only medium of communication with the outside world—that an entire sea lion rookery had been slaughtered near Rio Negro and that the story was all over the papers. Though poaching hasn't been eliminated, it is now front-page news—the first sign that those who are responsible will be held accountable for their environmental abuses in these remote regions.

I believe it was poet Gary Snyder who said that in order to promote the wild, we must have people living on the edge of wilderness. In fact, for this very reason—and despite repeated charges that the Tompkinses were trying to run people off the land—Doug and Kris planned to assist the colonos living in the area as part of the park project. The pioneering life is difficult. The soils are acidic from the heavy rainfalls, so pastures are depleted rapidly. Schools and medical facilities are few and far between and underfunded. And the increasingly global economy has slashed what little profit margin exists in traditional markets, like beef, lamb, fish, and wool. Settlers are caught in an economic cycle that forces them to clear more forest for diminishing returns. The average wage for a skilled laborer or carpenter is $12 to $20 a day, and underemployment remains a problem.

Doug and Kris employ more people than anyone in the province—170, as of early 1998—primarily for the park project. And contrary to accusations, settlers have gained titles to their land as a result of the Parque Pumalin Project agreement. They are not being forced to move.

Even though the government was still opposed to the park project in 1997, Doug and Kris began working on a model for what they hoped would become the park's five visitor centers. Rather than establishing park headquarters similar to what one might find in North American parks, they intended to create small demonstration farms. These fifteen- to twenty-five-hectare farms would be typical of many homesteads in the area. To broaden the skill base and perhaps develop some niche regional products that could put local colonos on the map, they would be run by some of Chile's leading practitioners of sustainable agriculture. Beekeepers, farmers, cheese makers, and other agro-ecologists have been slowly recruited to build up a competent team. "The idea here," said Doug, "is to develop a number of local cottage industries and to keep very precise records of how much it costs to establish them. Hopefully, we'll be able to do things for very little start-up costs that other settlers in the area can successfully replicate and earn, say, $3,000 per year in extra income, which will be just enough incentive for them to stay on their farms."

At Coleta Gonzala, at the southern end of the park, we walked to a recently completed row of bee houses, the beginnings of what Doug was confident would become a nationally famous source of honey, produced from the forests' flowering trees. There was a large garden of raised beds as well as a series of greenhouses, inexpensively crafted from wood, clear plastic sheeting, and string. Barns for lambing and for dairy cows had just been built. Chickens strutted in their own shelters, providing eggs and meat as well as manure for the organic garden. "Proper woodlot management also has to be emphasized," he said, shaking his head, "so settlers don't have to continue to raid the wilderness for basic fuels for cooking and heating."

These demonstration farms will also offer employment to people in the area. "Ninety-five percent of all the work here will be done locally. We'll of course have a number of park rangers to maintain the trails, meet the public, and keep order. But rather than the usual police-type rangers we have in North America, they will be hands-on farmers and craftspeople. The preserves will be assimilative to the local culture, not part of some national political orientation."

Coleta Gonzala also serves as a ferry station where the southern highway once again continues south. There we ate at a restaurant that serves homemade bread and simple meals. It appeared to be a rustic Chilote interpretation of a café in San Francisco that Doug had built from industrial materials in the mid-1980s. Large sepia photographs of alerce forests decorated the walls, and a glass case featured local crafts, including hand-knit sweaters and ponchos.

Twelve kilometers up the road, we walked a thirty-minute loop through an alerce grove on the Alerce Sendero, a gentle path carved through dense bamboo thickets. We had to strain our necks to look up at these huge trees, their trunks so stout that our three connected arm spans couldn't reach around them entirely. Their red shaggy bark reminded me of California's sequoias. Doug stopped at one tree whose bark had been stripped away from the first eight feet of its massive trunk. "This one's been poached," Doug said. "Fishermen use the *alerce* bark to repair their boats because the wood is incredibly moisture resistant. But in ten years the tree will be dead just from taking the bark away," he said. "We've made this part of our trail so people can learn about the fate of their national tree, which is increasingly difficult to find."

Toward the end of our visit in 1997, Doug, my wife, Quincey (Doug's oldest daughter), our son, Gardner, and I took a road trip around the Lake District in search of sunshine and to see a bit more of the country. In Puerto Riminahue, a retired couple approached us while we were enjoying a cup of tea. "Excuse me, are you Tompkins?" asked the man. Doug nodded. "We just want to say," said the woman, "that we fully support what you are doing down in the south. It is truly country worth saving, and you have the support of a lot of people in Santiago."

"Regardless of what the government and the newspapers say," the man continued, "you have to go on with the project."

"Oh, we intend to," said Doug. "We're fully committed."

Along the way, we met numerous people who recognized Doug and encouraged him to persevere.

On July 4, 1997, the administration of Chilean president Eduardo Frei Ruíz-Tagle endorsed a protocol laying the foundation for the Parque Pumalin Project. Doug credited the U.S. ambassador to Chile, Gabriel Guerra-Mondragon, for leading the way toward government approval of the park plan. Ultimately, a number of factors contributed to the government's about-face and acceptance of the park. Especially important was the public's approval of the Tompkins initiative, which had steadily gained momentum despite five years of government opposition and attacks from the press.

Doug was the first to admit that he had made some errors in his strategy that had helped to blow the situation out of proportion. His Spanish was not as good as it could have been when he began to appear in the media. Because he didn't want to raise suspicions by hiring a professional public relations person to handle his affairs, he spoke himself and, despite a good command of the language, at times may have been misunderstood. Certain government officials saw Doug as an arrogant Yankee and an environmental extremist, and they reacted accordingly.

Ironically, it may have been Chile's desire to preserve the sanctity of private property ownership (whether foreign or native)—and therefore economic development—that had the greatest influence on the government's decision to endorse the park project. "I was never really worried about the land being expropriated," said Doug, "because the government was very focused on restoring its reputation as a safe haven for foreign investment." In the 1970s, expropriation by foreign-owned facilities had prompted the coup against Salvador Allende, which resulted in two decades of military rule in the country. "There had been threats from certain ministries that our land might be taken away, and I made sure I told people about it each time the story came out in the press." This strategy put the necessary pressure on the government to act. Indeed, the press release concerning the park agreement emphasized that the government recognized Doug's rights to develop the property as a foreign investor.

Doug's conservation efforts are sometimes questioned because of his privileged station in life. With millions in the bank, some critics say, of course he can find comfort in the world's most remote corners. But I think that's an oversimplification; it doesn't take into account the larger economic forces that are increasingly commodifying the wild. Doug's vision is a grand one; he has been engaged in activism on a significant scale for some time now, not only purchasing land, but funding organizations, publishing books, and developing long-term strategies for more ecological approaches to forestry and agriculture. He is using his resources for what he considers to be best for the wild and, in turn, best for society as well.

"I make no apologies for my destiny," Doug wrote to me.

> I cannot undo the fact that I accumulated quite a lot of money. In some ways I am undoing it by having started various foundations and donated all this land. What I really object to is that one thinks that millions of dollars gives one isolation from difficulties or troubles. In my observation, the most troubled and unhappy people are those with all the money. I also feel tremendous responsibility put upon me because of the very fact that the system as it stands has allowed people like me to amass so much money. In return, to pay *my* rent for living on the planet, it's incumbent upon me to do something *in proportion* with my resources. This has made me, at a time when I could be basking in material well-being, work harder and worry more in matters of environmental and social causes.

Indeed, the Parque Pumalin Project and many other initiatives that have sprung from within the meeting rooms at the Foundation for Deep Ecology should serve as an example for others to do whatever is in their power to avert a future void of wild places. Such efforts prompt the question: Why aren't more people with significant financial means coming to the rescue of the wilderness in countries all over the world?

It was a noble act to fall in love with this wilderness and to take the land off the global economic market to preserve its integrity. At a time when investment and private property are gaining greater sovereignty regardless of the effects on communities or ecosystems, only this level of philanthropic commitment and this type of uncompromising intervention can save the world's remaining wildernesses. Should corporate ownership and industrial development be the only legacy of globalization? Given the failure of governments to resist multinational extractive industries, only acts like these can ensure that primary forests and all of the species that inhabit them will survive into the next millennium. Can ecotourism and sustainable forestry and agriculture help the locals who decide to continue to live on the fringes of the Parque Pumalin

Project? Only time will tell. However, only by persuading others in power of the long-term benefits of such wildlands philanthropy will we secure these remnants of the natural world. By keeping the last of the primary forests out of reach of the global industrial economy, we force ourselves to create ways to satisfy human needs without sacrificing these vestiges of the truly wild.

EDWARD A. WHITESELL

14 ———————— mapping the wild

Most international conservation organizations seem to have little to say about wilderness preservation anymore. To be sure, they still lead the charge against a wide variety of serious environmental ills. Prominent among these is the massive, ongoing loss of biological diversity all over the world. In fact, it almost seems as if the first impulse of the professional conservationist these days, when looking at a natural landscape, is to immediately start counting—the number of species, variety of ecosystems, and number of different kinds of genes in populations of flora and fauna.

It is now almost unimaginable to publish anything about natural-area conservation without using the word *biodiversity,* the term for such biological census taking. No one can deny the importance of the mass extinctions occurring today, but whatever happened to the words *wild* and *wilderness?* There are now countless office complexes filled with highly experienced, professional conservationists in places like Washington, D.C., and Gland, Switzerland, who design and promote conservation strategies for the entire planet, and yet among them there is no modern-day equivalent of a Henry David Thoreau, sternly admonishing modern society with the proposition that "in wildness is the preservation of the world."

Outside of conservation circles, wilderness preservation is hardly even an issue. If an advocate of wilderness preservation in the United States were to go abroad to survey public opinion about wilderness preservation all over the world, he or she would soon discover that most of the world's people would not even understand the survey questions. In many languages, the key terms in the parlance of the wilderness-preservation movement here in the United States—*wilderness, wild,* and *wilderness preservation*— cannot even be adequately translated in a way that conveys their exact meanings for wilderness advocates here. If it were explained to the survey respondents that the movement for wilderness preservation is fundamentally a movement of resistance to the domestication of every nook and cranny of the planet by humankind, it is conceivable that most of the world's people would either answer that wilderness preservation is a menace or that it is an exercise in futility.

Some ten thousand years ago, in widely scattered regions of the world, our ancestors took the first steps toward the domestication of other life-forms when they began cultivating and breeding varieties of plants and animals that eventually became partly or entirely dependent on people for their survival. We who are alive today are participants in the most advanced stage in that long historical process of the domestication of nature by one of its species. For centuries, we have been told that this is human progress. Only a misanthrope would not celebrate the tremendous prowess of humankind in its eradication of the dangerous forces of wild, untamed nature. Only the comfortable and callous could deny the rights of the masses of the world's poor to use natural resources wherever they are found so that they might attain a decent standard of living. Modern conservation, we are told, means wise use of natural resources and not the preservation of an imaginary wild nature that no longer exists.

Yet there are still, at the dawn of the twenty-first century, those of us who reject this view of progress and who are repulsed by the prospect of a completely domesticated earth. Perhaps we are slow learners, but is it not misanthropic to condemn all people to spend their entire lives in contrived environments? Even if most people would prefer to do so, we would echo the late Supreme Court Justice William O. Douglas, who, in *A Wilderness Bill of Rights* (1965), wrote that wilderness preservation is essential to protect the rights of the minority for whom the elimination of wilderness is an intolerable loss. Moreover, it is surely callous to measure the worth of all things by their utilitarian value to our own species. If this places us on the wrong side of public opinion polls, this is nothing new. The movement for wilderness preservation has always been, in essence, a critique of prevailing opinions about the role of people in the natural world, where we are one species among millions.

The Idea of the Wild

Once, in a casual, private conversation twenty-five years ago, the U.S. Forest Service's regional forester in Denver, Colorado, tried to persuade me that wilderness is all in the mind. At that time, which of course was long before the current hoopla in intellectual circles about the "social construction of nature" and the "deconstruction" of the idea of wilderness, this struck me as an odd and foreboding position. It implied that this powerful figure in the management of our nation's national forest system could see no valid reason to set aside any lands for wilderness preservation at all, since a "wilderness experience" was a figment of the imagination that could be had virtually anywhere. Less than a decade earlier, the 1964 Wilderness Act had mandated the Forest Service to gradually report and make recommendations to Congress on the suitability of specific parts of the national forests for inclusion in the new wilderness-preservation system. Hence, the historical context for this private conversation was nothing less than the very period in which the young National Wilderness Preservation System was initially being constructed.

There is now general acceptance among scholars that social and cultural lenses inevitably influence the way we perceive and understand the biological and physical communities of which we are living, breathing members. Therefore, there is nothing particularly insightful these days about the observation that the idea of the wild is just that—an idea. The social construction of nature has never really been the bone of contention between advocates and opponents of wilderness preservation, in this country or in any other. What has always been at issue is the critical question of *which* social and cultural spectacles we should put on in our efforts to achieve the actual patterns of land use and ecological relationships we desire.

Despite the adversarial relationship between the regional forester (who did everything in his power to minimize the amount of designated wilderness in the national forests of the Rocky Mountains) and myself (who, as the senior staff member of Colorado's only statewide wilderness-preservation organization, did just the opposite), we had developed a frank, professional relationship with each other. I know that he sincerely thought his point of view was insightful and true. I also know that if he had not been effectively blocked in the implementation of his beliefs, a great many of the undeveloped forests, streams, and meadows of the Rocky Mountains that westerners know and love would have been crisscrossed with roads, clear-cut, dammed, and mined by now. For that reason, I am proud to have taken effective action, along with many fellow preservationists, to thwart the full implementation on the public lands of what would now be called a "deconstructionist" line of thinking about the idea of the wild.

"Wild" is the quality of freedom from human control. Its geographic expression is wilderness. Wilderness may be identified as a place that is mostly wild, but, of course, different wilderness areas have different degrees of human control. The quality of wildness is manifested everywhere and in different ways. It will never be entirely lost but may be, instead, eliminated by degrees in the long historic struggle of humans to gain control over the natural forces that affect their lives.

We have still not domesticated most of life's tiniest representatives, including many pathogens, insects, and invasive plants, nor have we managed to tame such natural forces as the weather or the power of ocean waves and currents. Accordingly, we have dubbed such remaining challenges to complete human domination of the rest of nature with disdainful names like *germ, pest, weed*, and *natural hazard*. Moreover, try as we might, we will never completely control our own animal nature, which manifests itself in wild thoughts and acts that violate social norms for civilized human beings. So, let us not overestimate the ecological dominance of *Homo sapiens* by asserting that the planet has become completely domesticated.

Wildness may never disappear completely, but, with a total human population of six billion compounded by a rapidly escalating per capita consumption of resources and production of wastes, the last extensive areas of wild terrestrial ecosystems have long been on death row (with most executions proceeding unhampered by stays or pardons). Some say that true wilderness disappeared long ago, while others say that there are still important wilderness areas left to preserve. Definitively adjudicating such claims is impossible because this debate concerns subjective evaluations of a place as a whole more than direct empirical measurement of its characteristics. For example, one might ask whether the Arctic National Wildlife Refuge (ANWR) in Alaska is truly the last great wilderness in the United States, as is claimed by those engaged in the political battle to prevent commercial exploration for oil and gas development within the refuge. It is possible to gauge the biodiversity of such a place through biological surveys and to document its breathtaking landscape through photography, but it is not possible to measure how wild it is in any empirical sense. So, when forced to be as objective as possible in measuring the wildness of a place, we resort to using a variety of surrogate criteria, such as the amount and nature of human use, the extent of human alteration of landscape features, and the extent of human influence on ecological relationships.

Opponents of wilderness preservation have long argued that if there is any sign of people at all, then wilderness preservation is inappropriate. In the United States, this argument was used for decades by those who sought to keep the size of the National Wilderness Preservation System to a minimum. For many years, it was claimed that the sights and sounds of people—such things as Jeep tracks, nineteenth-century mining camps, or even views of distant highways and towns—should disqualify an area from eligibility for wilderness classification. This purist argument has been largely discredited in public land policy making in the United States, but now, in the international context, the same banner is waved by many scholars as if they had made a new discovery. For example, we are told in all seriousness that although preservationists naively assume the uninhabited portions of the Amazon rain forest to be a wilderness, research actually shows that previous human occupants caused noticeable changes in Amazonian ecosystems for thousands of years, through such practices as soil enrichment, transplantation or nurturing of valuable tree species, and small-scale, shifting agriculture.

Instead of perpetuating tiresome arguments about what a wilderness really is, perhaps the best way to respond is to simply bring the discussion back to earth by comparing how the preservation of areas with these sorts of previous human alterations would compare with the likely alternatives today, including such things as highway construction, conversion of forests to cattle pastures and soy plantations, open-pit mining operations, and the drowning of forests and poisoning of rivers by giant hydroelectric reservoirs.

Wilderness preservation is one of various forms of conservation. Far from being seen as a panacea for the world's environmental problems, it is advocated as only one essential component of conservation. Conservation as a whole includes a wide range of actions and policies designed to maintain or recover what is deemed to be a healthy or proper relationship between people and the nonhuman world. Even intensive forms of resource use, such as industrial-scale logging and the construction of giant dams, may be labeled conservation when they are designed to foster the maintenance of certain socially valued environmental conditions. Wilderness advocates in the United States have grown accustomed to their opponents declaring themselves to be the "true conservationists," while those in the wilderness-preservation movement are labeled "extremists." Even when advocating such extreme actions as logging the last old-growth rain forests in North America or damming every major free-flowing river in the West, they could proclaim themselves to be conservationists in the belief that these were the best ways to provide "the greatest good for the greatest number of people over the long run" (echoing the old dictum through which the so-called father of the U.S. Forest Service, Gifford Pinchot, justified utilitarian conservation in opposition to preservation).

Preservationists' principal objection to utilitarian conservationists is simply their assumption that all places should be exploited, managed, redesigned, or otherwise "man"-handled. Since the quality of wildness refers to the relative proportion of human as opposed to nonhuman influences, this can be seen as an issue of power relations, although not in the sense of the relative powers between social classes, ethnic groups, or men and women, as is commonly studied in sociology or political science. The idea of wilderness centers on the geographic concept of the power exercised by humans over the rest of nature in a particular place. Wilderness advocates seek to ultimately establish a different balance of powers between people and much of the rest of nature, in which the hubris of techno-scientific humankind is replaced by a good measure of humility and self-restraint. This objective raises hackles because it challenges and resists the widely accepted cultural perspective that the world belongs to *Homo sapiens* to refashion at will. Nevertheless, any conservation strategy that is so exclusive and intolerant as to deny a significant role to wilderness preservation reduces conservation to nothing more than ecological manipulation.

The conventional approach to wilderness preservation is the legal demarcation of places in which human occupation and use are restricted in certain specific ways, with the underlying tenet being that humans should be visitors who do not remain (to paraphrase the U.S. Wilderness Act). Unfortunately, the preservation of wildness within legally designated nature reserves is a tremendously difficult problem that is full of contradictions. The most fundamental of these contradictions is that land management designed to preserve wilderness is antithetical to the autonomous survival of the wild.

It was once thought that preservation simply meant reducing human manipulation of ecological systems and landscape features, in contrast to more intrusive forms of conservation management that refashion ecological systems to suit human designs. Now, that distinction no longer holds. Many wilderness reserves have become, for all practical purposes, human constructs. This is so for many reasons, ranging from the biological to the social. Science and history increasingly portray both natural and social systems as being more fluid, dynamic, and chaotic than previously understood, calling into question the whole idea that there is an ecological baseline, or a "traditional" culture and lifestyle, that defines the prototypical wilderness environment or the most adaptive human society for that area. Choices must be made regarding the ecological composition of a reserve and how humans should interact with it. For example, designated wilderness areas and similar reserves are usually managed to eliminate nonnative species and to restore some approximation of earlier ecological conditions. Because of tremendously increased appreciation for wilderness recreation, access roads, paths, and tourist facilities are usually installed, in accordance with the designs of professional landscape architects. Recreational users are distributed according to planned specifications for lowering environmental impacts and increasing the visitors' sense of having a "wilderness experience."

As officially designated reserves become ever more intensively managed to approximate human notions of their optimal composition, so-called protected areas do not, in reality, "protect" wilderness. That is because the wild quality of a place is not something that can be managed. *Wild* is the antithesis of *managed*. It is the condition of being completely free of control by humans. Yet conservationists and public-land managers unthinkingly bandy about the oxymoron *wilderness resource*. This is nonsense. As Jack Turner has so forcefully argued, "By preserving things—acreage, species, and natural processes—we believed we could preserve a quality. But collections of acreage, species, and processes, however large or diverse, no more preserve wildness than large and diverse collections of sacred objects preserve the sacred."[1]

This contradiction is inherent in any sort of preservation—of either wild or social spaces. For example, trying to preserve historic sites by cordoning them off from the evolving societies of which they had once been integral parts makes them static and lifeless. Are we to conclude, then, that the contradictions inherent in the idea of preservation make it futile to resist the domestication of the planet? Is the only reasonable conservation objective to which we can aspire in the twenty-first century the construction of so-called protected areas that are nothing more than scientifically designed and intensively managed arks to salvage as much biodiversity as possible from the deluge of humanity? Most current literature on international conservation proceeds from the assumption that the answer is "yes" and therefore seeks scientific and technical solutions developed by conservation biologists, park planners, and public-land managers. There is almost no formal discussion in international conservation circles today of how we might resist the disappearance of the wild both within and outside of so-called protected areas around the world.

To begin having such a discussion, we must understand that wilderness preservation requires not just a short-term agenda to create quasi-protected areas, but also the long-term promotion of social and cultural changes that might allow humans and all other creatures to once again share wild habitats over extensive portions of the earth. We must recognize that the establishment of protected areas is only an interim stepping-stone, while the overarching goal, the liberation of wildness, requires fundamental changes in the course of human development. Ultimately, therefore, the movement for wilderness preservation is a movement for social and cultural transformation and is not just a biological project (although even some of the most far-thinking wilderness preservation organizations in the United States have now virtually turned themselves

into the political arms of conservation biology). Wilderness preservation is, undoubt-
edly, a central tool of conservation biology because large areas of relatively unaltered
habitat are essential for the survival of many species, for the maintenance of wide
genetic variation within those species, and for the continuation of ecological and evolutionary processes. But those who mistakenly reduce wilderness preservation to a
biological program, ignoring its social and cultural dimensions, are trapped in what
Paul Shepard has called an "enclave mentality," which is ultimately self-defeating.

Mapping the Idea of the Wild

Where in the world might wilderness preservation be an appropriate conservation objective? To some, wilderness preservation appears to be culturally inappropriate in most
of the world because, outside of a few countries with some common historical and
cultural characteristics—like the United States, Canada, and Australia—most of the
world's cultures do not harbor the ideas (or social constructions of nature) that make
wilderness preservation understandable and desirable. For example, it is argued that
wilderness preservation should play an insignificant role in international conservation
policies because most of the world's cultures do not look upon human life and livelihood as things that are properly separated from the rest of nature, just as most of them
do not suffer from a longing to restore a lost Eden that never was. This line of thinking
would suggest that it is possible to plot on a world map a limited number of world
regions within which one would find the social construction of nature that produces
that odd duck, the preservationist.

Is something wrong with the idea of mapping the territorial range within which the
idea of wilderness preservation is endemic, just as a biogeographer delimits the territorial ranges of specific plants and animals? After all, this is only a different way of
stating what is commonly heard in denunciations of international wilderness preservation as a form of cultural imperialism. It seems to me that putting such allegations
into this sort of geographic perspective is a useful way of cautioning against an overly
static view of cultural processes and the landscapes they produce. Any map purporting
to block out regions within which wilderness preservation is culturally inappropriate
risks obscuring the important fact that the spatial distribution of ideas of the wild is in
flux. Environmental ethics and conservation strategies around the world are undergoing critical re-examination, experimentation, and change. The rapid and profound social and environmental changes denoted by the terms *development* and *globalization*

promote and facilitate much of this ferment. In short, there are various ideas of the wild, and these are evolving and mutually influencing each other in promising ways.

It is logically possible to differentiate ideas of the wild according to how universal or how culturally specific they are. Although very little research of this sort has been carried out, the practical significance of such investigations would be to facilitate the use of culturally appropriate ideas of the wild as the basis for wilderness preservation in different regions of the world, in much the same way that economic development may be approached through the use of what is known as appropriate technology.

Being based on the precept that the imprint of humankind should be minimal in at least some portions of the earth, wilderness preservation always entails prohibiting or limiting many sorts of human uses of a given area. This single objective is justified on a variety of grounds by different people. When designed to serve human needs and desires, preservation is a form of anthropocentric (human-centered) conservation. Frequently cited anthropocentric reasons for preservation include protection of wild relatives of valuable crops; maintenance of a diverse flora and fauna that might be found to harbor biochemicals useful as new medicines or pesticides; continuation of essential ecological functions that protect the quality of our water and air; maintenance of desirable climatic conditions; and the provision of opportunities for people to directly seek certain kinds of knowledge and wisdom that can never be mediated by human beings—knowledge and understanding of a world that we did not make but that, on the contrary, gave birth to us. Other justifications for wilderness preservation are based on what are believed to be the rights or interests of nature itself. An example of such a biocentric (life-centered) reason for wilderness preservation is the maintenance of habitat necessary for the survival of a species threatened by human disturbance, whether or not the existence of that species benefits humans in any discernible way. There are also religious reasons for preservation that may serve few if any human needs, as in the establishment of sacred groves of forest that are off-limits to exploitation in order to show respect to the divine presence in these places.

Designated wilderness areas may be understood as *cultural landscapes,* a term that refers to the view that the appearance of any given landscape tells us much about the human cultures that have occupied and used it over a long period of time. For a cultural geographer, the human handiwork and environmental modifications to be observed in rural and urban areas provide a wealth of information about the cultures responsible for those landscapes. Yet, nature reserves, too, are culturally revealing landscapes, not only by virtue of what people have done to them but also, significantly, by what they have deliberately refrained from doing. Innumerable permutations and combinations of the various reasons for wilderness preservation can differentially motivate significant numbers of people in different regions to preserve the places they care for in a relatively undeveloped condition. Thus there may be different cultural rationales for apparently similar cultural landscapes in widely scattered world regions.

Now, let us return to the earlier point that such rationales could theoretically be divided into those that are universal or potentially widespread versus those that are culturally specific or of limited range. In the first category would be at least the two ideas of sacred spaces and ecological reservoirs. For thousands of years, different cultures the world over have found religious reasons to preserve the environments of specific places, strictly limiting human ecological impacts. In fact, many of these sacred places have provided the ancient nuclei for modern-day national parks and similar reserves. Also widespread today is the scientific idea of an ecological reservoir, a term referring to the importance to society of large, undeveloped areas due to their value as the sources of irreplaceable plants, animals, genetic variation, and ecological services (regulation and purification of water and atmospheric gases, temperature regulation, protection of soils, and so forth). There is a wide variety of more culturally specific reasons for preservation, ranging from the necessity of wild places for spiritual, cultural, and psychological renewal, on one hand, to the rights of indigenous peoples who depend upon restricted public access to maintain their autonomy and self-determination as minorities with special territorial claims, on the other.

The important point to be made here is that such ideas about the relation between people and specific wild places are not static but are in flux. In the United States itself (home to a long line of archdruids and self-styled ecowarriors), preservationists are currently engaged in an unprecedented debate among themselves over the philosophical foundations, goals, and tactics appropriate for wilderness preservation in this country. Likewise, in developing countries, there are many deep divisions over questions of cultural change and traditional resource use in relatively wild areas.

Facilitated by satellite communications and greatly increased international linkages between nongovernmental organizations, elements of these domestic debates over the fate of undeveloped areas are being woven together, fostering a global diffusion of ideas about the proper relationship between people and the rest of nature. This results in both the spread of some U.S. ideas of the wild to developing countries and the selective adoption, in the United States, of conservation models from developing regions. For example, the idea of inhabited wild areas is gaining ground here in the United States in light of experimentation in other countries with innovative approaches, such as biosphere reserves and extractive reserves. The proposed Buffalo Commons, which would restore large portions of the Great Plains ecosystems, is one such idea. Likewise, there is now increasing pressure by Native Americans to recognize their rights to practice traditional uses in the portions of their historic territories that were incorporated into the U.S. National Park System.

It is evident that there will be a greater diversity of wildlands designations and policies in the United States in the years to come as a result of these changes in wilderness philosophy. Though taking a variety of forms and going by different names, what allows us to unify different kinds of restrictive land-use policies under the general rubric of *wilderness preservation* is nothing more complicated than their shared objective of placing geographic bounds, for whatever reasons, on the domestication of the earth. No single culture anywhere in the world has a monopoly on the capacity to ultimately attain such a level of ecological maturity.

The success of efforts to preserve wilderness through the creation of restrictive nature reserves depends, in part, on whether there are critical and honest examinations of such things as the political processes by which such reserves are established, the costs and benefits they bring to different social groups now and in future generations, the ecological ends they serve as compared to alternative conservation strategies, the human rights that might be violated by limitations on access to occupancy and resource use, the cultural changes that might ensue, and so forth.

The major international conservation organizations that have long dedicated themselves to the expansion of such reserves around the world are now under unprecedented public scrutiny concerning these questions. This is happening for good reasons, and it is long overdue. In many countries, international policies for the establishment of restrictive natural areas have conflicted with human rights. The large international conservation organizations now officially acknowledge the need for more democratic processes of land-use planning and zoning in places harboring the world's remaining wildlands. In practice, however, political power sharing remains highly imbalanced with respect to the many different social groups with a stake in the use of these lands.

This has brought us to a critical juncture in the evolution of international conservation policies. Ironically, at a time when the human capacity to radically alter the planet's lands, waters, and atmosphere is reaching unprecedented levels, influential organizations that have long worked for the establishment of restrictive protected areas are now advocating significant human occupation and local control over resource use within many nature reserves. As a direct consequence of ongoing shifts in global preservation strategies, heated debates and a great deal of uncertainty have arisen regarding the best course of action. While some conservation organizations recognize the rights of local people to shape conservation policies, even if that means the discontinuation of exclusionary preservation policies, most international conservation organizations still reject the prospect of a world in which human alteration of the landscape is ubiquitous. The choice of conservation strategies today will have lasting consequences for the remaining wild places, which can be lost by a misstep in either direction, either through precipitous policy shifts or through stubborn adherence to misguided policies.

Wilderness preservation is much more than the creation of quasi-protected areas. It necessarily includes this interim strategy, but wilderness preservation must also be examined from the long-term perspective of preserving the quality of wildness, both within and outside of such nature reserves. This is a social and cultural agenda—not a biological or technical project. The increasing effectiveness of international conservation organizations in securing the establishment of scientifically designed reservoirs of biological diversity masks the fact that they are losing the battle for wilderness preservation.

To maintain landscapes where ecosystems are minimally altered by human beings, such landscapes must have cultural and economic value for those social groups with at least some degree of influence over natural resource use in any given area. Therefore, lasting wilderness preservation in so-called developing countries depends on whether or not this "development" is of the sort that elaborates enduring cultural values and social institutions compatible with wilderness preservation. This suggests that those international conservationists who believe themselves to be working for the preservation of the wild will have to broaden their activities far beyond today's standard operating procedures. To make a long-term impact on the survival of wild landscapes, it will be necessary to promote social, political, and economic changes that will lead to that end. This is not a suggestion for greater cultural imperialism or political intervention by preservationists. It is simply a recognition of the necessity to build wilderness preservation on endemic social foundations, working in solidarity with the initiatives of local peoples who have alternative visions of development—development that is characterized by a sense of humility and self-restraint with respect to the rest of the natural world.

A self-righteous attitude in defense of one's own culture-bound view of nature against what is seen as the onslaught of a culturally homogeneous *Homo sapiens* is shortsighted and dangerous. So, too, is the pat assertion that preservation is green imperialism and, as such, has no place in a comprehensive set of international conservation policies. In short, international preservation politics must be approached with humility and re-spect for both other peoples and other (nonhuman) members of the natural commu-nity of life. The many inadequacies of current approaches to wilderness preservation, at home and abroad, demand innovation and the sharing of ideas of the wild among all people who would resist the domestication of the earth. Therein lies the best hope of forming what may someday become a world wilderness movement supported by a broad and politically effective coalition of the world's peoples.

NOTE

1 Jack Turner, "The Quality of the Wild: Preservation, Control, and Freedom," in David Clark Burks, ed., *Place of the Wild: A Wildlands Anthology* (Washington, DC: Island Press, 1994), pp. 176–77.

15 ———————————————— earth jazz

Over the past few centuries, our perception of nature has become narrowly visual. As a result, nature has taken on in our minds the frozen perfection of calendar photos, or the streamlined motion of television specials. Living in modern civilization, we see nature as an object to be manipulated or a view to be admired. We *hear* nature hardly at all. At the same time, we have come to hear music as a privileged language of human emotion, with no reference (except when the words or programs say so) to the world outside.

While it may be a modern specialty, the bias toward a visual perception of nature is hardly a modern invention. It is not even a human invention. As primates, we are profoundly visual creatures. Our eyes' precise stereoscopy suits us to size up the world, our hands' precision grip to seize it. We anatomize and butcher, have visions and build.

The eye is attuned to objects, the ear to process. The eye lives in space, the ear in time. It is no wonder that music, of all arts, lends itself most readily to improvisation. While the eye perches dryly at a certain point of view, the ear swims. Since the eye individuates while the ear unites, music has long been thought the art best able to give humans a sense of oneness with each other and with the universe. The word we unfailingly use for the reconciliation of unlike things is a musical word, *harmony*. Music is perhaps the most social of all arts, and one of the few that admits of group improvisation.

For Schopenhauer and Nietzsche, music was the voice of the cosmos itself. For many traditional peoples it depicts the cycles and moods of nature and often involves a delicate dialogue with birds and crickets, water and wind. By us it is bricked up in concert halls or living rooms, or blared from speakers that turn the outdoors into a living room. Meanwhile the sounds of nature are bricked out, glazed out, muffled by air conditioners and shredded by lawn mowers.

Both our perception of nature and our action upon it might be improved if we relied a bit less on sight and a bit more on sound. At least, we might use sound as a model. We might use sound in general, and one kind of sound in particular, as a model for our collaboration with nature.

What form should that collaboration take? The deep ecologists want us to sing one faint part among millions in nature's (imagined) harmony. The planet managers want to compose and conduct a planet-symphony of their own devising. Maybe there is a third possibility: a kind of *earth jazz*.

Its advice for humankind might go something like this: ditch your notated score—whether ascribed to nature or yourself—and learn to improvise. Respond as flexibly to nature as nature responds to you. Accept nature's freedom as the premise of your own: accept that both are grounded in a deeper necessity. Relax your rigid beat and learn to follow nature's rhythms—in other words, to swing.

A good model for the planet might be a bebop quartet led by a saxophonist. The style of each sideman pervades the whole, since the drummer, bassist, and pianist play almost all the time. Each player, though, also takes solos, stretches of music that he makes his own. During most of these solos the leader "lays out." But during the leader's solos the other musicians keep playing. In other words, they are indispensable and he is not—a sobering lesson for any leader, and one that man had better learn soon.

If you translate time into space, the sax player into humankind, and the three sidemen into other taxa—making the piano, say, the nonhuman animals, the bass the plants, the drum set a catch-all for fungi, protoctists, and bacteria—you get a lesson in how humans can work with nature. For humans to thrive, even the most humanized spaces must be inoculated with other species. Wildness, like swing, must flow through all things. But for other species to thrive, they must have some spaces to themselves: spaces from which humans discreetly withdraw, excuse, or recuse themselves, "lay out."

The leader of a jazz group takes a bird's-eye view of its music. On some level, he is aware of the sounds each player is making. That awareness shapes his own playing, which in turn nudges the others' in sundry ways. But he does not try to make each note that is played fit some preset scheme.

All life plays variations on the same few chord changes. Each taxon improvises, following certain rules but obeying no predetermined destiny. Each responds to the riffing, comping, noodling and vamping of those around it. Life makes itself up as it goes along. Withal, a certain unity emerges that no one has willed.

Now, it might be objected that jazz is only a small part of the world's music. Since it grew up on a few small patches of the earth's surface—the Mississippi River valley, the stockyards of Chicago, the steel cliffs of Manhattan Island—how can it claim to shed light on the relations of humans and nature in other places?

Jazz is not just any music but a mongrel of splendid pedigree. It is an urban music with deep rural roots. Its rhythms arise from the juxtaposition of chicken coops and locomotives, of bayous and steel mills, of tenements and penthouses. Most of all, it springs from the meeting of Africa and Europe—the tree where man was born, and the axe that would take it down—on the soil of a new world.

Another reason jazz fits the bill is that it is a music of exile. Born of the African diaspora, it gives voice to our nomadic urges as well as our longing for a home. The bedrock of jazz is the blues—a music of yearning, of anger, of dashed hopes that (like the twelve-bar form itself) always spring back. The blues are born of exile, oppression, and shattered love. While these are the special condition of the African-American, they are also, in a broader sense, the state of all humans outside Eden.

For modern people, maybe for all people, earth jazz begins with earth blues. Until you have felt in your bones what it is to be a species that cannot help but change the world—a species that in making its paradise unmakes Eden—your attempts at a joyful, playful dialogue with nature are bound to ring hollow. Until you have sat down and wept by the rivers of Babylon, you will not discover that they, too, flow from Eden. When you do make that discovery, the Lord's song will rise in your throat unbidden.

Jamming with the Goddess

"It don't mean a thing if it ain't got that swing"—Ellington's dictum fits earth jazz, too. What is swing? Pedants have gone gray trying to define it. For our purposes, we can think of it as a kind of suppleness, a looseness far more exact than mere exactness. To swing, one must be aware of the rhythms behind the rhythm. In nature, this means the chaos behind apparent order, and the order behind apparent chaos. A rhythm in jazz is like the coastline of Maine: no single measurement is possible—as you look closer, new convolutions appear. A good jazz solo can never be notated: you can get down to the level of dotted hemidemisemiquavers and still know that further layers of complexity lurk just beneath. Biologists trying to describe or model a natural system often get the same feeling. And Ralph Ellison may have had the same feeling about social systems when—using a Louis Armstrong record as his jumping-off point—he said of "invisibility": "You're never quite on the beat. And you slip into the breaks and look around."

We do not swing. Our science, our lifestyles are rigid. We deal with nature now as one who carries a mug of coffee in his right hand and a book wedged between his right elbow and his side. The arm is locked rigidly against the body, there is no give, the coffee sloshes wildly with every step. No wonder we lose so much.

How do you collaborate with Gaia if you don't know exactly how she works, or what she wants? You do it, I think, by playing earth jazz. You improvise. You are flexible and responsive. You work on a small scale and are ready to change direction at the drop of a hat. You encourage diversity, giving each player—human or nonhuman—as much room as possible to stretch out. You trade fours with the goddess: play four bars, listen to her response, respond, listen, respond. True, sometimes her response may not be clear for centuries. But then no one said this would be easy.

At any rate, it may be easier to accept our exile from Eden—and the need to intensify that exile, in a sense, by stepping back and giving Eden more elbow room—if we see it as the premise of a creative give-and-take. The music of Eden may have been gorgeous beyond our fluffiest dreams, but whatever it was it was not earth jazz. In that tangle of world and self, trading fours was not an option. Without difference, without distance, there is no dialogue.

Midnight at the Oasis

Jazzmen trade fours; shepherds in pastoral trade sixes, swapping hexameters in friendly strife. Both practices may go back to the games of real shepherds. While the static ideal of Arcadia may be a mirage, some of its ancient habits—of playful riffing, of shifting boundaries, of discord deftly harmonized—can serve us surprisingly well. Panpipes or saxophones, the basic point is the same.

Let me give some examples of missing the point and of getting the point. In the Sonoran Desert of Arizona, there is a place the Papago Indians call A'al Waipia where sweetwater springs trickle into a small pond, inciting a riot of green in a world of gray. For thousands of years, A'al Waipia was the site of Indian settlements. As late as 1957, Papago irrigation ditches fed more than a dozen acres of crops and orchards.

In that year, the National Park Service moved in. As one of the few true desert oases in North America, A'al Waipia had to be protected. With the connivance of an Indian who claimed title to the land, the Park Service summarily condemned the fields and buildings. The oasis was returned to its natural state so that its full value as a refuge of flora and fauna could be realized.

Things have not turned out quite as planned. Each year, the oasis looks less like an oasis. Each year, it loses plants and animals. When the ethnobotanist Gary Nabhan visited A'al Waipia in the early 1980s, not only had the fruit trees died; so had most of the "wild" trees. Only three cottonwoods remained, and only four willows. Summer annuals, too, were scarce. A survey Nabhan undertook with the help of ornithologists at three different times of year found a total of thirty-two bird species at A'al Waipia. At a similar oasis in the Mexican Sonora, the scientists found over sixty-five.

The Mexican oasis, known to the Papago as Ki:towak, is only thirty miles from A'al Waipia, but its aspect is very different. Resplendent with palms, cottonwoods, willows, elderberry, salt cedar, date, pomegranate, and fig; verdant in summer with squash, watermelon, beans, and other crops, and with wild greens coaxed forth by plowing and irrigation; its ditches rife with Olney's tule, the edible bulrush from which the oasis takes its name, Ki:towak offers plenty of food and shelter for teal, white-faced ibis, and dozens of other birds A'al Waipia no longer sees. For this is a cultivated oasis—cultivated in the thrifty, painstaking Papago way—just as A'al Waipia was before the Park Service arrived.

Nabhan quotes a Papago farmer: "When people live and work in a place, and plant their seeds and water their trees, the birds go live with them. They like those places, there's plenty to eat and that's when we are friends to them."[1]

Of course, I share the Park Service's presumption that ecologically sensitive places should be left wild or allowed to go wild whenever possible. But when indigenous people have been living in a place for thousands of years, chances are the "wild" things in that place have coevolved with them. Pulling them out of the ecological structure (if indeed we have the right to do so in the first place) may cause its collapse. A park service schooled in earth jazz would be flexible enough to avoid such an error, or at least to correct it once its effects become clear. Unfortunately, by the time the actual Park Service concedes this specific error, it may be too late, as there may be very few traditional Papago farmers left.

Avoiding the Nantucket Sleigh Ride

Similar problems arise when we think about "resource use." In the past couple of centuries, planet managers have convinced themselves that they know how to manage nature "sustainably." Scientists study a given renewable "resource"—fir, cod, what have you—and arrive at a consensus as to its growth rate, recovery rate, and so on. They determine the "maximum sustained yield"—the harvest that loggers or fishermen should be able to take every year, year after year, for all eternity—and the government sets its limits accordingly.

The only problem with this system is that it almost never works. For all the sophistication of their computer models, scientists have only the vaguest idea of what is going on in the woods and still less of what is going on under the water. The manifold factors that make fisheries, for instance, surge or ebb in cockeyed cycles—prey and predators, climate and currents, toxins and dams and a hundred things not yet identified—ensure that consensus stays slippery. Controlled, reproducible experiments are out of the question. With so much wriggle room, industry can always find scientists who will testify that a higher yield would be just fine, and politicians who will believe them. Even limits set in good faith tend to put too much faith in the compliance of fishing fleets. Worse, they put too much faith in the compliance of the fish themselves. If their population has been stable for several years, it is trusted to stay stable.

You might think that if a maximum sustained yield started to look unsustainable, it would be revised downward. In fact, just the opposite happens. What economists call a "ratchet effect" takes hold. In good years, extra boats go out and extra processing plants get built. But in the lean years that inevitably follow, those boats and plants are not put in dry dock or shut down. Instead industry looks to the government, which responds with subsidies of one kind or another. Boats are kept afloat, relentlessly fishing an ever dwindling fishery. More often than not, the net effect—seen in recent years in herring, cod, ocean perch, salmon, lake trout, sardine, anchoveta, and many other stocks—is collapse.

A society attuned to earth jazz would not let itself get locked into such patterns. Its scientists, knowing their own fallibility, would recommend limits below those that their computers spat out. They would be ready to revise them downward at the first sign of decline—that is, at the first sign not masked by the froth of natural variation—and would revise them upward only by small degrees. Policy makers, knowing a thing or two about human nature, would assume that the scientists knew even less than they said they knew. Nor would they wait for perfect consensus before taking action. They would hedge their bets and make their policies as supple and reversible as possible. Enlisting the help of business and labor, they would evade the grip of the ratchet effect by diversifying local economies and spreading risk. In such a society, communities would not be hostage to the leaping and diving of a single resource like whalemen on a Nantucket sleigh ride—a ride that ends in the destruction of one party or both. But the society as a whole would ride the waves of nature's changes, and humankind's.

Pick Your Eden

Whether we like it or not, the world culture of the near future will be, in large part, American. Both the best and the worst in American culture will be represented: the only question is, in what proportions? By speaking of earth jazz, I am trying to apply the greatest product of American culture to the greatest problem the world faces. It is not an answer to the problem, of course. Even to call it a model is stretching things a bit. When you come right down to the nitty-gritty of farming, industry, and the making of cities and villages, each region needs to work out its own answers. But as each of us hoes our own row (or nonrow, as the case may be), jazz may give us inspiration.

What seems at first glance to be vagueness may prove useful. Most visions of humankind's place in nature fail, I think, because they mark out too specific a place. One visionary likes the medieval city, another the nineteenth-century farming village, a third the desert Pueblo. It might make a good parlor game: "Pick Your Eden." The hunter-gatherer band; the Neolithic village; the putatively matrifocal culture of Old Europe; the "wild gardening" of South and Central American Indians; the "Old Planting Culture" of the South Seas; the elaborate mixed farming of East Asia; the wind-and-water technology of early modern Europe. . . . Each of these has been somebody's pick, and none has been everybody's.

While each Eden may have something to teach us, none can begin to address the wide range of problems we face. Worse, each makes the mistake of being an Eden—a world made whole, once and for all. Better, I think, to accept the exile from Eden, with all the division and instability that is its baggage. Better to take as your model not a thing, time-and-place, or state of affairs, but a process.

Rather than be hostage of my own tastes, I start with the rock-bottom fact—a fact shaped only slightly by my tastes—that we need wilderness. We need it not only for our psychological well-being (at least, this seems likely) but for sheer biological survival. The question then is, What is our proper relation to wilderness? How can we keep it alive, when our natural tendency is to overrun or smother it? Should we live in it, supposing that were logically possible? Should we live *like* it—use it, that is, as a template for our manmade world? If we cannot live exactly like it—if the manmade world has some rules of its own—how can we continue to enjoy the boons it confers on us and on all other creatures?

In seeking answers to these questions, I have tried to skirt the problems that cling to particular Edens by choosing a model that is not a place or a time or a kind of relation between humans and nature but something else entirely: a kind of music. Something else entirely—it is, after all, on a different ontological plane—but not something unrelated. For it seems to me that music, of all the arts, has the most to say about the relation of humans and nature. Music describes the workings of nature (including humans) at a level deeper than any particular landscape—deeper but not more abstract. It works on a different plane than the real world, but on its own plane it is just as specific and just as exact. That is why it can mirror some things in the real world more exactly than language, which is confined to the same plane as the real world and is constantly banging into the wrong things. Music, by contrast, shares the vast sonic plane with a fairly narrow set of natural sounds readily audible by humans. It has infinite space for maneuver, infinite shades of nuance.

Because of this, and because the vast ocean of the world's music is fed by rivulets from every landscape and every culture, music has something to say about the relation between humans and nature on every inhabited inch of the earth's surface. In this way it avoids the twin perils of vagueness on the one side and limited applicability on the other that afflict more literal models.

A model is not worth much unless it can serve, somewhere down the line, as a guide to action. So let us look at a specific, detailed example of earth jazz—in what we might call an acoustic, that is to say pre-industrial, style.

Gardening the Amazon

Anthropology is peculiar among the sciences in that its most out-of-date books are generally its best. The first, stumbling practitioners were the last to get a good look at the objects of study. It is as if the solar system had begun to disintegrate during the lifetimes of Galileo and Kepler and by Einstein's time consisted of the earth, the sun, and a cloud of dust.

Unfortunately, the first anthropologists did not take "primitive" farming very seriously. Its rituals, its "magic," the social roles it involved, the strange beliefs it seemed to imply—these were intriguing. Its efficacy, though, was presumed to be negligible when compared with that of modern agriculture.

For example, the most common agriculture of the rain forest, swidden or shifting cultivation, was long regarded as crude and wasteful. Its common name, "slash-and-burn," became a synonym for shortsighted mayhem. Only in the 1950s and 1960s, with the work of Conklin and Rappaport, did ethnographers begin to see just how deft a method swidden could be. New subtleties are even now coming to light, notably in Darryl Posey's studies of the Gorotire Kayapo.

The Kayapo are a fierce and ancient people who once roamed and ruled a portion of the Amazon Basin as large as France. Though their lands have been eaten away by ranches and plantations, they now live in a proposed reserve of some five million acres, which includes grassland and savanna as well as rain forest. A few generations ago, the Kayapo were seminomadic; the entire tribe would trek for six to eight months, relying only on wild foods. Though they are now settled in villages, they still go on frequent hunting and foraging trips—including treks of two or three weeks—and spend several months of each year living in Brazil-nut groves.

In clearing a plot of forest for a garden, the men in each family fell the largest trees standing near the center of the plot in such a way that they topple outward, bringing smaller trees down with them. The result is a circle of just under an acre, constellated like a wheel. Great tree trunks radiate from the center: toward the circumference is a tangle of branches and leafage.

While all this biomass is baking in the sun, getting ready for burning, the women find their way through the outer tangle and into the open lanes between the trunks. Here they do something that textbook slash-and-burn gardeners do not do: they plant about a quarter of their root crops *before the burn*. When the fire does come, the root systems of these yams, sweet potatoes, taro, and manioc will be ready to suck up the flush of nutrients it lets loose. Moreover, they will have a jump on the weed seeds that will also want a share of that bonanza.

A slow burn is the ideal. Moving from one pile of debris to the next, the Kayapo may take the better part of a day to burn a single plot. This way, the heat is kept low and the roots of the crops already planted are not damaged.

A few days later, when the ashes have cooled, the women plant the rest of the root crops. A week or so after that, the men gather the branches and twigs that have not been thoroughly burned, make piles, and set them alight. In the ashes the women plant beans, squash, melons, and other plants that are particularly hungry for nutrients. The staggered planting helps ensure a staggered harvest: a good thing where food storage is difficult.

Now the plot looks less like a wheel than like an archery target. Allowing for variations that take advantage of the plot's various soil types, the crops are mainly arranged in concentric rings. In the outer ring, which is richest in nutrients because it is where most of the foliage fell, papaya, bananas, cotton, *urucu*, tobacco, and beans thrive. The next ring is manioc, the next corn and rice. In the center are sweet potatoes and yams.

After a few seasons, this garden will no longer be planted. But it will not be "abandoned"—not in the textbook sense. True, it will be allowed to revert to forest. But it will remain useful to the Kayapo for decades. Though corn and rice disappear, sweet potatoes and yams keep bearing for four or five years, bananas and urucu for eight to twelve years, *kupa* for thirty or forty years. The volunteer plants that begin the process of succession include fruit trees, palms, and medicinal herbs. They also include berries that attract birds and other wildlife that the Kayapo like to hunt.

Once they are planted, the gardens will pretty much go of themselves. They have few pest problems, mainly because they are so small and widely scattered—in time and space—that large concentrations of pests can't build up. They can be left alone for months, and at later stages for years, which means they are well suited to a seminomadic (or hemiseminomadic) lifestyle. They can be visited and picked from during treks.

These gardens give high yields for very little work. In the balance sheet of calories invested against calories returned, they are triumphantly in the black: far more so than most modern fields. They also improve the soil of the rain forest. In fact, the "Indian black soil" found in certain places is aptly named, since it may well be an Indian creation. This, too, contradicts the textbooks, which tell us that swidden gardens lose their fertility after a year or two.

But then a question arises. If old plots are still fertile, why don't the Kayapo keep planting them? Why walk three or four hours to new gardens when you can replant old gardens that are just fifteen minutes away? In three or four years, admittedly, the nutrients released by the burn would be used up. But then why not do a new burn in a ten-year-old garden instead of waiting twenty years as the Kayapo do?

The reason has already been hinted at. Old fields that are returning to forest are full of plants directly useful to the Kayapo, as well as berries, fruits, and browse that attract birds and mammals. The latter factor may be the key. For all its abundance, the rain forest is not rich in meat. (That is why almost no pure hunter-gatherers live there.) The more widely the old gardens are dispersed, the greater the pool of game on which they can draw.

Resource Islands

The Kayapo have learned to play the forest's own game, and win. Yet the forest does not lose. While parts of the ecosystem are changed to meet the people's needs, the changes are subtle—so subtle that Western eyes can hardly detect them. The structural principles of the forest are respected, and the ecosystem as a whole keeps its integrity.

The contrast with modern agriculture, as practiced in the ranches and plantations that are carved out of the Kayapo's ancient lands, could not be more striking. Instead of an acre, thousands of acres are cleared at once. Deprived of the forest's parasol, the fragile soil is baked by the sun. Organic matter breaks down rapidly and is soon leached or washed away by the heavy rains. The rains also wash away the soil itself or pound it until it is hard as brick. In the space of a few years, forest has turned to desert.

Subtle as their swidden gardens are, the Kayapo have even subtler ways of playing the forest's game. Along their ancient paths through the forest, often near streamside campsites worn flat and hard with centuries of use, are patches of forest preternaturally rich in food plants. They did not get that way naturally (or rather, they did, if one grants that humans are part of nature). In these places, roots, tubers, stalks, and fruits foraged from the forest nearby have been replanted to form "resource islands." For a Kayapo it is second nature to replant an unfinished bit of food near where he shits.

Nor is it only the forest's game that the Kayapo play. In the *campo* (grassland) and *cerrado* (savanna) that are part of their range, and where for reasons of health they like to site their villages, there are islands of forest known as *apete*. These are much more common near the villages than elsewhere. At first glance, these patches of forest seem natural. Only recently have anthropologists caught on to the fact that some three-quarters of them are manmade. The Kayapo make them by building compost piles from branches and leaves, inoculating the compost with bits of ant and termite nests, planting trees they find especially useful, and then allowing "natural" afforestation to take over. After a few decades, this process can result in an apete as big as ten acres.

When Posey and a colleague collected 140 species of plants from apete near Gorotire, they learned that 138 of them were considered useful by the Kayapo and 84 had been deliberately planted. Besides serving as supermarkets, the islands are used as shelters in time of war and epidemic, as refuges from the midday sun, as studios for body painting, as playgrounds, and as motels for trysting lovers.

Formerly, it was believed that the only way indigenous peoples managed the savanna was by burning, to keep it open and encourage the growth of fresh grass. The

Kayapo do burn the campo, and one reason is to get fresh grass that will draw game. The other reason, though, is not to discourage trees but to encourage the growth and fruiting of certain fire-loving trees.

Naturally, the Kayapo's ways of playing with nature have stimulated new thought about the beginnings of farming. Most scholars have assumed that people would have to be settled in one place before the domestication of plants could get started. But the Kayapo (and other peoples lately studied) show us forms of semidomestication that mesh deftly with a seminomadic way of life. Indeed, if you could shield your eyes from the slash-and-burn farming on which they have lately come to depend more heavily, and look only at their ways of moving and manipulating "wild" plants, you might think you had found the missing link between gathering and gardening.

The irony is dense: the Amazon Basin, the one place on earth where nature and culture are most fiercely at odds, is also the place where the distinction between them comes to seem a fiction, thin as mist. But many other forms of wild gardening can be found in many other parts of the world.

Signposts in the Forest

To be sure, indigenous farming is not always good farming. Slash-and-burn, for example, is not always done as well as the Kayapo do it. Where population pressures are too great, fallow periods are often too short and patches too close together. In tropical Africa, the forest fallow has been largely abandoned in favor of a much shorter grass fallow. In such cases, the forest is destroyed more slowly but just as surely as it would be destroyed by Western farming. Nor are Western incursions always to blame. Misuse of swidden in Africa seems to have started in prehistory, shortly after the practice was introduced from Asia. Scientists have found that sickle-cell anemia occurs mainly in those parts of Africa where slash-and-burn farming is an ancient practice. The reason is that having a single, recessive gene for sickle cell is a defense against malaria. Where malaria is common, the gene is favored, even though people who have the bad luck to have two of them become anemic. Malaria is common in places where bad swiddening has caused compaction of the soil, creating pools of standing water that are maternity wards for mosquitoes.

Peoples that have lived in the same place for a long time without ruining it are not "natural." They are smart and they are lucky. And because they have lived in the same place for a long time, they have been able to fine-tune their dealings with nature. No primitive people that is still around today can really be primitive. All have thousands of years of trial and error under their belts. In many cases, they have had the same basic technology for centuries, which has allowed them to work out many of the kinks—the places where technology rubbed the wrong way against nature, or against people, or against itself. From this point of view, it is we who are primitive.

But non-Western societies have not always been models of ecological rectitude. The collapse of the Maya seven centuries before Cortés may have been caused largely by the felling of trees to fuel the fires in which they made lime stucco for their vast monuments. The volcanic highlands of Central Mexico seem to have lost soil at least as rapidly to pre-Columbian farming as they would when the Spaniards brought the plow. An animistic sense of oneness with nature did not prevent the Maoris from deforesting much of New Zealand and clubbing into extinction its flightless moas. The much-admired nature religion of the North American Plains Indians did not stop them from overhunting the buffalo as soon as they got horses and rifles. Nor did believing that Buddha-mind was in all things prevent Chinese monks from shaving the mountains to feed their funeral pyres. Asian medicine, with its shamanistic faith in animal powers, has brought the Siberian tiger, the Bengal tiger, the Asian bear, the black rhinoceros, and a host of other noble beasts to the brink of oblivion. Meanwhile the same culture that gave us Zen ink drawings is erasing with quick strokes many of the world's last forests, importing almost four times as much timber as any other country.

Suppose we grant, then, that non-Western peoples are not always perfect. Surely we have much to learn from those who, like the Kayapo, do certain things supremely well. Why not take the wild garden as our model?

We may do so, but with a grain of salt. In its purest forms, the wild garden is well suited to people whose wants are modest, whose tools are simple, and who are thinly scattered across the relatively wild terrain. Most of us do not fit that description. The wild garden takes us closer to Eden than we can wisely go.

Our way of learning from nature has to be more abstract; the systems we model on natural systems have to be more concentrated, less mixed up with the extant natural systems themselves. Since we can't trust ourselves to be as smart as the Kayapo—or rather, as much smarter than the Kayapo as our greater numbers and power would require—we had better mess with wilderness as little as possible. Jumping back to our basic metaphor, we might put it this way: our kind of earth jazz has to have a harder edge. If the Kayapo play a kind of New Orleans shuffle, the parts seamlessly bobbing and weaving, what we have to play is more like hard bop. The ideal would be to use our solo space—farms, gardens, factories—as boldly and economically as the Sonny Rollins of the mid-1950s used his.

Even so, we have much to learn from the Kayapo and their peers. Their paths are not our paths; but in the green depths of their paths are signs that may point our way.

NOTE

1   Gary Paul Nabhan, *The Desert Smells Like Rain: A Naturalist in Papago Indian Country* (San Francisco: North Point Press, 1982), p. 96.

DAMIEN ARABAGALI

16 on our taboos they trampled

(as told to Herbert Paulzen)

Damien Arabagali, a community leader in Toroba, north of Tari on Papua New Guinea, is one of the first generation of modern educated Huli. His grandfather was a Big Man (the traditional name for a man of sterling character—a warrior, magician, or orator; still called Big Men, they play a significant role in leading the tribes that lack a chief of their own).

Arabagali has written several essays about the changes his traditional society has undergone, and he has recently completed a book-length manuscript on the relation between the imported Christian religion and the Huli society. Arabagali often acts as mediator in conflicts involving material damage as a result of gold mining and oil and gas exploration.

In the Tari Basin in the Southern Highlands Province of Papua New Guinea, in a swampland area surrounded by dramatic limestone cliffs and bush-covered mountains, live the Huli people.

The Huli are one of the largest language groups of Papua New Guinea. Before the coming of the first white men some fifty years ago, there were about 150,000 Huli, divided into numerous tribes and clans. They were linked by many customs and trading relationships. They also had a common form of worship, centered on sacred places. They lived in what they themselves call "a perfect state of harmony" with their environment. As Arabagali notes, much of the traditional way of life has broken down since contact with white men in the 1950s and 1960s. The activities of missionaries not only destroyed aspects of the traditional spiritual way of life but also caused major damage to the natural and cultural environment.

The colonial administration fragmented the Huli "nation" with its new boundaries. The confrontation with the outside world has sped up since Papua New Guinea's independence in 1975. Now the area is the center of major oil, gas, and gold exploration that is likely to have a serious environmental impact.

The creation of the Earth started with the eruption of a volcano on the sun. Stones were thrown throughout the universe. One of the stones became the Earth. That's what our ancestors told us. Our belief tells us that the trees were created first on Earth. Then the Earth was populated by spirits, and the spirits became human beings. The environment we have lived in since is like a chain. The sun, the stars, the trees, the pigs, the birds, and all other creatures and men are all part of that chain, all interrelated. We all belong to the universe. We are offspring of the sun. We live in a spiritual world.

From the time of our ancestors, we had found complete unity and continuity. That is why nature has always been very much praised in all our traditional ceremonies. Our tribes and clans and families are all linked to other creatures, like eagles, pigs, or trees, or directly to the sun.

In sacred places we worshipped the spirits—in special forests, at special trees, on special lakes. In some places of worship we have found round stones, which we call the eggs of the sun.

No one, except our priests who had special knowledge of the spirits, was allowed to enter the sacred sites. We were not allowed to hunt there, to wander around, cut trees. We used to call these sites our heavens, because certain huge trees were used by our ancestors to go up—they followed the birds that flew in the direction of the opening in the sky.

There was complete harmony with nature in those sacred areas. Each tribe had such a place, and that place was protected by many taboos.

But not only in such places was there harmony. Rules regulated all our relations with our environment. Young trees and fruit trees were never cut. Herbal plants and trees that provided us with medicine were always protected. Certain animals were never killed. Dogs, cats, lizards, and possums were even regarded as brothers. All natural resources, like salt, oil, shining stones, and crystal, had special meanings for us. We used them to trade with our neighboring tribes or to decorate ourselves.

Every area was divided among tribal groups. And every tribal group used the land according to the traditional relationship with nature. Gardens were set apart from the hunting grounds. Only hardwood was used for building our houses. Hardwood and wood from fruit trees and of course from our sacred trees were never used for firewood. There was complete harmony between human beings and animals and nature. Men, birds, and spirits were especially interrelated. The survival of each was dependent on the other. That balance was a guarantee for survival. Continual and numerous ceremonies kept that relationship alive. Men never stood above nature. Each community felt part of the environment. The community sense was very strong. Everybody had his accepted place in that community.

But then the white men came, and the oneness of the community came face to face with an individual approach, which was completely alien to us. The "I" became the central point. The "others" became stepping-stones. "I" had to survive, "I" had to be independent, "I" had to decide for "myself." Very soon, the result of all that became clear: we call it greed.

A great confusion fell on our people. Our old men were watching and listening to the first white men very closely. How they ate, how they slept, what they did, and how they did it. The old men remembered the prophecies of our ancestors about the coming of the white men. Our people found the first missionaries very interesting. They gave them pigs to sacrifice. That was what our people always did. Priests had to sacrifice pigs to make the soil rich and fertile, the hunting abundant, and the weather favorable. But these white priests asked: "Why?" They did not accept the sacrifices and told our people that we were no longer allowed to do that.

Soon we were affected by all kinds of illnesses that we had never known before. Fighting broke out—more than we had known traditionally. There was complete confusion and disorientation. Our traditional places of worship were destroyed. The harmony disappeared. Trees that had been protected for centuries by our traditional laws and customs were felled. Sawmills were introduced. Pine trees in our special sacred places were cut to build mission houses. Our sacred places were called evil. Our trees were cut and dragged away, even out of the country, and these trees were never replanted. In this way, the missionaries contributed directly to the destruction of nature. We were also confronted with forced labor to construct roads that went straight through many of our sacred places, through mushroom areas, through hunting grounds, through breeding places of birds, through gardens. Along these roads Western-style buildings were constructed, so more and more timber was used.

New roads and airstrips in remote areas opened up the country, which had been isolated and cut off by tribal boundaries and taboos for generations. This brought together people who had been enemies before. That might have been a good thing, but this development caught us unprepared for the many abrupt changes in social life it brought with it.

Many of the traditional ways of life, especially religious, have broken down since the first contact with the white men in the 1950s and 1960s. The activities of the Christian missionaries not only destroyed aspects of our traditional spiritual way of life but also caused major damage to the natural and cultural environment. The colonial administration fragmented our people with new district boundaries.

Of all these impacts, the destruction of the sacred places by the missionaries is felt by many of us to have been the most serious. It has led to general outrage. All the magnificent stands of pines and other forest preserves that marked these sites have been cut down and sold to mission sawmills. The white men have taken our timber to build schools and hospitals but above all to build their own high-quality homes. Of course there have been protests, but the signatures of the leaders of our people on petitions have brought no response from the new provincial government or the missionaries directing these acts.

With the opening up of new areas, new values we did not understand came in. Taboos were trampled on. There was an enormous impact on our traditional system and on the discipline of our youth. There was a rush to the plantations on the coast. There, our people were faced with a whole set of new ideas, and when they came back to our communities they brought these new ideas with them. They returned to their homesteads with a different language and a different authority. The old values became vague. Conflicts, unthinkable before, arose between generations, between those who stuck to custom and those who were influenced by the customs of the white men.

Complete confusion! The elders did not understand all this. Their world changed under their very eyes and they could not stop it. Many were not able to cope with all those changes. The disruption of social life had really started and there was no return.

In traditional society, each person had a special role. Now it became the survival of the fittest instead. I, I, I, me, me, me—"I" can step on everybody to get what "I" want.

People tried to move beyond their limitations. The young felt more attracted by the wealth of the white men: axes, clothes, money. Especially money. Money changed our subsistence economy, and money became the road to all evil. The individualism brought in by the Europeans has not fully taken root yet; there's still a community aspect. But the traditional sharing of wealth is changing rapidly nowadays, especially among the better educated of our people.

The old sense of interrelation, the old traditional ways of respect and discipline . . . all that is vanishing. Look what we learn at school now. It's irrelevant. How to become a European!

No longer the sense of belonging to the group. No longer the feeling of going back to the land. The dream of many now is to go abroad, run after money. Get rich fast! Become somebody fast!

But look what is happening all over the country. The educated can't find jobs. They loiter around in towns and cities, frustrated, undisciplined. They become lawbreakers and create a safety problem everywhere, making traveling on our new roads dangerous, making walking about dangerous, which causes the police to shoot our own people, the foreigners to leave, the law-abiding citizens to hide themselves behind barbed-wire fences.

It's giving our young nation a bad name in the papers of the world. I think there's still a chance to stop that downward road and stop the destruction of the environment. Bring back discipline. Young people should come again to listen to our tribal leaders. Young people should be taught the traditional ways before going to modern schools. And those schools should be more land-oriented. Our young people should learn at school how to respect our nature, how to plant and protect trees, how to grow vegetables, how to look after drinking places, how to build their own houses, how to be a carpenter, how to be a farmer. Practical lessons. Relevant for rural areas. So there will always be a basis to return to. Education has to return to the land. Education has to be in harmony with the environment.

The system is here but no longer used. The government does not seem to see that. There should be more cooperation and coordination between government departments like forestry, public works, education. The school system should stop producing losers. Stop telling people: "If you fail, you are rubbish." That is why our old people think that school is a waste of time and money.

The future is in the hands of our present-day leaders. I, a Huli, want to contribute to the future. Now we have reached the turning point. If we find the right breed of leaders now, we might be able to stop the corruption that is standing in the way of real development. If not, our country will be running down the road to ruin. And once started, there will be no way to stop it. Today's situation is like a time bomb.

But there's still a chance. There are still grounds for hope and optimism. Somehow we have to find an improvement in life along the lines of our own roots and culture. There has to be unity. But we don't have peace now, and while there's no peace in this country we cannot achieve anything.

Unfortunately we don't know how to achieve peace. There's so much confusion, even right within my own group. How can we find the balance between Western and traditional values?

Is the Earth sick? Yes. Our ancestors prophesied that we would see the Earth turn sick. When the *kunai* grass in the swamps dries up. When we dig gardens where the pine trees used to grow. When the wild *pandanus* trees disappear. When the birds fly away. When the pigs and the children get smaller. When women have children who no longer look like their fathers. This is happening here. We are heading for a period when this land will say, "I can't produce anymore." Our land has been reused and reused. It can no longer reproduce. "I have had enough," says the Earth.

It looks like now is the beginning of a period of mass starvation. I see it before my eyes. The giant trees are disappearing. That is a sign. Look at our gardens. They are smaller than they used to be when I was young. Before, we could live from our gardens. Now these same gardens don't sustain us anymore. The gardens are worn out. We don't allow the land to refertilize because of the demands of our growing population.

The same with our forests. We need more and more material, for more houses, more roads, more factories. Land and forests don't get rest. And there's no more land to prepare. And because there are fewer and fewer trees, the rain washes the soil away. The time is fast approaching when our gardens will say, "Sorry, my friends, we can't produce anymore."

On our land lie mountains of gold. These mountains used to be covered with forests. Our people went there hunting for birds and wild pigs, and they used to gather nuts and herbs and mushrooms. From the mountains flowed many rivers that provided us with water to drink and water to fish in.

Look at what is happening now, since geologists discovered the hidden wealth of those mountains, and the government and the companies realized what this could mean to them. Mining started, regardless of what those mountains were to us. Greed brought our own people to dig in the ground in search of gold. Trees were cut. Big multinational mining companies brought up huge machines by helicopter and started drilling. Chemicals and other dirt started dripping into the waters of the rivers and into the ground. All kinds of waste are being dumped into the environmental system.

People drink from the water; people wash in the water, polluted water. Soon the pollution will enter their own systems and will stay there for generations to come. Not to mention the impact the mining has on our social life—the disruption of family life, the breakdown of morale, the use of alcohol, the fighting, the prostitution.

Now our people are complaining. There's no compensation for the destruction and damage to vegetation. All those trees and ferns and herbs that our people used to eat are gone. The area has been cleared. Slopes have been washed away. What will remain is a skeleton of nature.

We sacrifice the region and the environment for ten or fifteen years of development. But scars for millions of years to come will remain.

And who is benefiting right now? Not our local tribes. Not the local areas. It's not we who are able to benefit from the fruits of those mines. Nor our future generations. The money that is earned now by all that large-scale mining leaves the area and disappears into the hands of companies and institutions we cannot control. That money disappears quickly, but the scars remain, never to recover. All these places are being raped.

Our communities and environment are suffering from a development that does not benefit the local people. Oh yes, it's true, hospitals and schools are being built, and jobs are created. These are positive elements for sure. But if you take a closer look, then you see cheap labor and exploitation. The price we pay for a damaged environment is too high. We sacrifice our nature for quick money. Our leaders are selling out our land. Our natural richness is being plundered. We do not profit. And what remains are wounds that never heal. Is that development? And after that? Misery for our people. Pollution caused by chemicals has already killed pigs and even people. How many more will suffer?

It could be different. We could do the mining ourselves. Step by step. In a responsible way, with concern for the environment.

The white man sees man as the highest creature in the hierarchy. We see man as a link in the chain. And the chain is broken. Of course man is an important creature. But he is also responsible. If he is, according to the white man, the highest creature, man should also bear the highest responsibility. Animals, trees, birds, nature—they all have rights also.

I think Nature will pay back the disrespect shown to her. Look around you! It's becoming hotter, drier, more eroded. Here, in Huli country, people are hiding from the sun. They never used to do that before. The land is more barren than ever before. That's why people have to work harder. Look how skinny they are! And because of all this clearing of our forests we have floods, which we never had before. We see it here. Our fertile swamps, where we plant our *kaukau* and our sweet potatoes, they are drying out. Soon there will be no more swamps. What then? What's the cause of all this? I think it's greed. Something in humanity must be evil in itself. The ruthlessness and selfishness in a struggle for survival. The institutional organizations, big companies, and corporate bodies have become dehumanized. Profits at all costs, regardless of what that leaves behind.

I think it's still not too late. We still have a chance, if the proper leaders show their responsibility. But, of course, it's not a concern of leaders alone. The peoples of the world should rise up together—arm in arm—and act according to their responsibility for the Earth. The world should come together for the just cause. We must fight for the survival of our human society. We must fight together.

My people are naive. We, leaders and future leaders, have to make them aware of what is happening around them. And not only we, here in Huli land, but everywhere in our country, in the entire outside world. The time is ripe for a worldwide appeal. We should abandon our isolation here. We should be more connected, have more relationship to individuals and organizations and politicians and environmentalists from all around the world.

United, we should be able to pinpoint what and who is causing the most environmental damage, throughout the world. Information should be passed on about what is going on and where it is going on and who is doing what. And from that information action should be taken. We have to! We have to be aware about our survival. We have to think of our children. The language of action has to be spoken. A world environmental body should be set up, a global organization, an independent organization. Companies and governments that want to exploit natural resources should be obliged to hire independent environmental specialists. The advice of these independent specialists should be followed, not that of the so-called experts who are hired by the companies themselves.

I think if the United Nations takes responsibility for war to protect the interests of oil companies, then the United Nations has the responsibility to protect the environment of the nations of the Earth.

about the contributors

DAMIEN ARABAGALI is a community leader in Toroba, north of Tari on Papua New Guinea.

WILLIAM W. BEVIS is a professor of English at the University of Montana.

PHILIP CAFARO is a former ranger for the U.S. Park Service. He teaches philosophy at Colorado State University in Fort Collins, Colorado.

ANTONIO CARLOS DIEGUES is a lecturer at the University of São Paulo-Brazil.

EVAN EISENBERG has worked as a synagogue cantor, a music critic for *The Nation*, and a gardener for the New York City parks department. He is the author of *The Recording Angel* (McGraw-Hill, 1986) and *The Ecology of Eden* (Knopf, 1998).

KATHLEEN HARRISON is an ethnobotanist who studies the relationships between plants and humans, particularly as expressed in ritual and story.

DAN IMHOFF is a freelance writer who focuses on issues of design, the environment, and agriculture. He lives in northern California with his wife and two children.

VANCE G. MARTIN is president of the WILD Foundation, in Ojai, California.

ZEESE PAPANIKOLAS teaches cultural history and writing at the San Francisco Art Institute. His most recent book is *Trickster in the Land of Dreams* (University of Nebraska Press, 1995).

PRAMOD PARAJULI is a scholar of political ecology, anthropology, and social movements who has taught at Syracuse University and Lewis and Clark College. His current research centers on social-movement learning and ecological ethnicities. He is actively involved in various ethnoecological movements in his home country, Nepal, and in India.

IAN PLAYER, a former game ranger in the South African wilderness, is a leading conservationist and the founder of the Wilderness Foundation (South Africa). He continues to be involved with the WILD Foundation (USA) and the World Wilderness Congress.

SAHOTRA SARKAR is an associate professor of philosophy and director of the Program in the History and Philosophy of Science at the University of Texas at Austin. His laboratory is involved in nature reserve network design in several regions including Quebec, the Falkland Islands/Islas Malvinas, and southern India.

JOHN TERBORGH is James B. Duke Professor of Environmental Science and Botany and codirector of the Center for Tropical Conservation at Duke University.

TOM VANDERBILT is a contributing editor of *I.D.* and *The Baffler*. He is the author of *The Sneaker Book: Anatomy of an Industry and an Icon* (The New Press, 1998) and is currently working on a book about Cold War architecture.

MONISH VERMA is a senior researcher at Eco Monitors Society, which focuses on ecology and demography in the Indian Subcontinent. Its current project is an initiative on the demilitarization of the Himalayas as an ecological imperative. He also works as a freelance consultant in the fields of environment, energy, and education. He lives in New Delhi with his wife and two children.

DAVID WESTERN has been the director of the Kenya Wildlife Service since 1994. Formerly the Carter Chair of Conservation Biology and director of International Programs of the Wildlife Conservation Society, he teaches biology at the University of California, San Diego.

EDWARD A. WHITESELL is on the faculty of environmental studies at the Evergreen State College. He is writing a book called *Wild Habitats*, to be published by Arnold.

about the editors

DAVID ROTHENBERG is an associate professor of philosophy at the New Jersey Institute of Technology and the editor of *Terra Nova: Nature and Culture,* an award-winning journal published by MIT Press since 1996. His books include *Hand's End: Technology and the Limits of Nature* (University of California Press, 1993), *Is It Painful to Think? Conversations with Arne Naess* (University of Minnesota Press, 1992), and several edited collections, including *Parliament of Minds* (SUNY Press, 1999), interviews with leading philosophers in conjunction with the public television series of the same name, of which he is a coproducer. Rothenberg is also a composer and jazz clarinetist, and he has four CDs out: *nobody could explain it* (Accurate, 1991), *On the Cliffs of the Heart* (New Tone, 1995), *Unamuno* (1997), and *Before the War* (EarthEar, 2000). He lectures and performs all over the world.

MARTA ULVAEUS is the associate director of continuing Terra Nova projects at the New Jersey Institute of Technology. She was previously an editor of *TDR: The Drama Review,* at New York University, where she pursued graduate studies in jazz as performance practice. An avowed advocate of community radio, she produced and aired music programs for many years on radio stations KPFA and KDVS in northern California.

acknowledgments

Vance G. Martin, "Foreword: Whither World Wilderness?"; Pramod Parajuli, "How Can Four Trees Make a Jungle?"; Zeese Papanikolas, "The Unpaintable West"; Philip Cafaro and Monish Verma, "For Indian Wilderness"; Kathleen Harrison, "Roads Where There Have Long Been Trails"; Antonio Carlos Diegues, "Recycled Rain Forest Myths"; and Edward A. Whitesell, "Mapping the Wild" are all from *Terra Nova* vol. 3, no. 3 (Summer 1998). Published by the MIT Press and reprinted by permission.

Sahotra Sarkar, "Restoring Wilderness or Reclaiming Forests?" © 1997 by Sahotra Sarkar. Reprinted with the author's permission.

David Western, "In the Dust of Kilimanjaro," from *In the Dust of Kilimanjaro* © 1997 by David Western. Published by Island Press, Washington, D.C., and reprinted by permission.

John Terborgh, "Why Conservation in the Tropics Is Failing," from *Requiem for Nature* © 1999 by John Terborgh. Published by Island Press, Washington, DC, and reprinted by permission.

David Western and John Terborgh, "'Trouble in Paradise': An Exchange." Reprinted with permission from *The New York Review of Books* © 1999 NYREV, Inc.

Ian Player, "Zulu History," from *Zulu Wilderness, Shadow and Soul* © 1998 by Ian Player. Published by Fulcrum Publishing, Inc., and reprinted by permission.

William W. Bevis, "Bruno Manser and the Penan," from *Borneo Log: The Struggle for Sarawak's Forests* by William W. Bevis, and reprinted by permission of the publisher.

Dan Imhoff, "The Park of Ten Thousand Waterfalls," © 1997 by Dan Imhoff. Reprinted with the author's permission.

Evan Eisenberg, "Earth Jazz," adapted from *The Ecology of Eden* © 1998 by Evan Eisenberg. Published by Alfred A. Knopf, Inc., and reprinted by permission.

Damien Arabagali, "They Trampled on Our Taboos," from *Story Earth: Native Voices of the Environment* © 1993 by Inter Press Service. Published by Mercury House, San Francisco, CA, and reprinted by permission.

index

Franklin Pierce College Library

00143820

Terra Nova Books

The New Earth Reader

The Book of Music and Nature

Writing on Water

The World and the Wild

Terra Nova Books aim to show how environmental issues have cultural and artistic components, in addition to the scientific and political. Combining essays, reportage, fiction, art, and poetry, Terra Nova Books reveal the complex and paradoxical ways the natural and the human are continually redefining each other.

Terra Nova

New Jersey Institute of Technology

Newark, NJ 07102

973 642 4673

terranova@njit.edu

http://www-ec.njit.edu/~tn/